African
American
Women
in the
Struggle
for the
Vote,
1850–1920

Blacks in the Diaspora

Darlene Clark Hine, John McCluskey, Jr., and David Barry Gaspar

GENERAL EDITORS

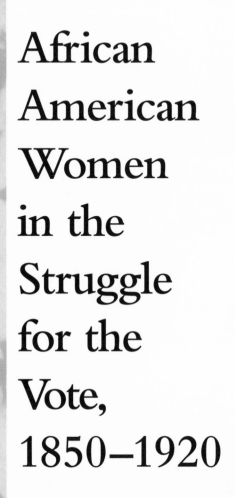

African American Women in the Struggle for the Vote, 1850–1920

Rosalyn Terborg-Penn

Indiana University Press
BLOOMINGTON AND INDIANAPOLIS

This book is a publication of

Indiana University Press
601 North Morton Street
Bloomington, Indiana 47404-3797 USA

http://www.indiana.edu/~iupress

Telephone orders 800-842-6796
Fax orders 812-855-7931
Orders by email iuporder@indiana.edu

Library of Congress Cataloging-in-Publication Data

Terborg-Penn, Rosalyn.
    African American women in the struggle for the vote, 1850–1920 / Rosalyn Terborg-Penn.
        p.   cm. — (Blacks in the diaspora)
    Includes bibliographical references (p.   ) and index.
    ISBN 0-253-33378-4 (alk. paper). — ISBN 0-253-21176-X (pbk. : alk. paper)
    1. Women—Suffrage—United States—History.   2. Afro-American women—Suffrage—History.   3. Suffragists—United States—History.   4. Afro-American women social reformers—History.   I. Title.   II. Series.
JK1896.T47   1998
324.6'23'08996073—dc21   97-41896

1 2 3 4 5 03 02 01 00 99 98

I dedicate this book to my parents,
Jacques Arnold Terborg, Sr., and Jeanne Van Horn Terborg,
and to my daughter,
Jeanna Carolyn Terborg Penn

CONTENTS

ILLUSTRATIONS

ACKNOWLEDGMENTS

Over the past twenty years while creating this book I met, worked with, and shared with so many people. To all of them I owe a debt of gratitude. I begin with special thanks to my mentors, both at Morgan State University where I have taught a generation of students, and at Howard University where I earned my Ph.D. At Morgan, I owe the deepest gratitude to the late Benjamin Quarles and Roland C. McConnell, both of whom mentored, inspired, and encouraged me. At Howard, I thank my late mentors, Harold Lewis, Dorothy Porter Wesley, and Lorraine A. Williams, all of whom I miss very much, and Arnold Taylor, who was the backbone of my dissertation committee. These six ushered me through my initial years of researching and conceptualizing an unchartered topic, always believing in my work and my role as pioneer in Black Women's History.

Friends and colleagues were important to me in my researching, conceptualizing, and writing. For reading drafts, critiquing my work, sharing material and ideas, and writing recommendations for grants, I thank: Elsa Barkley Brown, Lonnie Bunch, Bettye Collier-Thomas, Spencer Crew, Mary Dyer, Gerald Gill, Diane Glave, Ann Gordon, Debra Newman Ham, Sharon Harley, Nancy A. Hewitt, James Oliver Horton, Louise Daniel Hutchinson, Sylvia Marie Jacobs, Gail Lowe, Edith Mayo, Denise D. Meringolo, Cynthia Neverdon-Morton, Nell Irvin Painter, Jo Ann O. Robinson, Jacqueline Ann Rouse, Brenda Stevenson, Janice Sumler-Edmond, and Marjorie Spruill Wheeler.

I thank my students and interns who provided technical and research assistance: Maria DeLongoria, Stephanie Francis, and Tamika Mathews Lindsay from Morgan State University and Molly Jones from the National Museum of American History.

Over the years I have received financial assistance from several grant-giving agencies. I acknowledge the gracious support of a Berkshire Conference–Bunting Institute Fellowship, a Ford Foundation Postdoctoral Fellowship for Minorities, several Morgan State University faculty research grants and a sabbatical leave, a Smithsonian Institution Visiting Scholars Grant at the Anacostia Museum, and a Smithsonian Institution Faculty Fellowship at the National Museum of American History.

Without very special people I could never have completed this book. I especially thank Martha Vicinus for reading early drafts, forcing me to face my critics and work around the barriers, and for encouraging me never to give up. Exceptional thanks go to Darlene Clark Hine for having enough faith in my work to encourage me to submit my manuscript to Indiana University Press. My hardest-working supporters deserve my heartfelt thanks and gratitude because they shared material, read my entire manuscript, sometimes in different forms, and stayed with me along the way, especially during the last year of my struggle to complete my revisions. My deepest gratitude goes to my colleagues Adele Logan Alexander, Ellen Carol DuBois, and Vivian Njeri Fisher, and to my daughter, Jeanna Carolyn Terborg Penn.

African
American
Women
in the
Struggle
for the
Vote,
1850–1920

Chapter 1. Revisiting the Question of Race in the Woman Suffrage Movement

Legal status, class and economic status, organizational affiliations, region of residence, gender, racial identification, and generational affiliations determined the degrees to which African American women participated in the woman suffrage movement. Multiple forms of oppression, primarily slavery and later poverty, restricted many Black women's efforts to gain women's right to vote in government-sponsored elections. African American women persisted despite the many barriers to their political participation in public elections. The changes in the status of African American women over the course of the woman suffrage movement—from slave to free, from rural to urban, from illiterate to literate, from unskilled to skilled or to professional workers—can be seen as factors that encouraged Black strategies to achieve women's enfranchisement. One thing is certain: for various reasons, including multiple forms of consciousness, more and more Black women, like white women, joined the ranks of the suffragists as the movement progressed into the twentieth century.

Throughout the movement, similar fetters were common to all American women, and most African American men, preventing them from achieving political equity. However, during the seventy-two years of the woman suffrage movement, society limited Black women most severely. This book focuses on why African American women in the woman suffrage movement supported the "votes for women" campaign, and on the obstacles they met along the way to enfranchisement.

African American women contributed significantly to the passage of the Nineteenth Amendment, which enfranchised all American women in 1920. As a result, the history of the movement was shaped both by Black suffrage activism and by white racism. For middle-class white women, the movement's victory ended battles that had begun over seventy years before. For Black women, however, the struggle to maintain the vote continued for two generations after the passage of the woman suffrage amendment, as most were robbed of their ballots by the success of white political supremacy in the South. This is the story, however, of the first three generations of African American woman suffragists. Their long struggle for political equity spanned the years from the abolitionist movement of the antebellum period through the Progressive Era, when the Nineteenth Amendment was ratified and the majority of Black women attempted to cast their first votes as United States citizens.

Black women, in their struggle for the right to vote, fought racism and sexism simultaneously and revealed several things about the nature of their struggle as woman suffragists. First, although Black men appeared to be in the forefront throughout the duration of the movement, they occupied positions of prominence primarily during the first forty years. From the last decade of the nineteenth century to the end of the struggle for the Nineteenth Amendment, more Black women than men took leadership positions. Leadership was manifested in local and regional woman suffrage activities, although coalitions of African American women and men organized in the struggle for women's right to vote.

In addition, African American women developed multiple levels of consciousness in their political struggle, as Black women's support for woman suffrage often paralleled, yet developed differently from that of white suffragists, especially as the movement progressed. Although strategies were similar and there were coalitions between Blacks and whites, the experiences of the two racial groups differed. The existence of racism resulting in an anti–Black woman suffrage agenda and tactics among many whites, and the racial discrimination African American women encountered at the polls, reinforced differences among Black and white women suffragists.

Class was another factor that influenced women's participation in the organized woman suffrage movement. Just as the majority of white women who actively participated in the organized movement were among the middle class, the majority of Black women who were suffragists appear to have enjoyed higher status than the masses of women of their race. Because many of the activities of African American women participants were not recorded in the official histories of the movement, it is difficult to obtain statistics to ascertain that more middle-class Black women than working-class Black women were suffragists. Nonetheless, it seems likely that most of the Black woman suffragist leaders were among the educated.

Finally, the struggle for suffrage among African American women was different from that of white women and African American men, because racism did not limit white women and sexism did not limit African American men. Black male leaders publicly supported woman suffrage, especially those in the North who retained their right to vote after the ratification of the Fifteenth Amendment. For the most part, however, Black women rather than Black men were the ones who actively worked in the woman suffrage movement, but the women remained invisible, a mode of operation expedient in a sexist society. Consequently, they were limited politically.

The ever-increasing number of Black women involved in a struggle that culminated in what appeared to be a political victory revealed the steady growth of their political participation over time. This discussion of the issues that emerged during the seventy-year period of activism—from 1850 to 1920—seeks to capture the elusive history of African American women's political triumphs and travails. This history also serves as a revisionist interpretation of the traditional construction of the woman suffrage movement. Throughout, I attempt to find the voices of the African American woman suffragists, to have them tell their own stories. Consequently, in remembering African American women's history, I decenter white women and Black men from the history of the woman suffrage movement.

Debunking Myths:
Methodology and Theoretical Context

How does one go about reconstructing the history of African American women's involvement in the mainstream woman suffrage movement and specifically their own struggle for the vote? As a student at Howard University in the 1970s, I began researching and analyzing the Black role in the woman suffrage movement. In my 1977 study, "Afro-Americans in the Struggle for Woman Suffrage," I recovered sources relating to scores of Blacks, both women and men, who had publicly supported woman suffrage.[1] Until then, most of these individuals had been lost to contemporary studies of the movement, often because of myths about African American women's and men's relationship to woman suffrage issues. During the 1970s, feminist writers believed that, historically, Black women had been uninterested in feminist politics and that Black men had opposed feminist issues. Finding data that disproved these myths encouraged my further investigation of traditional and nontraditional sources for evidence to demonstrate that many nineteenth- and twentieth-century African Americans were suffragists.[2]

At the time of my research, there were very few published works analyzing even the mainstream of the woman suffrage movement. Nonetheless, biased accounts of the movement, written by white women who had been suffragists, were available and familiar to scholars of women's history.[3] Often when African Americans were mentioned in this literature, they were either described as opponents of the inclusion of women during the controversy over the Fifteenth Amendment (which enfranchised Black men) and as opponents of the Nineteenth Amendment, or as subjects of antisuffrage arguments, found mainly among white suffragists from the South, who sought to exclude Black women from state suffrage referenda. In my research, I found none of the alleged anti–woman's rights speeches or newspaper articles Black men had been accused of writing. I did find dynamic Black women feminists, not merely Black female victims.

Two studies were helpful in the early 1970s. One was Eleanor Flexner's *Century of Struggle*, in which she included several African American women. Yet Flexner concluded that African American women, when given the choice between fighting racism and fighting sexism, opted to fight against racism. Challenged by this view, and speculating that Black women could indeed fight both institutions at the same time, I continued my search for other historical analyses. The second study, Aileen Kraditor's *The Ideas of the Woman Suffrage Movement, 1890–1920,* confirmed my suspicions. Kraditor delved into the anti–Black woman suffrage argument among white southern suffragists and their northern supporters and noted that some Blacks protested the racism in the woman suffrage movement. Although Kraditor's study covered the white leadership in the movement and only the last thirty years of it, I theorized that Black women and Black men had remained in the woman suffrage movement throughout the struggle, fighting both racism and sexism simultaneously.[4]

To prove this thesis, I began with African American history rather than with white women's history. My most helpful secondary sources for the antebellum period were the books and articles written by Benjamin Quarles, who as early as 1940 had published an essay about Frederick Douglass and other African American men in the abolitionist movement who had supported women's rights issues.[5] I also read manuscripts, newspapers, journals, organizational proceedings, and biographies by and about nineteenth- and early twentieth-century African Americans, many of whom were abolitionists or civil rights activists as well as woman suffragists.

Continuing the process for the post–Civil War and Reconstruction years, then for "the Nadir" period in African American history, culminating with the World War I years and the passage of the Nineteenth Amendment, I used a similar methodology. The recovery of the names of Black reformers was important. The six volumes of *The History of Woman Suffrage* revealed the names of several men and women not recognized as African Americans by many historians of white women's history. In addition, sources contemporary to the woman suffrage movement were helpful, including the Susan B. Anthony Papers, *The Life and Work of Susan B. Anthony*, and the periodicals, *The Revolution* and *The Woman's Journal.*[6] In addition, some of the statements published in this history were contradictory and needed to be investigated further.

My search for quantifiable data about Black suffragists during the twentieth century met historical barriers. Although jurisdictions had kept voter statistics that reflected both race and gender, the two categories were rarely integrated. Hence, few data were available about Black women. African Americans were not separated in the statistics by gender, and women were not separated by race. Helen Woodbury had found a similar difficulty in 1896, when she analyzed the effect of woman suffrage on Colorado, one of the few states to grant women the right to vote in the nineteenth century.[7]

In researching her 1981 dissertation, historian Elinor Lerner faced a problem similar to the one Woodbury encountered. Lerner looked at the role of the ethnic vote during the woman suffrage campaign in New York City. Although she discussed the Black vote, finding some areas where African Americans resided to be prosuffrage and some to be antisuffrage, Lerner did not provide a voter analysis for Black neighborhoods, as she did for several European ethnic communities. One of the reasons she noted for her difficulty in analyzing racial voting patterns was her inability to distinguish the Black from the white vote in specific neighborhoods.[8]

In the early 1980s, as I set out to write the history primarily of the African American women involved in the woman suffrage movement, I reflected upon the perspective I had used in my earlier research. The issue was whether to take a Black nationalist perspective, which focuses on African Americans and how they define their own priorities, or a woman-centered perspective, which does the same from a gendered perspective, in this case with the focus on both Blacks and whites. I concluded that I needed both, because too many variables influencing the political experiences of African American women involved both race and gender. As a result, I developed a Black nationalist feminist perspective, in which I challenged other feminist approaches to constructing woman suffrage movement history. In this construction, I looked for the "metalanguage"—the alternative, racialized meanings in verbal expressions—of African American women and contextualized it by viewing the woman suffrage struggle from inside Black communities looking out, rather than looking from the outside in, through a "white filter."

In researching for my revised study during the 1980s, I looked at additional primary sources that treated African American women in the suffrage movement, and I read the scholarship about woman suffrage. Among the studies most helpful to me in the 1980s were those of historians Ellen Carol DuBois, Bettina Aptheker, and Elisabeth Griffith.[9]

DuBois's feminist analysis of the radical white suffragists of the post–Civil War era provided insight for characterizing the politics of Black women suffragists. Aptheker, who often disagreed with DuBois's interpretation of the radical feminists and their relationship to African Americans, provided an essay on abolitionists and suffrage, plus an essay on the Fifteenth Amendment controversy. Aptheker's analysis is a marxist feminist approach to the suffrage issues with a Black perspective, the only analysis to appear since my dissertation that has brought an approach different from mine to the roles of African Americans in the movement. Ironically, the two studies published in the 1980s by African American women, one by Angela Davis and the other by Paula Giddings, offered me little insight, because their research conclusions mirrored those in my dissertation.[10]

Finally, Griffith's biography of Elizabeth Cady Stanton included discussions about Stanton not only in her role as an abolitionist and suffragist, but in her relationship with selected Black and white reformers. Although Griffith admitted that her analysis was pro-Stanton, the data presented reinforced my belief that this pioneer woman suffragist was a racist. In using the term "racist," I mean a person of privilege who disparages and hinders the opportunities of others who are in a subordinate position, identifiable by skin color.

By the mid-1980s, I discovered new primary sources. These combined with the old supported my original thesis that, in their struggle for the right to vote, Black women fought racism and sexism simultaneously. Perhaps the most helpful sources were the antisuffrage literature and the extant copies of *The Suffragist,* the official organ of the Congressional Union, later renamed the National Woman's Party (NWP), housed in the National Museum of American History of the Smithsonian Institution. These findings confirmed my earlier belief about barriers to Black women's involvement in the woman suffrage movement. Of necessity, theirs was a unique strategy, which developed in conjunction with those of mainstream woman suffragists as well as those of disfranchised Black men seeking to regain their right to vote. Because of racial and gender differences in the politics behind enfranchisement, African American women's support for woman suffrage in the twentieth century also often paralleled, yet developed differently from, that of others who sought the vote.

Another decade passed before I could return to the project. By the mid-1990s, among the new studies about the woman suffrage movement, historian Marjorie Spruill Wheeler's was very helpful to me, for it detailed the southern white woman suffrage strategies in relationship to African American women. Further, Wheeler confirmed my assumptions that many northern white suffragists made their southern counterparts the scapegoats for the racism they shared.[11]

In addition, there was growing theoretical analysis of African American women's experiences by feminist historians. New questions were raised about interpretative voices, multiple levels of consciousness and of oppression, and additional venues for examining race, class, and gender. Specifically, theoretical constructs for analyzing Black women's history emerged by the 1990s from African American historians such as Adele Logan Alexander, Elsa Barkley Brown, Sharon Harley, Wanda Hendricks, Evelyn Brooks Higginbotham, Darlene Clark Hine, and Nell Irvin Painter.[12] Their ideas buttressed my attempts to view African American women's political and social milieu as similar to, but also different from, that of other oppressed groups who find alternative avenues for problem solving and community building.

A good example for constructing political participation is Elsa Barkley Brown's view of the Black women of Richmond, Virginia, during the last quarter of the nineteenth century. She reveals their political participation on two levels—in the external political arena of Republican Party politics and in the internal community arena of their own institutions, primarily churches. In both arenas, Brown found that African American women exercised their views informally and formally. At times they were challenged by Black men because of gender conventions. However, at times they were expected to participate, especially in institutions where women's monetary support was essential to institutional survival. Brown argues that Black women in the reconstructed South were quite conscious of venues for political participation and organized around them.[13]

As a result of new theoretical and research directions such as Brown's, I have reexamined my study and expanded it from a revisionist construct with a Black nationalist feminist analysis to include additional theoretical frameworks for seeking Black women's voices and for viewing their alternative meanings for Black women's participation in the woman suffrage movement over time.

Overview

The woman suffrage movement spanned a period that witnessed the changing status of Black women from the antebellum years when most were enslaved, to the post–World War I years when many asserted themselves in politics and the workplace. Black women's transfiguration in status and identity, plus their increasing participation in fighting for women's enfranchisement, influenced the transformation in goals of the wider woman suffrage movement.

The movement began officially at Seneca Falls, New York, in 1848 and ended with the ratification of what was called the Susan B. Anthony Amendment in August of 1920. For African American women, the battle to retain the vote, threatened by white political supremacy, began at this point. Beginning in the antebellum years, white manhood suffrage, not universal suffrage, characterized the growth of democracy in the United States. African Americans, both males and females, supported and argued for universal suffrage, for along with other groups of women, they too were denied political rights. Male leaders dominated the reform movements of this era. White women often worked behind the scenes in petitioning governments and in fund raising for the abolitionist movement and other early nineteenth-century reforms. This was also true of free Black women.[14]

After the Civil War, universal suffrage continued to be the goal of woman suffrage advocates, especially those who were Black. However, during the late 1860s, a split in the movement developed over strategy. Feminists who were disillusioned by the introduction of the word "male" into the United States Constitution first lobbied to exclude the word from the Fourteenth Amendment, but that strategy failed. Then they protested the Fifteenth Amendment, because it proposed to enfranchise Black males, leaving women disfranchised. The debate that ensued divided the universal suffrage movement into two camps, those who felt that Black men needed the vote even more than women, and those who were unwilling to postpone woman suffrage for the sake of Black males. The majority of African Americans who remained active in the movement affiliated with those who supported the enfranchisement of Black men, or what was called, "Negro suffrage."

Throughout the twenty years of the split, or during the period when the second generation of woman suffragists began to emerge in the movement, suffragists used two different strategies to gain the ballot. For a brief period, those of the National Woman Suffrage Association (NWSA) held that women should focus their efforts on challenging the Fourteenth Amendment by attempting to vote. The strategy was called the "new departure," and a handful of African American women affiliated with the NWSA attempted unsuccessfully to vote in the 1860s. For a while the NWSA focused on state referenda, but the organization eventually worked toward a constitutional amendment to enfranchise women. The members of the American Woman Suffrage Association (AWSA), who had supported the Fifteenth Amendment and universal suffrage, focused on local legislatures in attempts to obtain woman suffrage on state levels while continuing to petition Congress and support a constitutional amendment. A larger number of women, including Black women, were affiliated with this group from the 1860s through the 1880s, rather than the NWSA.

For this period of about twenty-five years, the recovery of evidence about Black women who had been lost to woman suffrage history is significant.[15] This era is important also for the development of Black women's clubs, many of which had goals and concerns unique to African American women. The changing status of African American women was becoming evident. Since emancipation, more and more Black women had become educated and were working to uplift their communities. However, throughout the nineteenth century, the majority of the nation's Black women had little opportunity to participate in organized woman suffrage activities. Those African American women who had the opportunity to become suffragists moved in two directions, identifying with the mainstream, white woman suffrage organizations on the one hand, and developing their own agendas in Black woman suffrage organizations on the other. By the end of the century, thousands of African American women joined clubs and lodges with affiliations in state federations. These women were primarily from the middle class, but working-class women also made significant contributions. Most clubs included woman suffrage as one of their goals. In addition, Black women developed their political and tactical skills as leaders of this movement.

By 1890, when the two national associations merged to form the National American Woman Suffrage Association (NAWSA), only one state, Wyoming, and one territory, Utah, offered full suffrage to women, although Massachusetts women had earned the right to vote for school boards in the 1870s. By the end of the century, women gained suffrage in only three states, all in the west—Colorado, Idaho, and Utah—as most white men in the East and in the South remained resolutely opposed to woman suffrage. Throughout this period, African American women participated in growing numbers in the suffrage movement, yet the probability of their achieving suffrage was far lower than that for either Black men or white women. Despite the fact that most African American men in the South had been disfranchised during the 1890s, those who lived in all regions outside of the South could still vote, and Black populations nationwide used a variety of tactics designed to reenfranchise Black males. As for the states where women had won full or partial voting rights, the Black female population was small. Enfranchisement in these states benefited white women for the most part. Nonetheless, African American, not white, suffragists continued to use strategies in support of universal suffrage, whereas white women for the most part campaigned for their own enfranchisement.

The growth of a nationally organized Black women's club movement, beginning in the 1890s, revealed the members' belief that votes for Black women would mean regaining votes stolen from Black men who had been disfranchised throughout the southern states by legislative action or constitutional amendments. National leaders of the Black women's club movement presented their views about enfranchising African Americans to white leaders whenever possible. In addition, they told Black women in their own networks how the strategy to keep Black women from obtaining the ballot would provoke the men who had remained silent about the issue to defend suffrage for their women. The coalition-building strategy was at work here, for African American women hoped that all three groups—Black women, Black men, and white women—could see the need to pull together in order to accomplish similar goals.

At the turn of the century, the third generation of woman suffragists emerged—the daughters and granddaughters of the first generation. Another exclusionary strategy developed among mainstream suffragists as several states legislated some form of literacy requirement. Among woman suffrage advocates, this trend was known as "educated suffrage," and was obviously meant to limit Black and foreign-born voters. Some historians maintained that this tactic impeded the cause, because it served to alienate potential supporters from the working class, noting that not until the First World War were middle-class suffragists able to realize that immigrant and working-class voters were not threats, as had been predicted. Other historians found that, in spite of support among working-class men and women in cities long before the First World War, the strategy of the conservative middle-class white suffragists was to play down the socialist, immigrant, and working-class voters in an attempt to recruit more middle-class, native-born, white male support.[16]

Conservative suffragists alienated Black women and Black men, claiming they were threats to the success of the woman suffrage amendment. In response, organized African American women publicly rebuked this tactic, speaking out in the Black press and at suffrage meetings about how African Americans did not oppose the movement. Despite the defamatory claims against them, Blacks vowed to continue their struggle for the vote as they criticized the white woman suffrage leadership for its discrimination.

Despite Black criticism, most mainstream white suffrage leaders acquiesced as southern whites attempted to cancel out the Black vote by writing African American women out of state and federal suffrage proposals. On the other hand, the efforts of white supremacists stimulated more Black men to join in the push for a Nineteenth Amendment, which would exclude no women. During the last eight years before ratification of this amendment, national and local coalitions of Black men and women worked to intensify support for its passage. The National Association for the Advancement of Colored People (NAACP) was the major association where this articulation centered.

While the politics of race divided the woman suffrage movement, some suffrage advocates of both races identified the absence of civil and political rights as barriers to the progress of women. At the turn of the century, a growing number of elite white women in particular argued that female reformers could better solve the problems of their society if they were armed with the ballot. This view was especially popular during the early years of the Progressive Era. Women reformers sought to address the societal ills of intemperance, political corruption, inadequate economic and educational opportunities for women, crime, and limited consumer protection.[17] Black female suffragists argued for most social reform issues during this period, even after middle-class white suffragists had abandoned many of them. However, white female suffragists did not include racial discrimination and the plight of disfranchised Black women in their priorities for social reform. They either avoided the race question or openly opposed including Black women in the suffrage ranks.

By 1918, of the forty-eight states in the union, only twenty-two provided for some form of woman suffrage.[18] Third-generation woman suffragists, for the most part, realized by the First World War that a national strategy, rather than a state-by-state approach, was essential to the success of the movement. White southern suffragists, in the meantime, held fast to the traditional states' rights argument that aimed to exclude Black women voters.[19] Consequently, national woman suffrage leaders expressed fear that suffrage initiatives by organizations representing thousands of Black women would create racial tension among southern members and jeopardize the passage of the Nineteenth Amendment. Consequently, they reversed their policy of prodding Black women outside the South to publicly encourage their men to support the woman suffrage amendment. Instead they encouraged Black women's organizations not to join the NAWSA.

Although opposition to woman suffrage failed to check the growth of the national movement, attempts to keep Black women disfranchised continued until both houses of Congress passed the federal amendment by June 1919. Ironically, by the time the amendment was ratified in August 1920, nine more states had granted woman suffrage through legislative enactment, including two southern states—Tennessee and Kentucky—where, for a period, Black women were enfranchised on an equal basis with white women.

For African American women, gaining the right to vote along with white women might not have been automatic. Just as Paula Baker theorized that woman suffrage might not automatically have come with changes in the nature of electoral politics without an effective lobby to include women, African American women also had to struggle to remain visible in order to insure electoral inclusion.[20]

As Black women became voters, they lobbied for political candidates, several of whom were women. In addition, African American women organized voter education groups in their own communities, ran for a variety of offices, and fought attempts by southern racists to keep them from the polls. In spite of efforts to implement their political rights, however, Black women in the South were disfranchised in less than a decade after the Nineteenth Amendment enfranchised them. The process took less than half the time it had taken for Black men to lose their votes after the ratification of the

Fifteenth Amendment in 1870. In addition, African American women outside the South lost the political clout they had acquired. As many Black female suffragists suspected, white women voters ignored their plight. Having earlier encouraged Black women to join the movement in order to bring Black male voters into the woman suffrage camp, white suffragists then abandoned disfranchised Black women. Similarly, some working-class white women believed that affluent suffragists had abandoned them after the passage of the Nineteenth Amendment. As a result, the coalitions established during the push for a woman suffrage amendment dissolved. Politically conscious women outside the mainstream became disillusioned with the goals and tactics of the new middle-class feminist leadership, whose ideological focus justified improving the position of women in their class, often by abandoning others in need of uplift outside of their race, class, or gender.[21]

In spite of the disappointing aftermath of the Nineteenth Amendment campaign, African American women suffragists had participated in the enfranchisement process and had learned lessons for the future. The Nineteenth Amendment victory was a shallow one for Black women, an anticlimax especially for those in the South who had dared to believe that winning the vote could enable them to participate in the electoral process. With these bitter lessons behind them, Black women redirected their energies toward other—race-centered—political goals.

Chapter 2. African American Women in the First Generation of Woman Suffragists: 1850–1869

> The colored women are as interested in politics as the colored men of the Republican Party.
>
> —"Laura," 1859[1]

The official birth of the woman suffrage movement occurred at the women's rights convention held at Seneca Falls, New York, in July 1848. In the formative years of this movement—its first generation—the number of suffragists grew slowly from a small group of reformers within the confines of abolitionist circles in the northeast to a more diversified, but still limited number of individuals and groups nationwide. Diversification occurred as individuals, both Blacks and whites, joined the movement from regions throughout the nation. During these formative years the majority of the participants came from the more affluent and educated white abolitionists, who can be classified among the mainstream reformers coming out of the antebellum era. Yet a handful of African American men and women added their color to the proceedings.

The early feminists who emerged from abolitionist circles held periodic conventions, wrote letters to editors, and sent petitions to government officials. Aside from their demand for woman suffrage, their activities were conventional compared to subsequent woman suffrage actions. Yet the political consciousness of the white women involved, and their ability to act upon their convictions, were much higher than for the majority of Black women, whether free or enslaved. Elite and middle-class white women did not normally work outside of the home. They did not have to contend with the realities of poverty, illiteracy, or menial employment, as did most Black women. Even the more fortunate Black women who were living in a quasi-free status outside of slavery, often had to work for wages or services.

Despite the disparity of lifestyles, African American participation in this movement began with the initiation of the struggle. Frederick Douglass, a former slave and Black abolitionist living in Rochester, New York, was at the Seneca Falls meeting. He became the first male of any color to advocate publicly for woman suffrage.[2] Black participation continued from that point forward, even after 1869, when the suffragists split into two camps and developed several strategies and goals that reflected the personal and political priorities of suffrage factions.

The Antebellum Era

For a little over a decade before the Civil War, the movement unfolded with limited definition and leadership. Elizabeth Cady Stanton, who helped organize the Seneca Falls meeting and initiated the radical cry for woman suffrage, attended none of the national meetings held annually from 1850 to 1861. Lucretia Mott, who had encouraged Stanton and helped organize the first convention, refused to take official leadership, though prodded to do so by the feminists.[3]

At first, the mainstream politicians did not take the feminist movement seriously, as revealed by unenthusiastic reporting in the press. Few newspapers wrote positively about the Seneca Falls meeting, and for a while suffragists were characterized negatively. The women were caricatured as "sexless old maids" and as "radical heretics." The men were ridiculed and branded "Aunt Nancy men" and "hermaphrodites."[4]

No African American women appear to have been present at that meeting if we rely on the records kept by the major players, who were elite white suffragists. I speculate that free Black women who lived in the upstate New York area—perhaps in cities like Rochester—attended the meeting along with the male abolitionists of color, but the chroniclers of the movement made no mention of them. However, there is evidence that, throughout the 1850s, a growing number of Black female abolitionists joined the small circle of suffragists. Identifying their names was tedious, but less difficult than recovering their ideas and activities as woman suffragists.

Aside from Sojourner Truth, the former New York slave and itinerant abolitionist preacher whose words were often quoted, the mainstream woman suffrage chroniclers did not identify most other women in the circle as African American. Early chroniclers were the women who edited the first three volumes of the *History of Woman Suffrage:* Elizabeth Cady Stanton, Susan B. Anthony, and Matilda J. Gage. The history writing began in 1876, when the women agreed to compile the data they had collected through the years. The data included personal reminiscences, biographical sketches, photographs, state reports, speeches, resolutions, excerpts from the *Congres-*

Sojourner Truth, the first known African American woman suffragist, was an illiterate, itinerant reformer originally from Ulster County, New York. *Moorland-Spingarn Research Center, Howard University*

sional Record, newspaper clippings, and items from the editors' personal files. The first volume was published in 1881, bringing the movement history from 1848 to 1860. Not one Black woman's photograph appeared in the volume, not even the celebrated Sojourner Truth. Aside from excerpts from Truth's speeches, the words of other Black female suffragists were all but absent. A function of the present study is to recover the Black women known to the contemporaries of the movement, but who became lost to later generations of woman suffragists and those who wrote about the movement.

In 1850 the first Massachusetts women's rights convention met at Worcester, and Sojourner Truth attended. Throughout the formative years of the movement, Truth attended women's rights conventions held in the North, earning her keep by doing domestic work, selling her narrative, performing the songs she composed, and making speeches. Unlike the other suffragists who made the women's rights circuit, staying with friends who in turn stayed with them on other occasions, Truth was homeless and had to provide for her own survival with little ability to reciprocate short of providing services. Perhaps her overwhelming presence and unique oratorical style prompted chroniclers of the movement to record her works, for the opinions of other Black women were rarely recorded. Or as Truth's biographer Nell Painter suggests, others such as Frances Gage constructed a view of Truth to support their political and feminist agendas.[5]

It appears that Sojourner Truth captivated even unwilling audiences, winning skeptics to the women's rights cause. In 1851 she attended the convention at Akron, Ohio, where she spoke on behalf of all women, despite attempts by white women to prevent her from taking the podium. Frances D. Gage presided over the meeting. She reported how fearful her colleagues were that allowing a former slave and an abolitionist to speak before the hostile audience would ruin the cause. Truth prevailed and delivered a heart-rending speech that resulted in "long and loud" cheers.[6]

In 1853 Truth attended the Broadway Tabernacle meeting in New York City, where she reportedly spoke about the legal disabilities that kept women downtrodden. Despite their low status, she believed all women would someday overcome the discrimination against them. An example of how the white women who remembered Truth's "classic style" reported it reads as follows:

> I've been look'n round and watchin' things and I know a little mite 'bout Woman's Rights too. I know that it feels a kind O'hissin' and ticklin' like to see a colored woman geet up and tell you 'bout things, and Woman's Rights. We have all been thrown down so low that nobody thought we'd ever get up again; but we have been long enough trodden now; we will come up again, and now I am here.
>
> Now women do not ask half of a kingdom, but their rights, and they don't get 'em. When she comes to demand 'em, don't you hear our sons hiss their mothers like snakes, because they ask for their rights; and can they ask for anything else? . . . But we'll have our rights; see if we don't and you can't stop us from them; see if you can. You may hiss as much as you like, but it is comin'. . . .[7]

Whether she spoke in the southern dialect reported is debatable, since Truth was born and raised and lived much of her life in what historian Margaret Washington has described as a Dutch-speaking region of the North. Nonetheless, Truth used what scholars of the Black Church call a classic African American preaching style, which has components of poetry, wit, and symbolism that stir congregations. Plausibly, she utilized that style effectively, and for the first years of the movement, her voice appeared to be a solitary one among Black females.[8]

However, by 1854, African American women's participation in the women's movement became more evident. Harriet Forten Purvis and her sister, educator and abolitionist Margaretta Forten, became two of the "chief actors" responsible for organizing the Fifth National Woman's Rights Convention, the first such gathering to be held in their home city of Philadelphia. The sisters were the daughters of the wealthy Philadelphia sail maker and Black abolitionist, James Forten, and his wife, Charlotte Forten, Sr. Students of the Black abolitionist movement recognize the Forten and Purvis families as prime movers among the African Americans in the movement. However, the Pennsylvania state suffrage records, which contained the names of the Forten sisters, did not indicate that they were Black. At the suffrage meeting, Harriet's husband, Robert Purvis, was chosen vice president for Pennsylvania, an indication of the movement's preference for Black male leadership. Consequently, it is not surprising that the Forten sisters would take an active, but behind-the-scenes, role in this event. They and their mother Charlotte were members of the interracial Philadelphia Female Anti-Slavery Society, many of whose members became active in the early women's rights movement. Like their white counterparts, the Forten sisters were educated and affluent. Unlike Sojourner Truth, who was illiterate, they had never been enslaved.[9]

The chroniclers recalled the 1854 convention as a large audience chiefly made up of women. They also noted "the colored people scattered through the audience," among whom was the free-born Nancy Prince.[10] A widowed seamstress and world traveler, originally from Massachusetts, Prince had returned to the United States nearly penniless in the 1840s after living abroad for many years, first with her husband in Russia, and after his death in Jamaica. By 1848 friends had come to her rescue, and encouraged her to write her narrative to sell for profit. Sale of the book, first published in 1850, enabled Prince to end her life of destitution and return to travel. Why she attended the Philadelphia woman's rights convention is debatable, for unlike the Forten and Purvis women, Prince did not appear to be a conventional feminist. Like them, however, she was an abolitionist and traveled in those circles. I speculate that Nancy Prince was probably among several African Americans who attended this meeting because Harriet Purvis and Margaretta Forten had invited them.

African Americans may not all have been driven to attend the gathering because they identified chiefly with the white feminist agenda. Perhaps people of color came to the convention as abolitionists with an agenda focused upon helping Black people, including Black females. I suggest this because of what Nancy Prince wrote in her own narrative. In commenting on her experiences as a missionary living in Jamaica in 1840, Prince wrote, "I do not approve of women societies; they destroy the world's conventions; the American women have too many of them."[11] At the time that she developed this view, Prince worked under the authority of white American women who were class-leaders in the Baptist missionary society that employed her.

It appears that like other African Americans of her times she used a meta-language, and when Prince spoke of "women," she meant "white women," not all women.[12] Prince's membership in a society with other women of color living in St. Petersburg, Russia, raised a question in my mind about the meaning of her language as a reflection of free Black culture in the United States. Language is a key to interpreting what may seem to be discrete meanings in African American communities of the times—what Evelyn Higginbotham referred to as metalanguage.

Prince's participation as it was reported by chroniclers, stated that she was "a colored woman," who after invoking the blessings of God upon "the noble women engaged in this enterprise," described why "she understood woman's wrongs better than woman's rights." The woman suffrage history writers then went on to summarize Prince's description of her harrowing voyage from the West Indies to the United States, illustrating "the degradation of her sex in slavery."[13] Chroniclers focused on a specific part in Prince's speech about a cargo of several hundred slaves in a brig on the Mississippi River. Among the slaves were said to be "a large number of young quadroon girls with infants in their arms as fair as any *lady* in this room."[14] Here again the word "lady," like the word "woman," refers to "white lady." Whether Prince truly made a speech about the degradation of enslaved women and men is not at issue. The debate is whether she truly focused upon the enslavement of quadroon women, or whether the writers interjected this dramatic scene in an attempt to focus the public upon the sexual abuse of enslaved women. Nell Painter warns about the way nineteenth-century white women reformers constructed Sojourner Truth in an image of their own making.[15] Similarly, the contemporary historians of the movement were representative of this group of reformers. They may have attempted to construct Nancy Prince in much the same way that they constructed Truth. However, we do have Prince's personal narrative to verify her own remembrances of her voyage. In her own narrative, Prince made no reference to enslaved quadroon girls. Yet, she did attend the convention and we can assume that she spoke out against the enslavement of women as an example of "women's wrongs" to the group assembled. The question remains, was she there solely to foster women's rights, or was she there also to campaign for abolition? I say she was there to do both. At a time when white abolitionist women were leaning more in the direction of feminist causes, Prince appears to have been both a feminist and an abolitionist, who can be characterized as an early Black nationalist feminist. Her goals supported women's rights and Black women's independent acts on behalf of communities of African Americans, distinguishing features of nationalist feminism.

Feminist sentiments characterized other free Blacks of the times. Charlotte Forten, Jr., a niece of Harriet Purvis and Margaretta Forten's, was a high school student in Salem, Massachusetts, at the time. In 1855, while living with the Charles Remond family, she was introduced to the women's rights movement, which she supported enthusiastically. Charlotte had been sent to school in Salem by her father, Robert Forten, because Black students were refused admission to the public schools in Philadelphia. The Remonds were noted abolitionists, who traveled within the network of Black anti-slavery circles. In 1858 Sarah Remond and her brother Charles spoke for the first time at a national women's rights convention. They attended the meeting held at Mozart Hall in New York City, where both were honored for their remarks in favor of woman suffrage. By the mid-1850s, in addition to the Remonds, Mary Ann Shadd Cary joined these other Black women in the movement. Her activities started when she returned to the United States from Canada to raise money for her antislavery newspaper, *The Provincial Freeman*. For at least twenty-five years thereafter, she attended woman suffrage conventions and campaigned for women's rights.[16]

During the 1850s, the politics of Black abolitionists, male or female, seemed compatible. Although males dominated the leadership positions in organizations that were not gender separated, females often agreed with the goals and participated in activities equally with men. The emigrationists— Blacks who organized to emigrate from the United States to Canada, the Caribbean, or African societies—and the radical abolitionists exemplified this trend, especially since they were outside of the preserve of the average white abolitionist. By the 1850s, the emigrationists held regular conventions in which women shared leadership positions with men. These movements were anomalies for white women reformers of the mid-nineteenth century. Among the radical abolitionists, the strategy to free fugitive slaves by any means necessary developed in reaction to white persecution of Blacks under the 1850 Fugitive Slave Act. Radical actions were shared by Blacks of both genders. The act was a component of the Compromise of 1850, legislation passed in the U.S. Senate as the political solution to the deadlock between the "slave" and "free" states. The Fugitive Slave Act allowed slave owners or their agents to pursue fugitives who had escaped to northern states where they lived free. Black abolitionists for the most part worked to subvert the efforts of slave catchers. Only a marginal number of white abolitionists participated in these activities.[17]

By the 1850s, white women undertook political action outside the traditional sphere of women reformers by becoming abolitionists in main-stream organizations. As a result, their tactics and ideology, though not as radical as the Black organizations that directly confronted the slaveholding authorities, rejected the early nineteenth-century notion of women's sphere and women's moral superiority over men. Women's sphere was an ideal developed by middle-class notions about placing females in the privacy of their homes, where they were believed to belong. The early woman suffragists who grew out of this abolitionist movement were radical in their attempts to oppose gender conventions by moving outside of the so-called women's sphere and acting independently in calling for their rights. Like Black women abolitionists, they had learned about political organizing, public speaking, and the use of tactics such as moral suasion to make political demands.[18]

However, some African American women learned the skills and tactics, used radical steps to oppose racism, and then took even more risky tactics to oppose sexism. In so doing, they fought both types of oppression, simultaneously. Mary Ann Shadd Cary, an emigrationist, exemplified such African American feminists. Although the *History of Woman Suffrage* editors made reference to Cary's and Sarah Remond's participation in the suffrage movement, they neglected to record these two noted abolitionists' views about women's rights. Cary's position on women's rights can be gleaned from the pages of her newspaper *The Provincial Freeman*. On numerous occasions she and her sister, Amelia Shadd, printed news items and editorials about women's struggle against slavery and against gender discrimination. According to the editors, "woman's work was anything she put her mind or her hand to do." They encouraged women to write letters to the editors of newspapers and to share their views as well as their accomplishments.[19]

Cary's affiliation with feminist leaders was evidenced by her words of excitement noting suffragist Lucy Stone's visit to Toronto in 1854. Cary published *The Freeman* from this Canadian city at the time when Stone arrived to lecture on women's rights. Cary reported that a crowd of Stone's supporters attended her lecture on "Woman's Rights." Lamenting that the number of Blacks in attendance was few, Cary commented that even in Toronto, "with the strong attachment to antiquated notions respecting woman and her sphere so prevalent, Stone was listened to patiently and applauded abundantly."[20] Shortly thereafter, Cary noted that feminist Lucretia Mott gave "generous donations" to *The Freeman*. Obviously Mott felt that the large Black community in Toronto was receptive to both antislavery and women's rights propaganda. Despite the contributions from generous donors and the vigor and efficiency of the Shadd sisters, the readers of *The Freeman*, the women lamented, found it difficult to accept female editors. Whether this attitude would have developed in the states, at a time when Black women were becoming more assertive in Black abolitionist associations, is not known, for there were no African American female editors of newspapers. In Toronto, Cary feared that the "public outrage" would destroy the paper. Putting the Black community first, Cary stepped away from the public view for the survival of the paper. In so doing, she was acting within a nationalist feminist framework. By mid-1855 she had recruited a man, the

Reverend William P. Newman, to edit the paper, while she continued as its owner. She bid her public adieu, but not before admonishing it for its sexism, and encouraging Black women to seek journalism as a career. At the time, Cary was a widow with two small children, receiving assistance from her family members as she toured various regions of the states, speaking about social issues while in search of *Freeman* subscriptions. In contrast, Elizabeth Cady Stanton, who was also a mother with young children, did not work outside of the home, yet could not allow herself to attend women's rights conventions during the 1850s because of family responsibilities.[21] The contrast in behavior between the two feminists reflected different assumptions about women's place in the public sphere as determined by differences in cultural and racial identity.

By 1859 the women's rights perspective was spreading among Blacks in the United States, as advocates made their philosophies known. At the New England Convention of Colored Citizens, held in Boston that year, Charles Remond declined a nomination to the business committee and said that it was time to elect women to leadership positions in the organization. As a result, several Black women accepted the challenge. Ruth Remond of Newport, Rhode Island, and another Black New Englander, a Mrs. Lawton, were elected to the business committee. One of the major demands that ultimately developed as a result of the convention was the call for universal suffrage, a position among African Americans that predated the woman suffragists' move in this direction a decade later. In the 1850s, most white woman suffragists focused their campaign in the direction of women's rights issues.[22]

Though the women's rights agenda continually drew support from Black reformers, the increasing oppression of African Americans during the decade before the Civil War divided their energies as survival became a major imperative. The effects of the Fugitive Slave Act, for example, led abolitionists of both races to respond spontaneously to calls for immediate aid for unfortunate fugitives being coerced back into slavery, some after living many years free in the North. In nearly all northern cities, hundreds of Blacks living free fled to Canada shortly after the passage of the infamous act. Others were not fortunate enough to leave the United States before recapture and reenslavement.[23]

The seizure of runaway Anthony Burns, a Baptist minister living free in Boston, was a case in point. The chroniclers of the woman suffrage movement noted how his capture and return to slavery stimulated sympathy among the delegates attending the New England Woman's Rights Convention held in Boston that June of 1854. The convention assembled June 2, the day Burns was returned to enslavement, despite radical abolitionists' attempts to foil his deportation. According to the convention reports, although many of the "friends of the woman movement" remained in the streets to witness the surrender of Burns to authorities, the convention hall soon became crowded with women's rights delegates, who decried the injustice to Burns. Not surprisingly, no names of Black delegates were recorded for this convention.[24] We can assume that African Americans were among the "friends of the woman movement," who remained in the streets to mourn the figurative passing of their colleague.

In such perilous times, African Americans, who were both suffragists and abolitionists, could ill afford to neglect issues of race in favor of concerns about gender. Charlotte Forten, for one, was so overcome by the events of the Burns tragedy, that the entry in her diary for that day reflected on the abolitionists' failure to rescue the fugitive. She made no mention of the women's rights convention, although I assume she would have attended it under different circumstances. Forten wrote, "A cloud seems hanging over me, over all our persecuted race, which nothing can dispel."[25]

Carter G. Woodson, the father of "Negro history," called this period in African American history the "Crisis." Yet Blacks responded openly to violations against their human rights, a consuming process that fostered radical behavior. Bettina Aptheker analyzed the reform politics of the times, finding that "the intersection of abolitionism and woman's rights" reinforced the radicalism of each movement. Both movements were revolutionary in Aptheker's opinion. Unlike most scholars of women's history, she found a revolutionary impulse among the individuals involved in both causes, which clearly motivated a feminist perspective.[26]

In the meantime, white feminists such as Susan B. Anthony worked in northern politics to promote both abolitionist and women's rights ideas. A Garrisonian abolitionist (one who followed the ideas of the radical William Lloyd Garrison), Anthony refused to support the Lincoln campaign in 1860, because the Republican Party merely wanted to check, not abolish slavery. Like Garrison and other radicals, Anthony adopted the political slogan, "No compromise with slaveholders. Immediate and unconditional Emancipation," and worked as an abolitionist organizer in her native state of New York. In conjunction with her antislavery work, she helped to organize a woman's rights convention in Albany, which successfully lobbied the New York state legislature for a woman's property rights bill. As a consequence of her radical position, Black women were attracted to Anthony, and a cadre of them worked with her in the suffrage movement. Nonetheless, if radical abolitionist actions conflicted with women's rights activities, Anthony participated in the latter.[27]

Elizabeth Cady Stanton, on the other hand, had never made the eradication of slavery a priority in her activism, although she identified herself as an abolitionist. Stanton was sympathetic to the plight of the slaves, but never really worked in their behalf, as had other women's rights activists such as Anthony, Lucretia Mott, and Lucy Stone. Stanton herself observed that "Mrs. Stone felt the slaves' wrongs more deeply than her own—my philosophy was more egotistical."[28] Nonetheless, Stanton adapted what biographer Elisabeth Griffith calls "the metaphor of bondage." This meant that Stanton considered elite white wives to be powerless, as were slave field hands (a position most scholars of African American history have not supported). Though Stanton depicted the plight of slaves and elite white women as similar, when given a choice between fighting these two oppressions, she always put white women first. When slavery was over in the 1860s, Stanton's position would serve to alienate her from many woman suffragists in both races, because she left no room for arguing for the rights of Black people.

With the coming of the Civil War in 1861, the Crisis period for Blacks seemed to subside, as abolitionists hoped that the conflict would bring an end to slavery. In addition, nearly all women's activities ceased as suffragists supported the Union effort. The status of Black women in the North did not change drastically during the war or immediately following it. For the most part, they continued to work in menial positions. In some urban areas such as the District of Columbia, they mobilized to assist the many newly freed African Americans who migrated to the cities.

The major change in Black women's status occurred in the South in 1863, when slavery ended in the rebelling states. The immediate priority of freedwomen was to find lost loved ones and to establish viable households, while attempting to counter white terrorism. Freed Blacks quickly attempted to establish two-parent and extended family households while working to meet the financial needs of their impoverished families. As far as voting was concerned, northern Republicans launched a campaign to give Black men, but not Black women, a political education.

Nonetheless, there appeared to be a movement among Blacks during the Reconstruction years to facilitate African American women's political empowerment in the South. Elsa Barkley Brown describes the political participation of southern Black women in the post–Civil War years as collective autonomy, wherein women and men developed institutions and "engaged in formal politics after emancipation." In reality, Black women's worldview was different from the assumptions of white women who engaged in the debates about disfranchised individuals. Brown constructs the world of freedwomen, showing how it functioned differently from that of middle-class women, whether they were Black or white. Freedwomen, she found, perceived suffrage as a "collective, not an individual possession." Consequently, women and men participated in mass political meetings to determine the Republican politics of the Reconstruction era so that it would provide the greatest benefits to the Black community as a whole rather than to one segment alone.[29]

Furthermore, as Benjamin Quarles found in researching the political activities of Blacks in the period, "In certain districts of the South Carolina elections of 1870 colored women, under the encouragement of Negro election officials, exercised the privilege of voting. By this act the Negro became the first practical vindicator of woman's right to the ballot."[30]

Quarles came to this conclusion when researching his dissertation on Frederick Douglass during the 1930s. His analysis is a significant indicator of the historiographical cleavages between the fields of Black history and women's history, as each field developed independently of the findings of the other. As Quarles saw African Americans as woman suffrage advocates, others outside of his field of "Negro History" viewed Blacks as opponents. The historiography surrounding the schism among universal suffragists, which occurred in the late 1860s, provides a good example of the different interpretations given to the period by those writing the Black history and those writing the women's history.

The Schism among Universal Suffragists

The schism that occurred among suffragists is a topic writers have debated since the 1960s. They usually focus on how male abolitionists abandoned the woman suffrage cause to make the enfranchisement of Black men—"Negro suffrage"—a priority. Writers argue that this suffrage strategy created discord in the ranks and led to the founding of the two rival woman suffrage organizations, which differed in personal, political, and philosophical ways. Although various authors differ somewhat in their analysis of the schism, focusing on specific individuals or groups or strategies, rarely has the schism been viewed from a Black perspective that addresses the question of universal suffrage. The aim of the present discussion is to do just that, while constructing a venue for acknowledging separate authentic voices revisiting this controversial event.[31]

In the North, the years immediately following the war brought a greater number of Black and white abolitionists and suffragists together as they united to work for universal suffrage. Several of the African Americans who had participated in the antebellum women's movement attained leadership positions in the newly organized American Equal Rights Association (AERA), founded in 1866. This group of African Americans included several veteran Black female suffragists—Harriet Purvis, Sarah Remond, and Sojourner Truth. Both Truth and Remond appeared at AERA meetings as guest speakers. Harriet Purvis served as a member of the executive committee.[32]

The suffrage activities of these women during this period were not limited to participation in the AERA. In Philadelphia in 1866, several Black men and women organized the interracial Philadelphia Suffrage Association. Harriet Purvis, along with several Black men, was elected to the executive

Sarah Remond was an abolitionist lecturer before the Civil War. A member of the American Equal Rights Association, she toured the Northeast campaigning for universal suffrage. *Courtesy Peabody Essex Museum, Salem, Mass.*

committee. Throughout 1866 and 1867, Sarah and Charles Remond lectured on behalf of woman suffrage throughout New York state in preparation for the constitutional convention to be held in 1867. Their efforts were unsuccessful, because the legislators failed to include women's enfranchisement in the new constitution.[33]

It was during this period that African Americans clearly identified the female reformer's quest for "rights" with the quest for the ballot. In his speech supporting woman suffrage in 1867, Charles Remond combined several political issues in his argument, which linked together the need for universal reform as well as the need for woman suffrage. In essence, he said that equal suffrage was essential to maintaining freedom for all Americans—Blacks, whites, and newly emancipated slaves. Although the words of most Black women suffragists were not included in the woman suffrage records, their association with such people as Charles Remond lends credence to the assumption that he spoke for the older generation of Black female suffragists as well as for the younger generation appearing on the scene.[34]

By the mid-1860s, the familiar names of the Remonds and others were augmented by those younger women such as Frances Ellen Watkins Harper and Harriet Purvis, Jr., known as Hattie. Frances Harper had been born free and educated in Baltimore at her uncle's Watkins Academy, the place where Frederick Douglass was believed to have secretly furthered his education. Despite her education, Harper's first job had been that of a domestic servant, because of the limited occupational opportunities opened to even skilled Black women. In this sense, she shared the status of the illiterate Sojourner Truth, who had worked as a domestic slave and later as a domestic servant. In 1852, Harper left the South to join the abolitionist lecture circuit. She married, but by the end of the war, she was a widow with a young child, sharing this status with Mary Ann Shadd Cary. A poet, Harper became known during the antebellum period and the post–Civil War years as an outspoken reformer among Blacks and among women. She spoke in behalf of woman suffrage at the National Women's Rights Convention in May 1866. It was at this convention that the AERA was founded. Hattie Purvis attended this meeting as well. As a youth she had participated in the Philadelphia Female Anti-Slavery Society, along with her grandmother, mother, aunts, and cousins. A hard-working member of the AERA, Purvis served alternately as recording and corresponding secretary for the organization from 1867 to 1869, the last year the AERA met. She never married. Like several of the young elite and middle-class reformers of the times, Purvis spent much of her adult life working with Susan B. Anthony in the woman's movement.[35]

The demise of the AERA began with its conception, as the conflict developed among members over "Negro suffrage" versus woman suffrage. A dispute occasioned by proposals for the Fourteenth and the Fifteenth Amendments prompted several male abolitionists to call for a moratorium on demands for woman suffrage until "Negro suffrage" was achieved. Subsequent histories of the schism in the ranks accused these men of abandoning the women's cause. However, even Susan B. Anthony, a prominent leader among the "woman-suffrage-first" faction, rejected making such accusations. She felt that, despite the differences of political opinion over enfranchisement, those who had repudiated the woman suffragists for taking an opposite position during the schism years still believed in the principle of women's right to the ballot.[36] Unfortunately, Black men could not truly say that all the women who repudiated them still believed in the principle of universal suffrage. Nevertheless, the universal suffrage movement was divided permanently by the end of the conflict.

For the most part, the white female suffragists, who balked and left the AERA, blamed male abolitionists for sacrificing the woman suffrage cause for the sake of expedience. Black and white abolitionists of both sexes felt betrayed by these women. Black women remained quiet or divided among the prevailing factions. The evidence suggests that they seemed caught between the proverbial rock and hard place.

Ellen DuBois saw the division as a significant turning point in the women's movement as the woman-suffrage-first faction, led by Elizabeth Cady Stanton and Susan B. Anthony, took a new political posture. They called for an independent, more radical women's movement, separate from the Republican Party abolitionism that had sustained the movement prior to the war.[37] Despite the revolutionary nature of this political feminism, the new strategy needed to achieve woman suffrage pitted Black men against women in a racist way.

The manner in which Black women responded to the factionalization of the movement revealed how they were often torn between identifying with racial priorities or with gender priorities. The literature on the schism rarely refers to African American women, and when it does they are mentioned in passing. On the other hand, Black men as a topic has been a dominant theme. In discussing this literature, Bettina Aptheker noted that not only was sympathy for the Stanton-Anthony position evident in much of it, but a "racist current" was also apparent. She referred to Alma Lutz's perception of the schism specifically, wherein Lutz described Black men as "ignorant and utterly untrained in the principles of government." As a member of the third-generation woman suffragists, Lutz published an undocumented biography of Stanton in 1940. Lutz appeared outraged because Black male rights were given priority by the Republican Party over those of white women. As a result, she felt that men humiliated suffrage leaders such as Stanton and Anthony. Lutz concluded that women leaders learned that they had to fight their own battles without the help of former male allies. Like Aptheker, I have problems with Lutz's tone. More disturbing than Lutz is that feminist writers of the 1970s and 1980s took cues from her interpretation, justifying racism as expedient behavior on the part of white women, but often not justifying the pro–"Negro suffrage" male behavior as expedient. The parties most highly criticized in this debate are Black men.[38]

Elisabeth Griffith, looking at the question of racism over 100 years later, defended the behavior of Stanton during the controversy. Griffith felt that Stanton, who was one of the women to initiate the protests against the Fifteenth Amendment, became hostile toward Black men because she perceived them to behave exactly like white men. Griffith believed that to Stanton all men wanted to keep women subordinate. As a result of this assumption, Stanton attacked Black men on account of gender rather than race.[39] I disagree. The facts do not support this argument.

As early as 1865, signs of the factionalization in the universal suffrage movement could be observed. Name-calling and anti–Black male suffrage sentiments were heard frequently from whites, of whom the most outspoken were Elizabeth Cady Stanton and later her Democratic Party supporter George Francis Train. Name-calling was never directed against white men, however. In Stanton's letter to the *Anti-Slavery Standard*, she said, "In fact, it is better to be the slave of an educated white man, than of a degraded ignorant Black one."[40] During the heated 1867 Kansas debate over "Negro suffrage" and woman suffrage, Train argued before a largely Irish audience that giving the vote to Blacks was absurd, especially if white women were not enfranchised. It was in Kansas that Train decided to finance Stanton and Anthony's woman suffrage newspaper *The Revolution*, which frequently expressed anti-Black and anti-Republican sentiments.[41]

The 1867 Kansas campaign of woman suffrage was especially bitter, revealing the disillusionment of some African Americans as well as the positions on either side of the debate that they began to develop. Conflicting reports about Black support came from suffragist Lucy Stone. During April 1867 Stone appeared in Lawrence, Kansas, a community with a large Black population. She wrote Stanton that Black men there supported woman suffrage as well as "Negro suffrage," but she also made reference to "an ignorant Black preacher named Twine," who campaigned against woman suffrage.[42]

By the time the controversy over African American men and the woman suffrage campaign had reached the pages of the *History of Woman Suffrage* over a decade later, a subhead in chapter 19 set the tone for future readers—"Black men opposed to woman suffrage." This chapter on the 1867 Kansas suffrage campaign was written in the 1880s by suffragists who had been in the Kansas campaign, and from Stanton's and Anthony's recollections. It appears that many scholars and students of American women's history have taken this chapter at face value without looking at both sides of the controversy. On the other hand, students and scholars interested in discerning the effect of the Kansas campaign on African American history should detect a significant anti-Black bias among the editors of the *History of Woman Suffrage* as well as among the white suffragists whose recollections and letters contributed to the chapter. Constant reference to "ignorant and degraded black men" certainly must have alienated African Americans in Kansas, who were reported to have supported the woman suffrage referendum early in 1867.

Interpreting the 1867 Kansas suffrage campaign raises questions about which voice is authentic. The key to the answer is to acknowledge that there are several voices rather than just one, whereas some students in the past have acknowledged the white feminist voice as the only true voice. In Charles Langston, from the perspective of the African American struggle for human rights after the Civil War, another voice in the Kansas controversy is revealed.

Perhaps the most prominent African American male leader in Kansas at the time, Langston became disillusioned by the controversy between "Negro suffrage" and woman suffrage. A former slave from Virginia, he had been manumitted in 1834 after the death of his master, who was his father. Both he and his younger brother, John Mercer Langston, were among the noted Black abolitionists of Ohio, the state where they had settled after manumission. Charles attended Oberlin College for two years, becoming well known in the reform and Underground Railroad circles. After the Civil War, he migrated with his family to Kansas. In a biographical sketch of his life, Frank R. Levstik noted that Langston "advocated Negro suffrage and to a lesser degree, votes for women."[43]

Nonetheless, in 1882 suffragist Olympia Brown wrote Susan B. Anthony that she recalled Langston to be the orator who "added his mite of bitter words to make the path a little harder for women, who had spent years in pleading the cause of the colored man." Although Brown admitted that she had not maintained a diary or kept records about this campaign in Kansas fifteen years before, her references to Langston have led contemporary scholars of the woman suffrage movement to interpret him as being opposed to votes for women in Kansas. Interestingly, feminist scholars did not construe Brown's negative remarks about enfranchising African American men to be prejudiced and anti–Black civil rights. Nor have scholars believed that Lucy Stone was opposed to "Negro suffrage," when she made comments about Republicans who criticized those who opposed "Negro suffrage" as "unutterably contemptible from the lips or pen of those whose words, acts, and votes are not against ignorant and degraded negroes, but against every man's mother, wife, and daughter."[44] There appears to be a double standard for evaluating the rhetoric of those caught in the politics of the suffrage controversy, with the bitter words of Black men found unjustified and the defamatory words of white women found justifiable.

The question remains—why would Charles Langston speak bitterly about woman suffrage? Eugene H. Berwanger may have the answer in his research about Langston and the Black suffrage campaign in Kansas. He noted that Langston began his push for "Negro suffrage" in 1863, the year he organized the equal suffrage movement in the state. At a Black-sponsored convention held in Leavenworth in January of that year, Langston delivered a dramatic address that moved the participants to petition the legislature for the right to vote. The white legislature felt the issue was so controversial that they wanted to wait for the votes of the Kansas soldiers who were still at the battle front in the Civil War. This excuse was merely a stalling tactic, because when Langston led the petition effort again after the war, in 1866 the legislature felt the movement to enfranchise Black men was premature. Throughout 1866 Langston tried various approaches, from lobbying the

Republican state convention to lobbying the Republican candidate for governor, Samuel Crawford. None of these approaches succeeded; however, after his election, Crawford asked Kansas to vote on three different franchise propositions: one for the removal of the word "male" from the constitution, one for the removal of the word "white," and one for the disfranchisement of persons suspected of disloyalty during the Civil War.[45]

Senator Samuel Wood, a suffragist known to Stanton and Anthony, had originated the woman suffrage proposition to remove the word "male." Although white suffragists such as Henry Blackwell and his wife Lucy Stone praised Wood as a man who had not only supported women's rights, but had helped "more runaway slaves than any man in Kansas," they could not understand why Blacks disliked and distrusted him. Equal suffrage advocates, on the other hand, felt that Wood was aware of this political reality. African Americans specifically suspected Wood's motives. Their fears that Wood's primary focus would be toward winning woman suffrage at the expense of "Negro suffrage" came to pass with the activities of the Impartial Suffrage Association. As a result, Blacks were dismayed when nationally known woman suffragists invited by Wood canvassed the state on behalf of woman suffrage, while ignoring "Negro suffrage." Of the women, Olympia Brown was especially criticized in the white Republican press for first refusing to comment on "Negro suffrage" and then "disclaiming against placing the dirty, immoral, degraded Negro before a white woman."[46]

With the Black perspective on the suffrage controversy in mind, Langston's "mite of bitter words to make the path a little harder for women," seem more directed to Olympia Brown than to the idea that women should not have the right to vote. To make matters worse, Langston believed Wood deliberately attempted to discredit him in the eyes of the woman suffragists. Despite the fact that Langston had publicly supported woman suffrage and had persuaded a convention of Blacks in Highland, Kansas, to pass a resolution advocating "impartial suffrage without regard to sex or color," Wood charged that Langston opposed woman suffrage and had accused the white suffragists of attacking equal suffrage. In response to this charge, Langston wrote Wood, "You misrepresent me when you intimate that I think the friends of female suffrage are opposed to negro [sic] suffrage. . . . There is no antagonism between me and the friends of female suffrage [who] are seeking the defeat of colored suffrage." In addition, Langston threatened to hold Wood, not the white women, responsible if the "Negro suffrage" referendum was defeated. According to Lucy Stone biographer Andrea Moore Kerr, Sam Wood had voted against "Negro suffrage" in the Kansas state legislature every year since 1862. Wood was indeed against enfranchising Black men.[47]

How Black women in Kansas felt about the controversy remains to be determined. Berwanger does not discuss other persons in the equal suffrage movement, nor those in attendance at the Black conventions held in the state. The editors of the *History of Woman Suffrage* do not discuss the politics of Black women in Kansas either. Nonetheless, the rhetoric of the woman suffrage advocates, or the supporters of impartial suffrage on the one hand, and the advocates of "Negro suffrage" or equal suffrage on the other, was powerfully charged with distrust and emotion. Indication of disillusionment among Black universal suffragists outside of Kansas is also apparent. None of them joined the Kansas suffrage campaign, though Frederick Douglass and Frances Harper had been invited. Both refused to go to Kansas. Interestingly, Stanton criticized Douglass, not Harper, for not going to Kansas to support woman suffrage. This failure to admonish Harper revealed that Stanton really felt Douglass, a Black man, to be more important to the movement than Harper, a Black woman.[48]

In the meantime, during the summer of 1867, the AERA convened in New York City, where several women expressed anti–Black male sentiments similar to the ones voiced in Kansas. Sojourner Truth was the only Black woman noted among this group. Chroniclers reported her fear that the enfranchisement of Black men and not Black women in the South would leave the men "masters over the women, and it will be just as bad as it was before." Furthermore, Truth was alleged to have accused the freedmen of being lazy while she described the freedwomen as hard-working. However, unlike several of the white women who spoke, such as Frances Gage and Stanton, Truth argued, they recalled, for the enfranchisement of Black men and Black women.[49] It is not surprising that Stanton and Anthony would remember Truth's sentiments, because except for her pro–Negro suffrage argument, Truth was reported to have aligned with the editors' position.

Truth's alignment with the pro–woman suffrage faction appeared to be evident earlier that year, when she was alleged to express her impatience with abolitionist newspaper editors Horace Greeley and Theodore Tilton. Both men supported women's rights, but during the Kansas controversy over "Negro suffrage," neither man publicly advocated the woman suffrage platform. According to the chroniclers, Truth said that if she could write, she would publish "Sojourner Truth on Suffrage," and that her great desire was to "sojourn once to the ballot-box before I die."[50]

Once again questions must be raised about why white female suffragists continued to quote Truth. They seemed to find an illiterate Black woman more compatible than the several educated ones in the universal suffrage movement. Could it be that whites felt they could not manipulate the voices of literate Black women as easily as they could the voice of one who could not read?

Despite the controversy during the 1867 AERA convention, it closed

with the officers signing a memorial to Congress calling for the enfranchisement of all women and Black men. Although the delegates appeared to have
departed from the convention in harmony, the battle continued. By September, George Train was campaigning in Lawrence, Kansas, the town where six
months earlier Lucy Stone had noted that Black men supported the woman
suffrage referendum and "Negro suffrage." Train repudiated Republicans
and "Negro suffrage" and called Black men ignorant and degraded. In the
meantime, Stone was back in New York City running the AERA office. She
begged Anthony not to use AERA funds to assist George Train in campaigning against "Negro suffrage," but Anthony ignored Stone. This tactic alienated all the Republicans in the state of Kansas. With the controversy and
factionalism, both "Negro suffrage" and woman suffrage referendums failed.[51]

By the 1868 AERA convention in New York, the gap had widened.
Stanton and other suffragists in Kansas had apparently angered most AERA
members, mainly because they insisted on primacy for woman suffrage
instead of universal suffrage. In anticipation of a bitter fight during the 1869
convention, Stanton reported promising Anthony that she would send letters
to all the old friends of the movement asking them to forget the past. Despite
the efforts toward reconciliation between the abolitionists and the feminists,
expediency characterized the tone of the convention. Even then, very little
was heard from the Black women other than words reported about Sojourner Truth, although African American females were present during the proceedings. It was at the 1869 meeting in New York City that Frances Harper joined the controversy, taking the "Negro suffrage" position. The
inability of the leaders to compromise forced delegates like Harper to take
sides publicly. In the process, she risked alienating the pro–woman suffrage
group of white women.[52]

Harper was not alone among women at this convention who expressed disagreement with the position that women should be enfranchised
before Black men. Lucy Stone and abolitionist feminist Abby Kelly Foster
were among the few white women who spoke in favor of the Fifteenth
Amendment (although Stone seemed less favorable to enfranchising Black
men when she was in Kansas). Nonetheless, Harper appears to have been the
most outspoken Black woman present at the convention. Her comments
revealed her disillusionment with the priorities set by the white feminists,
who often attempted to speak for African Americans. Harper agreed with
those Black male suffragists who felt the political climate of opinion in
Congress was most favorable to the enfranchisement of African American
men, but not women. Although she dearly sought the ballot, Harper was
quoted as having said, "When it was a question of race [I] let the lesser question of sex go. But the white women all go for sex, letting race occupy a
minor position."[53] This nationalist position reflected concerns expressed

years before by Nancy Prince, and set the stage for future nationalist feminist sentiments to come.

Harper's statement applied well to women such as Susan B. Anthony, who felt hurt by the stand her dear friend Frederick Douglass took in favor of the Fifteenth Amendment. On the other hand, Harper supported Douglass throughout the convention, as he took issue with the anti-Black name-calling on the part of radical suffragists and their refusal to stop attacking Black people and the Fifteenth Amendment. When white suffragist Paulina W. Davis attacked the amendment because she felt that it would result in a "race of tyrants" raised above the women in the South, and that Black women would be treated worse by Black men than by whites, Douglass and Harper disagreed vehemently. Harper's final recorded response came after Stanton declared that she could not allow "ignorant Negroes and foreigners to make laws for her to obey." In noting Frances Harper's answer to Stanton, the AERA recorders wrote, "If the nation could only handle one question, [Harper] would not have Black women put a single straw in the way, if only the men of the race could obtain what they wanted."[54]

Bettina Aptheker has analyzed the Fifteenth Amendment controversy and believes that the effect of the amendment could have rebounded to the benefit of women. However, the self-interests of different oppressed groups prevented them from realizing how to use the AERA to support both a Fifteenth Amendment to enfranchise Black men and a Sixteenth Amendment to enfranchise all women.[55] Needless to say, self-interests prevailed.

Significantly, Black women represented both oppressed groups, forcing women like Harper to choose between nationalist and feminist issues when they were in conflict. In this battle, Harper felt compelled to take a nationalist position, which she clearly articulated to her cohorts. Nell Painter has discovered speeches Harper delivered during the AERA conventions that were not published in the official proceedings. Painter analyzes the difference between Truth and Harper in relationship to what the chroniclers of the woman suffrage movement chose to print about each woman. Painter concludes that Harper refused to separate her race from her sex. Furthermore, Harper challenged the elitist views and goals of the white women leaders. Unlike Truth, Harper did not fit the image of Black womanhood that these feminists wanted to project to the American people. Consequently, the chroniclers excluded Harper's speeches from their published proceedings.[56]

By the close of the convention, Stanton led the minority of anti–Fifteenth Amendment women away from the AERA to form the National Woman Suffrage Association. Although Stanton and Anthony, leaders of the newly formed woman suffrage group, opposed accepting males, several unnamed women refused to join the organization unless men could also be admitted. The leaders compromised by accepting male members, but no man ever held an official position in the organization. Discord among suffragists continued, and by November 1869 Lucy Stone and Henry Ward Beecher had founded another group, the American Woman Suffrage Association, in opposition to the political views and strategies of the NWSA. The larger of the two groups, the AWSA was in reality an outgrowth of the New England Woman Suffrage Association, founded with a pro–Republican Party and abolitionist platform. The organization attempted to keep the woman suffrage issue from interfering with the Republican Party–supported "Negro suffrage" cause. The AWSA platform was similar. On the other hand, the NWSA divorced itself entirely from the Republican Party and the "Negro suffrage" question, concentrating on woman suffrage and other issues of concern to feminists. In reality the AWSA argued that universal suffrage should be the goal. With the ratification of the Fifteenth Amendment in 1870, the AWSA turned exclusively to suffrage issues—the gaining of woman suffrage and universal suffrage. In looking at factors of representation, including size of membership, budget, and political impact, Stone biographer Kerr challenges modern-day historians who fuse national woman suffrage history with the NWSA. Kerr finds the AWSA to be more representative of woman suffragists.[57]

The response of veteran Black female suffragists to the split varied. Frances Harper became a founding member of the AWSA and apparently did not attend NWSA meetings. On the other hand, Harriet and Hattie Purvis continued to participate with their old friend Susan B. Anthony in the NWSA, with Hattie in later years becoming the first African American woman to be elected vice president of the association. This is not surprising, for her father, Robert Purvis, was one of the few outspoken Black men to criticize the Fifteenth Amendment for failing to include women. Sojourner Truth frequented AWSA and also attended some NWSA meetings, whereas Sarah Remond appeared to be disillusioned by it all and became an expatriate in Florence, Italy, where she studied medicine. The remaining old guard of African American females continued to take a more militant feminist position than did others during the 1870s.[58]

As the decade of the 1860s came to an end, there was evidence of twenty years of African American woman suffrage activism among fifteen women representing two generations. Several of them were related—sisters, mothers and daughters, or aunts and nieces. Several had joined with their husbands, fathers, or brothers, in the struggle for universal suffrage. The known African Americans in this first generation of woman suffragists included the following women, several of whom were related to one another:

Mary Ann Shadd Cary and Amelia Shadd (sisters)
Margaretta Forten, Sarah Forten, and Harriet Forten Purvis (sisters)

Charlotte Forten and Harriet (Hattie) Purvis, Jr. (Forten nieces)
Frances Ellen Watkins Harper
Nancy Prince
Sojourner Truth

Conclusion

As the era of the first generation of woman suffragists drew to a close, several competing voices emerged. There were middle-class white woman suffragists who focused on "woman suffrage first." There were middle-class whites and African Americans of the Republican Party who focused on universal suffrage. There was the voice of Sojourner Truth, which was often manipulated by others who represented her in ways they created, rather than as she really was. The voices of other Black women, like Frances Harper and Sarah Remond, who were literate and often spoke to issues of race as well as gender, appeared to be silenced by the woman suffragists who later reconstructed the history of the movement and recorded it for posterity.

The dichotomous representations of African American women and the conflicting representations of Black men who were suffragists have been filtered into the historiography of both women's history and Black history so that interpretations have developed that appear to be oblivious of one another. In the conflicting historiography, Black histories of the past saw African American men and women as advocates of the early woman suffrage movement. Women's histories, especially those of the recent past, historicize African American women in ways that often distort their voices and participation in the movement.

In attempting to reconcile the dichotomy, I have heard the metalanguage of African Americans, for which others often see opposing meanings. I have heard the silenced voices of African Americans, which provide evidence of their positions about woman suffrage and universal suffrage that disagree with the interpretations chroniclers and histories have provided. In addition, the evidence raises questions about how white woman suffragists in particular were imprisoned by the sexist society they challenged, especially when they found the words and actions of African American men, such as Frederick Douglass and Robert Purvis, more important to record and critique than they did the actions of their African American women peers, like Sarah Remond and Hattie Purvis.

As the nineteenth century entered its last quarter, African American women's voices began to be heard and read. Whether because of their previous omission, or because of their developing actions as nationalist feminists, new Black women's voices with messages similar to, but often different from those of their white cohorts, became evident.

Chapter 3. African American Woman Suffragists Finding Their Own Voices: 1870s and 1880s

Day after day did Milly Green
  Just follow after Joe,
And told him if he voted wrong
  To take his rags and go.

—Frances Ellen Watkins Harper, 1872.[1]

In the period following the collapse of the American Equal Rights Association, African American women's voices became more evident as their views about woman suffrage began to differ from those of white women. Even the watersheds in the movement differed for the two groups. For white women, the schism that had resulted with the birth of two rival national woman suffrage associations ended in 1890, when the two organizations reunited to achieve votes for women. For Black women the turning point began in the 1870s and 1880s, as their suffrage arguments took on new meaning, more closely identified with their unique status as women of color. They never abandoned the universal suffrage cause, as did many mainstream suffragists. As a result, African American woman suffrage strategies combined demands for Black women's right to vote and civil rights for all Black people. Even when African American women adopted the strategies of the larger woman suffrage movement—demanding suffrage based on the citizenship clause of the Fourteenth Amendment, or calling for a federal amendment to enfranchise women—they included caveats specifically designed for the needs of Black women. The present discussion, in seeking to identify authentic Black women's voices, looks at the differences in how Black women and white women perceived suffrage goals in the 1870s and 1880s.

The New Departure

Following the split that caused the demise of the AERA, the woman-suffrage-first faction became more militant in its strategy to obtain

Frances Ellen Watkins Harper was a founding member of the American Woman Suffrage Association. *Moorland-Spingarn Research Center, Howard University*

the vote for women. During the first five years after the split, from 1869 to 1874, the strategy this faction adopted aimed to reinterpret the Fourteenth Amendment, which had introduced the word "male" into the Constitution, yet had guaranteed the right to vote to all citizens of the United States. Missouri suffragists Virginia Minor and her husband Francis took the lead in developing a controversial strategy, the "new departure," which was an attempt to use the Constitution and its definition of citizenship to enfranchise women. Elisabeth Griffith notes how Elizabeth Cady Stanton remained in the midst of this controversy, stimulating women-centered awareness, yet alienating former friends and allies with her offensive statements. Nonetheless, militant suffragists, both Black and white, mobilized to implement the new ideas fostered by Stanton and others.[2]

Even before the implementation of the new plan, suffragists had used a modified strategy, which can be described more as a mock political exercise to dramatize women's desires to vote as citizens of the United States. In 1868, the women suffragists of Vineland, New Jersey, set up voting tables across from the platform where the election officials were accepting male ballots. The women had tried unsuccessfully to cast their votes, and when rejected decided on a unique strategy to indicate their protest against disfranchisement. On that election day, 172 women cast mock ballots. Of this group, four were Blacks.[3]

The 1868 New Jersey case appears to have been an isolated event;

however, by 1870 Stanton testified that women should challenge the Fourteenth Amendment. She urged women to register, to vote, and if necessary, to go to court and to jail in defense of their right to the ballot. Significantly, Stanton was unable actually to practice this confrontational strategy. It took a charismatic person like Victoria Woodhull to restate the Stanton argument at the 1871 NWSA convention in the District of Columbia, and to incite Black and white suffragists to implement the strategy. Woodhull also called the tactic the "new departure."[4]

Like the NWSA leaders, several African American women were impressed with the new strategy. At least three Blacks can be identified by name, Mary Ann Shadd Cary of the District of Columbia, Sojourner Truth of Battle Creek, Michigan, and Mrs. Beatty of Portland, Oregon.

Veteran suffragist Mary Ann Shadd Cary had many talents as a journalist, teacher, politician, and law student. In 1869, at the age of forty-six, she had decided to study law and became the first woman student at the newly founded Howard University Law School. She studied in the evenings and taught in the District of Columbia school system in the daytime. During the early 1870s, Cary earned additional income as an agent for *The New National Era,* Frederick Douglass's Black newspaper in the District of Columbia. On summer trips sponsored by the *Era* throughout the South and the East, Cary carried the news about reform and Republican Party politics. Her articles offered feminist strategies aimed to educate public opinion, and feminist commentary upon the economic and the political conditions of African Americans in the District of Columbia. Her speeches, and the items about her in the local Black press, revealed her ideas about woman suffrage.[5]

Although listed in the Howard University law class of 1871-72, Cary was not permitted to graduate because the District legal code limited admission to the bar to men only. Charging sex discrimination, she temporarily ended her law school study. In the meantime, Charlotte E. Ray of New York City completed the law course at Howard. Fortunately for her, the District code struck the word "male" as a qualification for bar admission by the time of her graduation. Yet to be on the safe side, when her name was submitted by Howard University officials to the bar for acceptance, the school, remembering the problems Cary had with sex discrimination, recommended "C. E. Ray," instead of listing her full first name. Bar officials did not realize that Ray was female until after accepting her name. In the meantime, Cary, after suffering for a decade with financial problems, finally returned to Howard University and graduated with her law degree at the age of sixty.[6]

Invoking the ideas of the "new departure," but with a race-specific twist, Cary's unpublished testimony before the House Judiciary Committee contains her views on woman suffrage. In arguing for the right to vote in

Mary Ann Shadd Cary was an advocate of the "new departure" and was perhaps the first African American woman suffragist to organize a suffrage association for Black women. *Moorland-Spingarn Research Center, Howard University*

1872, Cary clearly applied the Fourteenth and Fifteenth Amendments to Black women, as well as to Black men. She believed that with emancipation, Black men and women realized the same responsibilities needed for survival. Although Cary felt the amendments were "otherwise grand in conception," they left the women of her race only nominally free because they were denied the right to vote. In this nationalist context, Cary's woman suffrage ideology related specifically to African American women. However, she shrewdly redirected her argument in keeping with the mainstream suffragists by noting how all women were discriminated against as long as the word "male" remained in the two amendments. Consequently, Cary called for an amendment to strike the word "male" from the Constitution.[7]

Cary's speech had the sound of a legal argument, reflecting her professional training. Her testimony spoke specifically about why Black women in the District of Columbia needed the vote. Using herself as an example, Cary noted that she was a taxpayer with the same obligations as the male taxpayers of the city. Therefore, she felt suffrage should be her right just as it was theirs. Cary noted that many women of her race in the nation's capital supported woman suffrage and that they too called for the striking of the word "male" from the Constitution.[8] Her position was definitely an NWSA stand against the interpretation of the Fourteenth Amendment. Cary's reference to other Black women who supported her position, however, is an important clue to the fact that more than the three identifiable African American women had welcomed the "new departure."

Other NWSA women challenged the Fourteenth Amendment by attempting to register to vote. The most celebrated case occurred in 1872, when Susan B. Anthony and several Rochester, New York, women registered and attempted to vote. Anthony and her colleagues were all arrested for registering "illegally," found guilty, and fined. The same year Sojourner Truth went to the Battle Creek, Michigan, polls on election day to assert her right to vote; however, she did not succeed in her effort to cast a ballot. Truth and her grandson had managed to acquire enough money to purchase a small house in Battle Creek, where they lived when not touring the country. In addition to Truth in Michigan, Abigail Scott Duniway and two other white suffragists joined Mrs. Beatty (referred to by the chroniclers as a "colored" woman) in their unsuccessful attempt to register. Like Truth and Beatty, Cary was unsuccessful in her attempt to register to vote in 1871. However, Cary and sixty-three other Washington, D.C., women prevailed upon the elections officials to sign affidavits indicating that the women had tried to vote. Unlike the Rochester women, the Washington women were not arrested for asserting their right to the ballot, and the elections officials gave them the requested affidavits.[9]

Several reasons may account for the differences in how the Rochester and Washington women were treated. First, Susan B. Anthony was a nationally known figure, who publicized her attempt to register to vote. The white men in political power felt the need to set an example by her imprisonment and conviction. On the other hand, by 1871 the District of Columbia had obtained home rule; large numbers of Black men voted, and several of them served on the city council, including Frederick Douglass. Perhaps the election officials were sympathetic to the women and their cause. Indeed, in 1870, the Black election officials in certain districts in South Carolina had encouraged Black women to register to vote.[10] Black District of Columbia election officials may have been influenced by these events.

One strategy used by Blacks as well as whites to obtain the ballot for women was an appeal for female enfranchisement based on the Fifteenth Amendment. In 1872, white suffragist Mary Olney Brown of Washington state wrote a letter to Frederick Douglass, editor of the *Era*. Offering an emotional plea for African American male support of the vote for Black women, Brown argued that the Fifteenth Amendment, which had enfranchised Black men in 1870, should be applied to the enfranchisement of women because it did not exclude them in the definition of citizenship. Douglass printed the letter, wherein Brown encouraged voting Black men to support her strategy. This appears to be the first of many efforts by white suffragists to reestablish the political coalition they had severed with African American men. The rarity of their attempts at rapprochement with African American women reveals the degree to which white woman suffragists believed Black men to be more influential than Black women.[11]

Brown's strategy to demand suffrage as woman's legal right, a strategy frequently employed in the 1870s, could very well have come from journalist Mary Ann Cary. She was an example of the women Ellen DuBois calls radical feminists, who emerged in the 1870s as independent suffragists.[12]

Radical suffragists abandoned the "new departure" strategy with the losses of the Anthony case and, more important, the Minor voting rights case. Virginia Minor, president of the Missouri Woman Suffrage Association, and her husband, Francis, sued the St. Louis registrar for refusing to allow Virginia to vote in 1872. The couple took their case to the United States Supreme Court, but lost the suit in 1874. Afterwards the NWSA suffragists realized they needed another strategy. By 1877 they had returned to seeking a new constitutional amendment to prohibit disfranchisement based on sex. This time, it was a call for the Sixteenth Amendment to enfranchise all women. The goal was a woman suffrage amendment, not a universal suffrage amendment, which in itself should have been troubling to African Americans and others who were committed to this broader amendment. Ellen DuBois analyzes the new goal and its implementation to be "elitist and racist."[13] Indeed, the strategy elicited less resistance from the body politic as a whole because of its more conservative character.

Continuing her fight for woman suffrage, Mary Ann Shadd Cary wrote the NWSA in 1876 on behalf of ninety-four Black women from the District of Columbia. Her letter requested that their names be enrolled in the July 4th centennial autograph book as signers of the Woman's Declaration of Sentiments, which called for the immediate enfranchisement of American women. Although the editors of the *History of Woman Suffrage* made note of the letter, the names of the Black women were not included. Hence they remain anonymous. Yet there appeared to be growing political awareness among African American women, at least in the nation's capital. By the 1878 NWSA convention, Cary announced that African American women were determined to obtain the right to vote and that they "would support whatever party would allow them their rights, be it Republican or Democratic." Cary, who had been a staunch Republican since after the Civil War, reflected the disillusionment of African Americans, rather than the disillusionment of white suffragists. The Hayes Compromise of 1877 brought Reconstruction to a final end and signaled the laissez-faire policy toward the South, which ended the growing political influence of African Americans nationwide. Cary continued to develop a Black nationalist feminist perspective, using her own voice—one that reflected the interests of her people, especially the women.[14]

African American Woman Suffragists in the Postschism Era

Little remains of any published data about the views of Black female suffragists during the postbellum period. Nonetheless, several new names can be added to the growing list of African American feminists from throughout the nation. From 1865 to 1875, African American women—both veteran suffragists and new recruits—affiliated with the two rival national associations. Despite the assumptions modern-day writers have about Black women's participation in the two groups, a larger known number selected the AWSA than the NWSA.[15] Of the known African American women who participated in the two national organizations during the 1870s, nine selected the AWSA and six selected the NWSA:

AWSA: Charlotte Forten
        Frances Ellen Watkins Harper
        Mrs. K. Harris★
        Caroline Remond Putnam★
        Charlotta (Lottie) Rollin★
        Louisa Rollin★
        Josephine St. Pierre Ruffin★
        Sojourner Truth
        Frances Rollin Whipper★

NWSA: Naomi Talbert Anderson★
        Mrs. Beatty
        Mary Ann Shadd Cary
        Harriet Purvis
        Hattie Purvis
        Charlotte E. Ray★

★Women new to the woman suffrage movement.

Whether even more Black women affiliated is not clear, since the trend among white suffrage leaders to write-out the views of Black female suffragists continued. For the most part, African American women's opinions were not recorded, and some women remain anonymous. Of the new names, two came from Massachusetts, where Blacks as well as whites campaigned for woman suffrage. In Massachusetts, unlike many other northern states, notably New York and Pennsylvania, Black men retained the right to vote throughout the antebellum years. During the 1860s and 1870s, six African

Josephine St. Pierre Ruffin, abolitionist and journalist, joined the Massachusetts Woman Suffrage Assocation in 1875. *A New Negro for a New Century (1900), Anacostia Museum, Smithsonian Institution*

American men served in the Massachusetts House of Representatives. All of them represented predominantly Black districts, and all supported the various woman suffrage bills that came through the legislature, but failed.[16] It appears that there was a politically motivated Black community living in Boston in particular, and that woman suffrage was an issue consistently supported by the African Americans living in the respective voting districts. Although Black women, as all women, could not vote in Massachusetts, it is safe to say that by the postbellum period they were more politically aware than those in other areas of the nation, because their men could vote. For this reason, it is surprising that more names of African American suffragists were not found for Massachusetts during this period. Perhaps unknown Black women attended meetings without official positions in the woman suffrage organizations. Nonetheless, the two who participated in leadership positions in the state woman suffrage movement were Caroline Remond Putnam and Josephine St. Pierre Ruffin, both educated, affluent women from prominent African American families.

Putnam was a sister of Charles and Sarah Remond. A successful businesswoman, she operated a ladies' hair salon and wig factory in Salem, where most of the clients were white. As a delegate from Salem, Putnam attended the founding meeting of the Massachusetts Woman Suffrage Association, an affiliate organization of the AWSA. This group was organized in January 1870, under the auspices of the AWSA, with Julia Ward Howe, a white abolitionist, as president. Putnam was elected a member of the executive committee of the first board; however, her views about suffrage were not recorded. Presumably she continued her activities in this suffrage association until 1885, when like her sister Sarah, she became an expatriate in Italy.[17]

The Remond sisters' departure from the United States suggests the hopelessness they must have felt about African American women ever achieving equity in their homeland. Unlike most Black women, the Remonds could afford to leave America, as could their brother Charles. However, he remained with his family in the United States and died in Salem in 1874.

Ruffin began her association with the Massachusetts Woman Suffrage Association in 1875. The wife of George L. Ruffin, one of the pro–woman suffrage representatives from Boston in the state legislature, Josephine had been noted as an abolitionist before the Civil War, and would later become a journalist and a Black women's club leader. In later years, she explained that she affiliated with the Massachusetts suffragists because of the warm welcome she received from Lucy Stone, Julia Ward Howe and other movement leaders. Ruffin noted that these white women were wise enough to "include no distinction because of race with no distinction because of sex," as prerequisites for membership in their suffrage organization.[18] These words, spoken in Ruffin's own voice, indicate in a subtle way that African American women were reluctant to seek membership in white women's organizations, fearing rejection. There should be no question about whose was the authentic voice in this case when an African American woman contemporary to the times raised the issue of racism among some persons in the organized woman suffrage movement.

Unlike Massachusetts, South Carolina was not a traditional feeding ground for abolitionists and woman suffragists. Nonetheless, once Reconstruction enabled Blacks to participate effectively in government, several men and women championed woman suffrage. As in Massachusetts, by 1868 Black men could vote in the state; they retained that right until disfranchised in the 1890s. Not surprising, the first South Carolina delegate to a national woman suffrage convention was a Black woman. She was Charlotte Rollin, known as Lottie, of Charleston, who along with her sisters, Frances and Louisa, influenced Reconstruction politics in the South Carolina state capital of Columbia during the late 1860s and 1870s. Frances married William J. Whipper, who as a delegate to the South Carolina Constitutional Convention of 1868, pleaded for the enfranchisement of women as well as Black men. Louisa Rollin spoke on the floor of the South Carolina House of Representatives in 1869 to urge support of universal suffrage. By 1870 Lottie Rollin had been elected secretary of the newly organized South Carolina Woman's Rights Association, and in 1871 she led a meeting at the state capital to promote woman suffrage. The following year she represented South Carolina as an ex officio member of the executive committee of the AWSA.[19]

The South Carolina suffrage group's affiliation with the AWSA was predictable because the political strategy and the membership of the two groups were similar. Like the AWSA, the South Carolina Woman's Rights Association was Republican in party affiliation and included male as well as female members and officers. Of the fifteen delegates cited as either speakers or elected officials, at least three were Black men and four were Black women. In addition to Lottie Rollin, Mrs. Alonzo J. Ransier and Mrs. Robert C. Delarge, the wives of African American Congressmen from South Carolina, were elected vice presidents. Mrs. K. Harris, the wife of a Black Charleston minister, was elected treasurer.[20]

The coalition among African American men and women suffragists in South Carolina is not surprising. The African American men of the state had been enfranchised before the ratification of the Fifteenth Amendment; hence the final goal of this universal suffrage organization remained the enfranchisement of women.[21] With this goal in mind, Lottie Rollin addressed the chair of the 1870 convention, held in Charleston. Her words became the first from an African American woman, other than Sojourner Truth, to be preserved in writing by the chroniclers of the national woman suffrage movement leaders. Rollin exhorted,

> We ask suffrage not as a favor, not as a privilege, but as a right based on the ground that we are human beings, and as such entitled to all human rights. While we concede that woman's ennobling influence should be confined chiefly to home and society, we claim that public opinion has had a tendency to limit woman's sphere to too small a circle, and until woman has the right of representation this will last and other rights will be held by an insecure tenure.[22]

Rollin's words reflected the traditional African American rationale that women were second-class citizens who needed the vote to improve their status in society. It also revealed a significant recurring theme among the voices of Black feminists—the concern with human rights, or in this case universal suffrage, rather than identification with women's rights exclusively.

The goals of the South Carolina Woman's Rights Association exemplified the model Bettina Aptheker used for examining how effective a universal suffrage coalition of men and women could be if gender primacy was not the suffrage goal. Although the Black men in the South Carolina organization had achieved the right to vote with the writing of the new state constitution and women had not, their focus was then directed to enabling their women to obtain that right. When women did not obtain the right to vote in 1868, they did not reject the men who had the ballot, but combined to work for it with those sympathetic to their plight. Nonetheless, the existence of a woman suffrage association in one of the reconstructed former confederate states was unique for the period. An association of men and women with Black female leadership was also quite significant for the times. However, when considering that Louisiana and South Carolina were the two most progressive southern states with sizable Black leadership, it is not surprising that delegates from these states would be among the first to attend AWSA meetings in the 1870s. Whether Laura L. D. Jacobs, the Louisiana delegate to the AWSA Convention in Cleveland was Black or white, I do not know.[23] Nonetheless, no female delegates from reconstructed states appear to have attended NWSA meetings immediately following the founding of the rival woman suffrage organizations. The fact that the AWSA had supported the Fifteenth Amendment may have been one reason why Republican suffragists in the former confederate South were more attracted to the AWSA than to the NWSA, for the Fifteenth Amendment had been the brainchild of the Republican Party. Besides, during this period, the AWSA leadership seemed more interested than the NWSA in recruiting suffrage associations from the South.

However, affiliating with one of the national woman suffrage organizations was not the only strategy used by African American woman suffragists living in the South. Independent suffragists used traditional strategies such as petitioning the federal government in coalition with their men. A good example of this strategy is found in a petition in the National Archives, circa 1870. The document holds several clues to the ways in which the African American elite in the District of Columbia identified themselves and exerted political influence. The petition was addressed "To the Senate and House of Representatives" on a form with spaces to be filled in by the group of individuals who signed the petition. This format indicated that several of the documents, "Petition for Woman Suffrage," had been reproduced and circulated. The petition read:

> The undersigned, Citizens of the United States, Residents of the *Dist. of Col.*, County of _____, Town of *Union Town* earnestly pray your Honorable Body to adopt measures for so amending the C onstitution as to prohibit the several States from Disfranchising United States Citizens on account of Sex.[24]

The petition form divided the signatories by gender, a customary practice of the times. However, the signers wished to identify themselves by adding the word "Colored" to the categories for "men" and "women." Frederick Douglass, Jr. and his wife, who signed her name "Mrs. Frederick Douglass, Jr.," headed the lists. Only one other woman used her husband's name, and she was Mrs. Nathan Sprague, Frederick Douglass's daughter Rosetta Douglass Sprague. However, seven additional women used the titles "Mrs." or "Miss" before signing both their first and last names. There were no "x" marks in either column, indicating that all of the signatories were literate, probably elite African Americans who lived in the affluent Anacostia suburb of the city. There were eighteen names of women signers. All were new to my list of African Americans, and appeared to be independent woman suffragists. In keeping with the characteristics of earlier Black woman suffragists, several of these women were relatives of other petition signers. This rare find revealed how elusive are the records of Black women suffragists of this era; however, it confirmed my suspicion that there were many more of these women to find in southern cities like Washington:

Mrs. Frederick Douglass, Jr.	Mrs. Nathan Sprague
Mrs. Julia Dorsey	Mrs. Eliza A. Spencer
Mrs. Sarrah A. Jones	Mrs. Mary V. Berry
Harriette H. Lee	Caroline Burnett
Jane Lawson	Alice Scott
Rozie Harris	Miss Celia Gray
Miss Elizabeth Chase	Mrs. Caroline Chase.

I can only speculate about these women's feminist and political sentiments. However, they appeared to be in the Frederick Douglass family network, where there was strong support for the Republican Party, the ratification of the Fifteenth Amendment, and universal suffrage.

Support for the Fifteenth Amendment and interest in southern women probably convinced Frances Ellen Watkins Harper to affiliate with the AWSA. In 1873, after returning from a tour of freedmen's communities in the reconstructed states of the South, she delivered the closing speech at the AWSA convention held in New York City. Harper declared that as "much as white women need the ballot, colored women need it more." Hence, she initiated a rationale that African American women would use in future arguments, distinguishing themselves from suffragists who were white. In addition, Harper indicted what she called the "ignorant and often degraded men" who subjected Black women in the South to arbitrary legal authority. Unlike the white women who used this term, Harper was referring to white authority for the most part. Acknowledging the progress already made by women of her race, Harper pleaded for equal rights and equal access to education for the African American women of the nation. Although there is no written record of Harper's address at the 1873 AWSA convention, she did attend, seated on the platform with the honored guests as a delegate from her state of birth—Maryland.[25]

Harper's call for equal rights and equal access to educational opportunities for Black women may appear to be a conservative matter, but for the AWSA's one-issue politics—woman suffrage—adding Black women's economic and social plight must have seemed radical or inappropriate to some of the membership. Because Harper presented her case at the close of the 1873 convention, there may not have been time for discussion. Nonetheless, the AWSA records show no further discussion about this issue during subsequent conventions. Yet Harper and other Black women spokespersons considered the points important to the survival of their people. Theirs was a nationalist position, a Black survival issue.

The postbellum years had uprooted many Americans, especially the freedpeople, whose lives were often characterized by social disabilities. As a result, Harper was not alone in her concerns for her race. Sojourner Truth revived many of the old political remedies for new social ills as she observed the plight of the poor freedpeople who lived in the District of Columbia. Truth reasoned that instead of the District government spending money to imprison vagrants, officials could use the funds to provide adequate housing and education for them. Reportedly, in her narrative, she regretted that women had no political rights, for she believed that if "the voice of maternity" could be heard, "the welfare not only of the present generation, but of future ones, would be assured."[26] While in Topeka, Kansas, she spoke against the evils of intemperance, because like many Black women reformers of the times, Truth connected alcohol abuse to the political corruption of her people. Her strategy for solving this problem included politically empowering Black women. She asserted that they needed the suffrage and equal rights in order to succeed in correcting the evils of government. In this case, temperance laws would discourage politicians from using alcohol to buy votes. By 1871 Truth was in Battle Creek with other African Americans who celebrated the anniversary of the emancipation of the slaves of the British West Indies. On that occasion, she called for the enfranchisement of women. Her continuous connection of women's rights and Black rights was characteristic of African American women of the times, although it was not the goal of the major woman suffrage organizations with which Truth affiliated.[27]

Perhaps for this reason, not all Black female suffragists of the times identified with the AWSA, whose single goal was woman suffrage. Others who focused more on broader feminist issues and women's adversities remained independent or participated in the NWSA as the leadership directed the campaign and recruiting into the Midwest and the Far West. For example, in 1869 the NWSA called a convention in Chicago, where Naomi Talbert (later to become Naomi Anderson) was recruited from among the Black women and spoke from the platform. Anthony and Stanton published excerpts from her speech in *The Revolution*, but, true to tradition, identified her merely as a "colored woman." Talbert, who spoke in the classic Black oratorical style, addressed the convention:

> And gentlemen, I warn you no longer to stand out in refusing the right for which we contend; in trying to withhold from these noble ladies here and their darker sisters the franchise they now demand. Miss Anthony and Mrs. Stanton, with their high moral and intellectual power, have shaken the states of New England, and the shock is felt here today. . . . Woman has a power within herself, and the God that reigns above, who commanded Moses to lead the children of Israel from out the land of Egypt, from out the house of bondage, who walled the waters of the Red Sea, who endowed Samson with power to slay his enemies with the jawbone of an ass, who furnished Abraham Lincoln with knowledge to write the emancipation proclamation, whereby four millions of Blacks were free—that God, our God, is with and for us, and will hear the call of woman, and her rights will be granted, and she shall be permitted to vote.[28]

Talbert's identification with Stanton and Anthony, at a time when they severely criticized Blacks and the pending Fifteenth Amendment, offended many of the African Americans of Chicago. Talbert's biographer, Monroe Majors, noted in the 1890s that she was severely censured as a result. In an attempt to vindicate herself, Talbert wrote an article on woman suffrage that was published in the *Chicago Tribune*. Ironically, the article was quite similar to her speech at the convention, which probably did not endear her to her critics. Her position was radical for Blacks at the time, revealing her identification with white feminists on one hand, yet using words reminiscent of Sojourner Truth's religious exhortations on the other. Talbert seemed caught in her attempts to deal with the problems of racism and sexism at the same time. Nonetheless, both her speech and her newspaper article reflected nineteenth-century African American oratory and writing, in which religious symbolism was often connected to political issues.[29]

Characteristic of several Black feminists of the times, Talbert struggled throughout the 1870s to support her ailing husband and her family. She moved from Chicago to Portsmouth, Ohio, and learned the hairdressing trade. Carrying on another long nationalist tradition among African American women, she combined work and service to Black communities. In

Portsmouth she organized a home for orphaned Black children and continued to write and speak about the merits of temperance as well as woman
suffrage. Widowed before the end of the decade, by 1879 Talbert had
moved to Columbus, Ohio, where she met and married Lewis Anderson and
continued to lobby for women's rights.[30]

Similar to Talbert's growing awareness about the plight of Black
women, Mary Ann Shadd Cary continued an even more militant attack
on the oppressive system of racism and sexism. Unlike Harper, after the
demise of the American Equal Rights Association, Cary affiliated with the
NWSA and attended all the national conventions held in Washington during
the 1870s. While a law student, she met Charlotte E. Ray, daughter of
abolitionists Charlotte B. and Charles B. Ray of New York City. During
the 1860s, the elder Rays had been members of the AERA. It was perhaps
Cary's influence that stimulated their daughter to affiliate with the NWSA
rather than the AWSA, for Mr. and Mrs. Ray's names disappeared from the
national suffrage scene with the collapse of the AERA. Regrettably, few
details of the younger Ray's participation as a suffragist have survived. She
was reported to have participated in the NWSA discussions during the 1876
convention held in New York City, to ˉ .hich she returned after a failing law
career in the District of Columbia. Cary by this time had been an active
suffragist for twenty years. She was respected by the leadership and appointed
to the business committee in 1877.[31] Within a few years, however, Cary's
name no longer appeared among NWSA leadership.

In the meantime, NWSA affiliations began to spread among suffragists in the Pacific Northwest, as Susan B. Anthony traveled west to recruit.
In 1873 Mrs. Beatty attended the first annual convention of the Oregon State
Woman Suffrage Association. The convention met in Portland, and Beatty
was among the platform guests who addressed the body as woman suffrage
advocates. Her speech was not recorded; nonetheless, her presence indicated
the involvement and presence of Black women on the western woman
suffrage frontier during the formative period.[32] The question remains about
why Beatty's first name has not been found in any of the extant woman
suffrage reports. Two possible reasons come to mind. First, the invisibility
of Black women in general may have contributed to informants' inability
to remember her full name. Second, during the postbellum period and
the emancipation of all the enslaved, African American women sought the
respectability that mainstream society had denied them. Many, like the
women of Union Town outside of the District of Columbia, were reluctant
to use their first names, preferring to simply use the title Miss or Mrs., or
their first initials, with their last names, or to add Mrs. to their husband's
name. In this manner, white people in particular could not casually use the
women's first names as was the custom. I suspect Mrs. Beatty herself pro-

tected her first name by not making it known publicly. Certainly she was not an anomaly among African American suffragists in the West. However, nearly twenty years passed before additional written sources emerged that told of Black women suffragists west of the Mississippi River.

As the woman suffrage movement progressed into the 1880s, independent African American woman suffragists emerged, such as Mary A. McCurdy and Gertrude Bustill Mossell. McCurdy, like Sojourner Truth and Frances Harper a decade before, viewed intemperance as a major barrier to the uplift of her people. McCurdy edited a temperance newspaper while she lived in Richmond, Indiana, in 1884. A firm believer in woman suffrage, she saw the franchise as the means to prohibit the liquor traffic.[33] Unlike white women who joined the temperance movement in the 1880s and supported woman suffrage as a means to prohibition, McCurdy, like Black women before her, specifically viewed intemperance as a government ploy to keep Black people powerless. Nonetheless, her rhetoric was in keeping with the reform strategies mainstream suffragists developed during the times.

Another journalist, Gertrude Mossell, was consistent with other married African American women of her era and often wrote using her husband's initials—Mrs. N. F. Mossell. In 1885 she used traditional woman suffrage arguments when she initiated a woman's column in T. Thomas Fortune's Black newspaper the *New York Freeman*. Fortune, who was born a slave in Florida, had migrated to New York City after the Civil War. Like Frederick Douglass, he supported woman's rights activities by writing editorials that complimented his women columnist's ideas. Mossell was from a prominent Philadelphia antebellum, free Black family and was married to a physician. She can be characterized as among the Black elite. Her first article for the *Freeman* was entitled "Woman Suffrage," and in it she encouraged Blacks to read the *History of Woman Suffrage* (which had been published for the first time in 1881), the "New Era," the essays of British woman suffragist John Stuart Mill, and other works about woman's rights that would familiarize Blacks with the woman suffrage movement. Mossell praised Senator Henry W. Blaire of New Hampshire, who had sponsored a bill in the United States Senate calling for an amendment to enfranchise all citizens, regardless of sex. Consequently, Mossell was in step with other woman suffragists of her race who were calling for a federal amendment. In addition, Mossell encouraged other men to join Blair, and noted that most housewives had already embraced woman suffrage.[34]

Although Mossell's frame of reference was taken from the mainstream views in the woman suffrage movement, like McCurdy, she directed her argument to the Black community, via the Black press. Gertrude Mossell was born into the same circle as was Hattie Purvis, who was a teenager when

Gertrude was an infant. In addition, Mossell was a cousin of Sarah Douglass, an African American who had been a member of the Philadelphia Female Anti-Slavery society along with the Forten-Purvis women. Although younger than the abolitionist women, Mossell had traveled in similar arenas among white reformers. Hence her frame of reference initiated in their world. As an affluent mother of two, as well as a professional writer, like Stanton, she could relate to the middle-class views of housewives who were feminists. Nonetheless, by the 1880s, Mossell directed her argument to the African American women readers of the *Freeman*. It seems as though some of her words could have been spoken by Hattie Purvis, whose experience in the woman suffrage movement would have been extensive by the 1880s. Purvis was a member of the executive committee of the Pennsylvania Woman Suffrage Association in 1884, and between 1883 and 1900 she served as a delegate to the NWSA, and after the merger of the NWSA and the AWSA in 1890, to the NAWSA.[35] Unlike Mossell, who made her voice heard through the Black press, Purvis apparently did not. As a result, her views about woman suffrage remain unheard.

Conclusion

As the end of the 1880s approached, so did the formative years of the woman suffrage movement and a generation of Black women's involvement in the struggle. As the pioneers were joined by new recruits, at least thirty-five known Black women had petitioned for suffrage or participated actively in the movement during the first generation, with another 100 or more whose names remain unknown. By the mid-1880s, Nancy Prince, Margaretta Forten, Harriet Forten Purvis, and Sojourner Truth were dead. Sarah Remond had emigrated to Europe, with her sister Caroline Remond Putnam soon to follow. Other aging suffragists, such as Charlotte B. Ray, seemed to disappear from woman suffrage activities with the demise of the AERA. As the first generation of Black woman suffragists began to decline, however, a new more militant few began to emerge.

Nonetheless, during the last few years of the formative period, the names of African American women who were once prominent in the woman suffrage movement on a national level started to disappear from the national reports of the woman suffrage leadership. Several possible factors could have caused this trend. Either the white female leadership began not to need the support once sought from early Black suffragists, and leaders refrained from recruiting Blacks; or the African American women suffragists saw less benefit from affiliating with white suffragists whose political priorities differed from their own; or there was a combination of both factors at work, provoked by the growing racial polarization in the United States during the late nineteenth century. This polarization stimulated separate political directions among the woman suffragists of the two races. Despite the ideological split in the woman suffrage movement that divided even Black women in the early 1870s, before the 1880s the realities of racism and sexism brought African American women who were feminists to a new political awareness that was more nationalistic in character. As this politicization occurred, Black women remained woman suffrage activists, working with the mainstream suffragists on some levels, but also organizing on local and national levels among themselves. These organizations also brought their leaders into public view on local and national levels. What made the 1870s and 1880s significant, nonetheless, was the emergence of verifiably authentic Black women's voices, which reflect the growing Black nationalist feminism of the era.

Chapter 4. Suffrage Strategies and Ideas: African American Women Leaders Respond during "the Nadir"

> The Colored American believes in equal justice to all, regardless of race, color, creed or sex, and longs for the day when the United States shall indeed have a government of the people, for the people and by the people—even including the colored people.
>
> —Adella Hunt Logan, 1912[1]

From the late 1870s until the eve of the passage of the Nineteenth Amendment, African American women leaders in Black communities responded to feminism and currents observed in the woman suffrage movement, then developed their own strategies and ideas. Because the women were leaders in their communities, for the most part their voices were recorded and disseminated in print on local and national levels. Thus, they left a legacy of their political views during "the Nadir." Among scholars of African American history, this roughly forty-year period was known as a low rugged plateau in the history of Black people living in the United States. It was an era when race relations were extremely strained—the political period marked by presidential administrations from Rutherford B. Hayes to Woodrow Wilson.[2] For woman suffragists generally, this period witnessed not only the unification of national woman suffrage associations, but the rise of the Progressive Party and the First World War. African American woman suffragists seemed less focused on these issues and more concerned about solving the problems in their own communities through the political empowerment of their women.

For some, primarily those who spoke out in the late nineteenth century, suffrage strategies and ideas reflected those of middle-class white suffragists. Others can be characterized as more radical suffragists, in terms of

Adella Hunt Logan was a southern-born intellectual, a professor at the Tuskegee Institute, and a member of the National American Woman Suffrage Association. *Twentieth Century Negro Literature (1902), Anacostia Museum, Smithsonian Institution*

either their race chauvinism or their feminist views. For the most part, these were Black women who came of age at the turn of the century. Nonetheless, all the African American suffragists manifested principles designed to improve the status of Black women and their communities. As the woman suffrage movement progressed into the early twentieth century and the racial oppression of Black people intensified, African American women suffragists moved further away from the abstract nineteenth-century argument that suffrage was a human right that all people deserved, to focus more on what they perceived as the real issue—that African American women needed suffrage even more than white women, because Blacks were more heavily oppressed. Because their opinions were sought by other African Americans, these women reached a large audience, recruiting both men and women in Black communities to support woman suffrage. A look at the views of prominent African American spokeswomen, often expressed in their own voices, reveals the evolution of their ideas and strategies for winning the vote.

As the Reconstruction era ended, new awareness stimulated new strategies among all the suffragists. For the AWSA members, the state-by-state woman suffrage referenda strategy still appeared to be the best device for enfranchising American women; however, they also looked to a federal amendment as a strategy. African American women who affiliated with the AWSA sought venues for improving the lives as well as the political status of women of their race, finding the AWSA to be the more conducive of the two national groups for coalition building. As the Fourteenth Amendment strategy waned, Black women lobbied for a separate constitutional amendment that would include them as well as white women as voters. This argument was implemented in the late 1870s as the major strategy of the NWSA. For a decade, from 1877 to 1887, the suffragists pushed forcefully for a Sixteenth Amendment, finally abating this strategy with the fifth defeat of the congressional bill to propose a woman suffrage amendment.[3]

From then until 1890, suffragists acknowledged that they needed to unite in order to persuade Americans that woman suffrage was essential to democracy. As the rival suffrage associations united in 1890 to form the National American Woman Suffrage Association, they developed a compromise that brought more conservative strategies, which moved away from various feminist issues, to focus on women winning the vote. One of the strategies was to ignore the priorities of Black women, an expedient tactic designed to bring in white southern women who did not relish the idea of encouraging Black women to vote. Despite the movement to alienate African American women, several Black women continued to attend NAWSA meetings, while others concentrated their efforts on convincing their people that gaining political rights for Black women was a means to solving social and economic problems of the race. As the movement progressed into the twentieth century, African American women's voices clearly targeted their own political agendas.

In the meantime, Black institutions—the press, the church, the college—gained significantly during this time of "the Nadir," when racism became institutionalized nationwide. It is not surprising then, that the growing suffrage movement among Blacks was observable through African American women in these institutions. As Elsa Barkley Brown discovered for Richmond, Virginia, where Black men and women operated in both external and internal social and political arenas, so did African Americans in other jurisdictions all over the nation.[4] The woman suffrage movement was gaining national momentum, and with it the leadership sought to recruit white middle-class, native-born women at the expense of Black women, immigrant women, and working-class women of all races. As a result, many Black female suffragists were shut out. Some responded with more radical agendas that connected suffrage and the economy with the status of Black women.

For this nearly forty-year period, the complexity of woman suffrage strategies and ideas can be traced through the various experiences of the African American spokeswomen of the second and third generations of suffragists. They continued to reflect priorities secondary to middle-class white suffragists, who did not face the triple oppression of race, class, and sex discrimination.

Black Institutions as Venues for
Disseminating Woman Suffrage Ideas

From the last quarter of the nineteenth century through the early years of the new century, a growing number of educated African American women expanded their limited economic opportunities through employment in Black institutions that provided services to African Americans and also gave professional Black women visibility they could not have had in the mainstream society. These institutions included newspapers, churches, secondary schools, and colleges. Prior to the period, middle-class Black women were teachers in primary schools, with a few others as entrepreneurs and orators, mainly in reform and religious circles. The significant rise in the founding of Black colleges and universities such as Howard University, the Hampton Institute, Atlanta University, and the Tuskegee Institute, created not only a cadre of college-trained Black women by the end of the century, but also women previously educated in institutions such as Oberlin College serving as secondary school and college instructors.[5]

For the most part, the earliest African American suffragists in this group had been born free into families in which the men were skilled craftsmen, entrepreneurs, or professionals. These men had gained political and public experience from the abolitionist movement of the antebellum years and had educated their daughters. Yet women of slave lineage obtained education and leadership positions in Black communities within two decades after slavery was abolished. Consequently, as the nineteenth century drew to an end, a third generation of African American woman suffragists emerged. Like the first, it was diverse, yet the majority of the women were born into middle-class families. Unlike the whites of the third generation, who were often far removed from the reform tradition known to earlier suffragists, African American women were connected to the tradition in nationalist ways. They were eager to struggle for women's right to vote and to uplift their communities.

The testimonies of Frances Ellen Watkins Harper in 1873 and Mary Ann Shadd Cary in 1878 predated Black women's new course. As African American women shifted from the mainstream woman suffrage rationale, however, they constructed strategies designed to convince Blacks that African American women needed the vote to help their communities. With this approach, more and more Black female suffragists included the arguments of white female suffragists, but clearly defined race as a significant variable in the denial of women's rights, a view expressed by Nancy Prince as early as 1854.

Ida B. Wells was an activist journalist who early promoted the value of women's political mobilization. *Moorland-Spingarn Research Center, Howard University*

Spreading the woman suffrage word was a significant strategy. Often the best audiences were among the readers of various Black newspapers, which emerged in significant numbers during the last quarter of the nineteenth century, or among readers of Black college and church periodicals. The work of African American women journalists, like Mary McCurdy and Gertrude Mossell, appeared in these publications, and Black institutions encouraged their women to speak out during an era of heightened racial segregation.

By the 1890s, the growth in the number of Black women journalists with feminist perspectives writing for Black newspapers became more evident. Among these women in the public sphere was Carrie Langston of Lawrence, Kansas. The daughter of civil rights activist Charles Langston, she later became the mother of Harlem Renaissance poet Langston Hughes. Before her marriage, however, she wrote for a family-operated newspaper, *The Atchison Blade*. In 1892 Carrie Langston refuted what she called "the male notion" that females were contented with their lot. She criticized men who attempted to relegate women to an inferior position in society, and she encouraged Black women to become involved in politics. Her words seemed to be aimed at the Black men in her community who continued to maintain traditional notions about women and their place in society. It appears, however, that she had been influenced by the politics of her father, who had supported the 1867 woman suffrage effort in Kansas.[6]

Carrie Langston's sentiments were not unique at the time, for other African American women journalists became active in politics. Ida B. Wells was one. A militant Memphis journalist, in 1892 she was forced by whites to leave her home and abandon her paper, *Free Speech*, because she dared to take a stand against lynching and racial proscription in the city. Using the pen name Iola, Wells wrote for several Black papers including T. Thomas Fortune's *New York Age* and Ferdinand Barnett's (Chicago) *Conservator*. After several years touring the United States and western Europe on behalf of the anti-lynching crusade, Wells settled in Chicago and married Barnett. Shortly thereafter, Ida B. Wells-Barnett became active in the Women's Suffrage Association of Illinois. Unlike journalists Gertrude Mossell and Carrie Langston, Wells-Barnett had been born into humble circumstances. Her parents were Mississippi slaves who migrated to Tennessee after the Civil War and become sharecroppers. Wells was among the first generation of Black women out of slavery, who had been educated in Freedman's Bureau schools from the primary school to the college level, and thereafter set out to uplift their race.[7]

By the 1890s, Mary McCurdy was living in the South, where she continued her career as an activist and journalist. Her views echoed the changing rationale for woman suffrage exemplified by racial and gender identification. Like Wells, McCurdy personified the growing number of southern women who sought political means to solve the social ills of Black communities. While living in Rome, Georgia, McCurdy was president of the local Black women's temperance union and an official in the state temperance organization. She also edited the *National Presbyterian*, a temperance paper published in 1890. Not only did she blame white men for keeping the ballot from the women of the nation, she also blamed them for the political corruption in the South, an issue debated among African American woman suffragists into the twentieth century. McCurdy felt that the majority of African American men who had voted after emancipation in the South had been robbed of that right, or had allowed their ballot to be purchased. Taking a gendered position common among the middle-class whites and elite Blacks of the time, McCurdy presumed that the females of her race held a moral authority often lacking among the males. African American women, she predicted, would never allow their votes to be bought.[8]

Along with Black female journalists and writers, there was a small cadre of African American women teaching in southern Black colleges and universities. Among these were Adella Hunt Logan and Margaret

Murray Washington, both Atlanta University graduates who taught at the Tuskegee Institute in Alabama. Like Lottie Rollin of South Carolina, Logan was a southern-born woman who early championed Black women's right to the vote and published her ideas. She was listed as the only life member of the NAWSA from Alabama in the 1900 edition of the *History of Woman Suffrage*. It is quite possible that some white women suffragists of her state thought she too was white. Her paternal granddaughter, historian Adele Logan Alexander, says that Logan used to go to the white suffrage meetings with her friend and fellow suffragist Georgia Stewart (later to become Alexander's maternal grandmother). Both passed for white as spies for the Black suffragists at Tuskegee. A native of Sparta, Georgia, who joined the Tuskegee Institute faculty in 1883, Logan contributed much to the philosophy of Black woman suffrage before her early demise in 1915. As a member of the Tuskegee Woman's Club, she was influential in developing woman suffrage as a major concern among the club members, of whom Margaret Murray Washington was the president.[9]

According to Alexander, Logan was inspired to become a suffragist by Isabel and Emily Howland, two white suffragists who were frequent visitors and financial contributors to the Tuskegee Institute. Julia Ward Howe and Susan B. Anthony, both supporters of Tuskegee, also influenced Logan, and by 1895, she was an active member of the NAWSA. Along with Margaret Murray Washington, Booker T. Washington's third and last wife, Logan was one of three women in Alabama to subscribe to the NAWSA *Woman's Journal*.[10]

By 1905, Logan's views were published in a comprehensive argument that combined the traditional woman suffrage rationale with African American woman suffrage tenents. Her essay included the classic reasoning, heard as early as the Seneca Falls convention:

> It is the purpose of this article to direct thought to the justice and desirability of placing the ballot in the hands of the other half of the American people, their women citizens. Government of the people is but partially realized so long as woman has no vote.[11]

But to this logic Logan added the dimension of race. She addressed her views to the Black reading public via a Black journal, the *Colored American Magazine*:

> If white American women, with all their natural and acquired advantages, need the ballot, that right protective of all other rights; if Anglo Saxons have been helped by it—and they have—how much more do Black Americans, male and female need the strong defense of a vote to help secure them their right to life, liberty and the pursuit of happiness? And neither do the colored citizens of the Republic lag behind in the fundamental duties of

tax-paying and using the elective franchise. The price of their freedom as far as that freedom has progressed, was too dear a price to be treated lightly.[12]

Logan very aptly combined the arguments of Black suffragists of the past such as Mary Ann Shadd Cary, Sojourner Truth, and Frances Ellen Watkins Harper, with the views of Black activists of her time who decried the disfranchisement of Black men. What none of these women verbalized publicly was that for Black women, protection against rape and other forms of sexual abuse should be included in the argument for Black enfranchisement. Darlene Clark Hine speculates that this silence was a dimension of women disassociating themselves from issues foreign to respectability, such as slavery. Because by law enslaved women could not be raped, the assumption after slavery included the myth that African American women encouraged racial liaisons with men outside of marriage, especially with white males. African American women's challenge to those who defamed their character was not unique to the women who met in Boston to found the National Federation of African American Women in 1895. The debate was rooted in the abolitionist era and continued long into the twentieth century. Nonetheless, women printing articles about rape and sexual abuse was not quite accepted in turn-of-the-century Black literary venues.[13]

Logan, however, answered every anti–woman suffrage myth that was popular at the time by discrediting the belief that women really did not want to vote, that women were ignorant of civics and unable to participate in politics, and that if women participated in the political process by voting, their babies would be neglected. Finally, like other Black and white suffragists of the past, Logan commented about how "the right of suffrage is withheld from women largely by ignorant and vicious men."[14] Significantly, Logan's comprehensive woman suffrage ideology predated the progressive era views Black suffragists articulated nearly a decade later.

All but one of the five women discussed in this section had southern roots or lived in the South at the turn of the century. Their networks included white women who were suffragists; however, the messages they sent about why Black people should support the drive to enfranchise African American women came from Black institutions. For the most part, access to the public came through cooperation with Black men. Langston published her views in her father's and brother's newspaper, McCurdy's essay was published in James Haley's encyclopedia about Black life, Wells-Barnett, like Mossell before her, published her views in T. Thomas Fortune's Black newspaper. Both Logan and Washington taught at the Black institution headed by Booker T. Washington. Logan published her article in a nationally circulated Black journal, the *Colored American Magazine*, which received financial support from Booker T. Washington. However,

Boston fiction writer and feminist Pauline Hopkins was the Black editor at the time Logan's essay was accepted for publication.[15]

African American Suffragists in the District of Columbia

By the turn of the century, the District of Columbia had drawn a number of single and married Black women to the city, several of whom were feminists and suffragists. Some of these women came with male family members, who sought to provide professional services to the growing Black bourgeoisie of this racially segregated, southern city. Others came alone in search of higher education or civil service and teaching positions, or to build institutions of their own. This cohort of educated women provides one of the few cases for prosopagraphical study among African American suffragists who span nearly three generations. In looking at their views and experiences, we can see issues about gender and politics discussed and debated within the context of nearly thirty years, from 1890 to the First World War.

Veteran abolitionist and suffragist Charlotte Forten, for one, came to Washington in the late 1870s. She worked there in government and as a teacher before she married Francis J. Grimké, a former slave and a nephew of the white abolitionists and feminists Sarah Grimké and Angelina Grimké Weld. The sisters had financed the education of their nephews, Francis and Archibald, who studied the ministry and the law, respectively. Charlotte and Francis Grimké left Washington, but were recalled to the city from Florida in 1889 by the 15th Street Presbyterian Church, a congregation of distinguished African Americans, where Francis served as minister for many years, and Charlotte worked with the women of the church. After a difficult first pregnancy at the age of forty-three and the death of her infant, Charlotte Grimké suffered from failing health; however, she mentored younger women reformers such as her niece Angelina Weld Grimké and her niece's friends like Anna J. Cooper.[16]

By 1905 Archibald Grimké moved with his daughter, Angelina Weld Grimké, from Boston to Washington, where they lived with Charlotte and Francis Grimké. Archibald became a Republican Party diplomat and then a civil rights activist, the president of the Washington NAACP. His daughter taught physical education at Armstrong Manual Training School for Black students, and then English at the Dunbar High School (formerly called the M Street High School), the first academic high school founded for African Americans in the segregated District of Columbia. Like her aunt Charlotte, Angelina was a well-educated writer and became a feminist and suffragist. A single woman, she remained very close to her father, and her

Angelina Weld Grimké
was a District of Columbia
feminist, lesbian, dramatist,
poet, and educator from a
family of distinguished
women reformers, including
the Fortens and the Grimkés.
*Moorland-Spingarn Research
Center, Howard University*

biographers believe she was a lesbian who suppressed her sexuality because
her father disapproved. Biographers believe that Grimké's poetry expressed
her frustration and despair over lost sexual opportunities. This may be
correct. However, I find her circumstances to be more complex than some
presume. Her plays reflected despair among elite African Americans living in
a society dominated by white supremacists who perpetuated the myth of
Black inferiority.[17] Perhaps she did not make her sexual preferences known
publicly during this era when elite African American women particularly
sought to protect issues surrounding respectability. Nonetheless, we cannot
assume that her preoccupation with themes about rejection and despair were
just the results of suppressed sexual emotions. The violence and discrimination against Black people in her times were enough to cause despair among
heterosexual, as well as lesbian African Americans.

Angelina Grimké was part of the social and intellectual circles of
Mary Church Terrell and Coralie Franklin Cook. Both Terrell and Cook
had migrated to the District of Columbia in the late nineteenth century as
single women to seek educational careers. Terrell, then Cook, became the
first and the second African American women appointed to the District of
Columbia school board, and both were active members of the NAWSA as

well as leaders in the Black women's club movement. Terrell was from an affluent African American family of Memphis. Her father, Robert Church, was a former slave who had become a wealthy landowner after the yellow fever epidemic of the post–Civil War years depopulated the city of Memphis. Mary Church was educated at Oberlin College, and after completing her master's degree there, she moved to Washington to teach at the M Street High School. There she met and married the principal, Robert Terrell. Coralie Franklin came to Washington from West Virginia to teach oratory at Howard University, and later became a professor at the Washington Conservatory of Music. Like Terrell, Cook married a professional man, Howard University professor George W. Cook. Both women settled in the District of Columbia, and by the turn of the century had become prominent social and civic leaders among the African American female elite, who like the younger Angelina Grimké despaired about the plight of their people.[18]

In addition to this group of elite African American women, others of modest upbringing and exceptional talent and aspirations for community building also came to the District of Columbia. Anna J. Cooper was one of these contemporaries. Like Mary Church Terrell, Cooper earned an A.M. degree from Oberlin College in 1884 and came to the District of Columbia to teach at the M Street High School. Cooper's life, however, had been much more difficult than Terrell's. Cooper's mother had been a slave in Raleigh, North Carolina, and had struggled to educate her daughter, the result of a liaison with her master. When Anna Cooper arrived in Washington, she was a widow and remained so, a former instructor at both St. Augustine's College in North Carolina, and Wilberforce College in Ohio. Like Terrell, Cooper became a social activist and clubwoman, a mentor to women students such as Angelina Grimké and Nannie Helen Burroughs.[19] Cooper exemplified the formerly enslaved woman who had managed through travail and triumph to become college-educated during "the Nadir."

Nannie Burroughs, like Cooper was raised by a single mother of humble circumstance. Born in Orange, Virginia, of slave parents, Burroughs came to the District of Columbia with her mother, who sought employment for herself and education for her children. Nannie Burroughs was fortunate enough to attend the M Street High School, where such feminist teachers as Mary Church Terrell and Anna J. Cooper became her role models. Unable to find suitable work after high school, however, Burroughs left Washington to seek employment elsewhere, eventually becoming involved in the Black Baptist Convention. By the turn of the century, at the age of twenty-one, she had become a national leader as one of the founders of the Black Baptist Women's Convention. It was this organization of African American women, many of whom became woman suffragists, that made it possible for the founding of the National Training School for Women and Girls in the District of Columbia, with Burroughs as the president.[20]

More than any other southern city of the times, Washington was home to a significant number of African American woman suffragists, who networked in various ways. Perhaps because these women lived in the nation's capital, their views were heard in the white and in the Black public spheres, and their ideas were recorded for posterity. Of the six women noted above, Charlotte Forten Grimké was a generation older than the others. Her public life was limited to church activities because of poor health. However, Terrell, Cook, Cooper, Angelina Grimké, and Burroughs—the youngest among them—remained in the public eye during the first two decades of the twentieth century. They exemplified the third generation of African American woman suffragists who related to both the Black and the white worlds.

Mary Church Terrell's name first appears in the *History of Woman Suffrage* for 1898, twenty years after Mary Ann Shadd Cary and Charlotte E. Ray became the last Black female participants noted in national woman suffrage convention proceedings. Although no portion of Terrell's address was recorded, the editors noted her topic, "The Progress of Colored Women," and that she was the president of the National Association of Colored Women (NACW). However, excerpts from the text of Terrell's address to the delegates of the 1900 NAWSA convention appeared in the proceedings, the first of several published examples of the ideas and the strategies of this Washington African American woman suffragist. Like Adella Hunt Logan, Terrell felt many problems could be solved if Black women were enfranchised, and she used several strategies designed to convince African Americans to join the cause and white suffragists to support their entry.

In addressing the audience of the NAWSA convention, Terrell may have seen a large number of Black faces, for the more I recover lost African American suffragists, the less I can assume that the District of Columbia conventions were attended primarily by whites. Nonetheless, the leadership was white, and Terrell appeared to assume two roles with this in mind, if we can rely on what was printed about her in the convention proceedings. First she related to the mainstream feminist ideas and woman suffrage strategies, when she said,

> When one observes how all the most honorable and lucrative positions in Church and State have been reserved for men, according to laws which they themselves have made so as to debar women; how, until recently, a married woman's property was under the exclusive control of her husband; how, in

all transactions where husband and wife are considered one, the law makes the husband that one—man's boasted chivalry to the disfranchised sex is punctured beyond repair.

These unjust discriminations will ever remain, until the source from which they spring—the political disfranchisement of woman—shall be removed. The injustice involved in denying woman the suffrage is not confined to the disfranchised sex alone, but extends to the nation as well, in that it is deprived of the excellent service which woman might render.[21]

Like Logan, Terrell refuted the argument that it was unnatural for women to vote, calling the belief "as old as the rock-ribbed and ancient hills." Women, she believed, owed a responsibility as citizens to the state, just as did men. Terrell's second role was to remind white suffragists that denying the franchise because of race was equal to denying the vote because of gender. Not surprisingly, this side of her argument was not included in the NAWSA published proceedings, but it did appear in a local Washington newspaper account of her talk. She said,

The elective franchise is withheld from one half of its citizens, many of whom are intelligent, cultured, and virtuous, while it is unstintingly bestowed upon the other, some of whom are illiterate, debauched and vicious, because the word "people," by an unparalleled exhibition of lexicographical acrobatics, has been turned and twisted to mean all who were shrewd and wise enough to have themselves born boys instead of girls, or who took the trouble to be born white instead of black.[22]

This of course seemed to be a controversial statement for white woman suffragists to hear. Perhaps that is why the chroniclers refrained from recording this portion of Terrell's words in the proceedings.

In 1904 Terrell spoke again at the NAWSA meeting, which she attended in Washington. She was then a national figure, and her challenging words to white suffragists were recorded by the movement leadership. She felt that Black men were being unduly condemned for selling their votes. Terrell was reported to have said, "They never sold their votes til they found that it made no difference how they cast them," noting also that there were many cases of African American men who were tempted, yet never sold their right to the ballot. Furthermore, she exhorted, "My sisters of the dominant race, stand up not only for the oppressed sex, but also for the oppressed race!"[23]

Like others before her, Mary Church Terrell responded repeatedly to white women's criticism of the Black men in the South who had allegedly sold their votes, and for this reason should remain disfranchised. Although white women complained about political corruption in the South and in immigrant communities in the Northeast, they were usually on the offensive with their criticism of others. African American women, on the other hand, were always on the defensive, defending their race as well as criticizing the ills that kept many former slaves powerless. As early as the 1870s, white women had pointed to the irresponsibility of the Black freedmen. Despite the protests of prominent Blacks like Frederick Douglass and Frances Harper, white suffragists clung to this attitude, and by the 1890s had transferred it to all Blacks, both men and women.[24] From this time into the first decade of the twentieth century, the idea of Blacks as the source of political corruption was a constant charge that African American women faced and discussed all over the nation, not just in Washington.

For example, in 1891 Mary A. McCurdy felt that southern governments owed Black people political rights because of the way freedpeople had been abused. She saw the hope of the South resting in the hands of female voters because white men were dishonest and unprincipled since they either denied or bought the Black man's vote.[25]

While touring the South during the Reconstruction years, Frances Harper had observed the results of political corruption. Years later while living in Philadelphia, she expressed her sentiments against political corruption, when she published her 1896 collection of poetry, *Sketches of Southern Life*. Harper acknowledged the problem to be widespread in the South, but unlike McCurdy, she did not trust that most white women suffragists would treat Black people any better than had their men. Harper spread the blame among both white and Black men. She spoke in dialect through "Aunt Chloe," who said,

> Of course, I don't know very much
> About these politics,
> But I think that some who run 'em
> Do mighty ugly tricks.
> When we want to school our children
> If the money isn't there,
> Whether black or white have took it,
> The loss we all must share,
> And this buying up each other
> Is somthin worse than mean.
> Though I think a heap of voting,
> I go for voting clean.[26]

Like McCurdy and Harper, Terrell spread the blame for political corruption among whites and Blacks and talked about Black stolen votes. Among the Washington suffragists, however, there was no consensus about who was to blame for political corruption and the buying and selling of Black men's votes. Some resented being placed in the same category with those of the race who were considered to be irresponsible, especially men who had sold their votes. Feminist Anna J. Cooper, on the other hand, focused her discussion on the females, not the males, and made no excuses for Black men. In 1892 she wrote in her book *A Voice from the South* that Black women in the South had been known to have left their husbands for selling their votes and "repudiated their support" for disloyalty to the race. Moreover, she commented, "You do not find the colored woman selling her birthright for a mess of pottage."[27]

As late as 1915, Nannie Burroughs echoed Cooper's sentiments in an article W. E. B. Du Bois solicited to publish in the *Crisis,* the official organ of the NAACP. Burroughs argued that Black women needed the ballot to protect themselves and the race, and that unlike Black men who had "bartered and sold" their ballots, Black women knew the value of the vote. She declared, "The Negro woman, therefore, needs the ballot to get back, by wise use of it, what the Negro man has lost by the 'misuse' of it."[28] Here we see Burroughs taking the position of one mentor, Cooper, over that of another, Terrell. Perhaps the difference reflects the radical feminist views of Cooper and Burroughs—two independent single women—over the less feminist, more race-centered views of Terrell, who also straddled the politics of both the white and Black worlds during "the Nadir."

An example of Terrell's attempt to operate in both arenas is when she was asked by white suffragists to write a memorial in 1906, at the time of Susan B. Anthony's death. Terrell praised Anthony for attempting to fight for the rights of Black women as well as white women. Two years later, Terrell attended the sixtieth anniversary meeting of the women's rights convention at Seneca Falls, New York. At this gathering, she spoke again about the need for all women including Blacks, Jews, and other minorities to have the right to vote.[29] In both instances, Terrell assumed the role of the racial or minorities protagonist, a position she seemed to take in most of her opinions about woman suffrage strategies. Few African American women wrote publicly about the similarity between racial and ethnic oppression. Consequently, Terrell's 1908 reference to the many white native-born suffragists who attempted to eliminate the foreign-born immigrant voters, many of whom were Jews, and the southern-born Blacks, seemed controversial to the mainstream movement, to say the least. On this issue, her position was radical. The strategy she challenged was called "educated suffrage," wherein nativists proposed a woman suffrage amendment that would limit the vote to women who could read and write English.

"Educated suffrage" was not new. Elizabeth Cady Stanton and Henry Blackwell had argued this strategy nearly twenty years before, winning support from xenophobics and white supremacists who were reluctant to join a suffrage movement that included all women. The "educated suffrage" strategy was symptomatic of "the Nadir" and the polarization in America based upon class, ethnic, and racial differences.[30] In reality, "educated suffrage" was a mainstream woman suffrage strategy, but its very nature made it an anti–Black woman suffrage argument (a subject to be discussed in greater detail subsequently).

In the meantime, Coralie Franklin Cook was also traveling in the inner circles of the NAWSA. In 1900 the program announcing the celebration of the eightieth birthday of Susan B. Anthony indicated "greetings from colored women." Cook brought the greetings at the celebration that was held in the Lafayette Opera House in the District of Columbia. Like Terrell, Cook was an active member of one of the oldest Black women's clubs in the nation, the Colored Woman's League of Washington, and she felt strongly that the cause of Black women was not a priority among the white women in the suffrage movement. As the token Black woman, Cook was the only member of her race to make an official statement at the Anthony celebration, although many white female suffragists were listed on the program. (Even Hattie Purvis, Anthony's longtime friend, was not acknowledged.) In her address, suffrage chroniclers reported that Cook praised the work of Anthony and noted how the woman suffrage movement had awakened women throughout the world to realizing their responsibility to others and their potential political power. Cook emphasized the need for interracial empathy in the woman's movement when she said, "no woman and no class of women can be degraded and all woman kind not suffer thereby." While she made no accusations printed in the proceedings, Cook nevertheless established the point that Black women as well as white women looked to the day when they all would possess the ballot. It appears that Cook chose her words with diplomacy, as this analogy reveals:

> Not until the suffrage movement had awakened woman to her responsibility and power, did she come to appreciate the true significance of Christ's pity for Magdalene as well as of His love for Mary; not till then was the work of Pundita Ramabai in far away India as sacred as that of Frances Willard at home in America. . . . And so Miss Anthony, in behalf of the hundreds of colored women who wait and hope with you for the day when the ballot shall be in the hands of every intelligent woman; and also in behalf of the thousands who sit in darkness and whose condition we shall expect those ballots to better, whether they be in the hands of white women or Black, I offer you my warmest gratitude and congratulations.[31]

Terrell and Cook were among the few African American suffragists recognized by the NAWSA hierarchy, because both women were educated, professional, middle-class women, or the image of the "intelligent" women Stanton had hoped to see enfranchised. Nonetheless, their ancestors had been enslaved, not the Puritan elite to which Stanton usually referred. Although the chroniclers of the woman suffrage history recorded and edited her words, Cook appeared to echo sentiments heard from Terrell and earlier Black suffragists, which reminded elite white women that they should not ignore the political rights of the less fortunate. Thus, it was up to women like Terrell and Cook to become the conscience of the conservative woman suffrage movement.

On the eve of the World War, diverse feminist voices were heard among Washington African American women. Radical feminist Angelina Weld Grimké wrote for several journals, including Margaret Sanger's periodical *Birth Control Review*. A close friend to Anna J. Cooper, Grimké combined traditional woman suffrage ideas with the new ideology of both Black and white feminists. For example, her literary works expressed vividly some of her views about the pain and violence Black women endured during the second decade of the twentieth century. Politically, Grimké's greatest qualm was with the double standards imposed upon women by the courts, in education, in employment, and particularly in marriage, the institution in which she felt some females were reduced to slavery. True to her views, Grimké never married. "When women become equal with men," she reasoned, "the injustices will end." She argued further, "it seems to me that this will occur when she gains the ballot, for to me the ballot is in a Republican democracy the signer of absolute equality."[32] Like many other radicals, Grimké seemed to shy away from joining more conservative women's clubs and woman suffrage associations, remaining independent.

Instead Grimké's words were spoken in an address to a group of Washington African American women prior to the passage of the Eighteenth Amendment, which implemented prohibition. Her ideas reflected the sentiments of white suffragist Winnifred Harper Cooley, who in 1913 defined radical feminism. Cooley believed that radical feminists called not only for the ballot, but for "the abolition of all arbitrary handicaps" designed to keep women from economic, political, and social independence.[33]

In remaining single, Grimké maintained her teaching position on the Dunbar High School faculty for many years, because all over the nation the rules of the times forced married women to abandon their careers as primary and secondary school teachers. As a result, married women like Terrell and Cook left the classroom and developed their cohort relationships with other suffragists in clubs and associations instead of in formal work situations as educated single women did. Grimké's radicalism may have been characteristic of the relationship she had maintained with other single women who were intellectuals, literary figures, and activists. Some of these women, like Grimké, were lesbians, such as fellow playwright and Dunbar colleague Mary P. Burrill. Both Grimké and Burrill had studied drama under Montgomery T. Gregory and Alain Locke at Howard University. Black theater scholar Kathy A. Perkins describes Gregory and Locke as race men who promoted "folk plays" to bring Black drama and dramatists to national attention. Grimké and Burrill wrote plays with race propaganda messages, performed by the university's Howard Players. In addition, both women wrote fiction for the special issue of *Birth Control Review* that dramatized the need for Black women to practice birth control.[34] Before going to teach at Dunbar High School, Burrill, like Cook, taught at the Washington Conservatory of Music. Although Burrill was a nationalist feminist who must have been a woman suffragist like her cohorts, she left no known published evidence of it. The subject of Grimké's love poems, Burrill enjoyed an intimate relationship with her when they were both teenagers and perhaps longer; however, as a mature adult, Burrill lived for many years with her companion, educator and suffragist Lucy Diggs Slowe (whose suffrage views I will discuss subsequently).[35]

Like Grimké, Nannie Burroughs's motives for supporting woman suffrage reflected the more radical view of African American women. Burroughs had little patience for men who did not treat women as equals. As corresponding secretary of the Woman's Convention of the National Baptist Convention, she was responsible for writing annual reports, which reflected support for woman suffrage for several years. Perhaps she made the most direct and forceful argument against the sexual abuse of African American women when she envisioned the use of the ballot as a strategy to combat the evil. Unlike other women before her, who talked around the issue, Burroughs, like Grimké, addressed it directly, defying the "culture of dissemblance." Darlene Clark Hine describes this course of action among Black women of the period, who avoid discussing their sexual vulnerability so as to conceal threats to their respectability as a group. Burroughs noted that Black women had been the "prey of every race" for years, despite attempts to resist sexual abuse. She wrote,

> The Ballot, wisely used, will bring to her the respect and protection that she needs. It is her weapon of moral defence. Under present conditions, when she appears in court in defence of her virtue, she is looked upon with amused contempt. She needs the ballot to reckon with men who place no value upon her virtue, and to mould healthy public sentiment in favor of her own protection.[36]

Views of these radical District of Columbia feminists of the early twentieth century would not have been strange to the first generation of woman suffragists, yet the primarily white cohorts of this group could not have foreseen a distinct twentieth-century group of middle-class, African American women whose social and economic disabilities were greater than their own. Angelina Grimké, for example, was a talented short story writer, a dramatist, an orator, a Wellesley-educated woman. She was born into a comfortable, middle-class environment, but like most Washington, African American women of her class, she found that her career opportunities during the early twentieth century were largely limited to teaching in Black institutions.[37]

The nine prominent African American cohort women from Washington all traveled in some of the same circles, yet their feminism ranged from the conservative to the radical. They shared race chauvinism, and community activism that was woman centered. All were connected in some way to either Dunbar High School or Howard University. For the most part, their feminist and woman suffrage views were published in Black periodicals like *The Voice of the Negro* and the *Crisis*, or in books they published themselves. However, as "the Nadir" began to draw to a close, white feminist journals sought Black voices. Even the women who had come from humble origins, by the time they interacted in the District of Columbia, were among the Black elite, yet their career choices were limited by sexism and racism. Despite new opportunities, as the nation approached the First World War, Black women, particularly in Washington, became more aware of their low economic status and tied their disabilities to the lack of political rights.

Suffrage Strategies to Solve Economic Problems

Using votes as a means to organize on behalf of uplifting the economic status of Black women was first proposed by radical feminist Mary Ann Shadd Cary, when she addressed the Black congregation of Mt. Pisgah Chapel in Washington. In 1880 Cary urged the women in the audience to join her in efforts to "obtain the ballot and look alive after the welfare of both girls and boys in the training of the youth, working promptly to extend the number of occupations for women."[38] Cary's strategy was unique to Black and white women of the time, and can be characterized as one of the more radical suffrage arguments to be used. Only a handful of suffragists like Cary and Susan B. Anthony were actively involved in the labor and woman suffrage movements of the late nineteenth century, connecting the suffrage arguments to the needs of working women. However, by the early twentieth century, suffragists included immigrant working-class women, middle-class socialists, and middle-class African American women applying various strategies to the solution of economic problems in their communities. Among Blacks the strategy included: educating the Black reading and voting public about the economic value of having African American women as voters; convincing Black women themselves that the ballot in their hands

Maria L. Baldwin was the principal of the Agassia School in Cambridge, and voted with other woman suffragists in Massachusetts school board elections. *Boston Teachers Newsletter (February 1949), Moorland-Spingarn Research Center, Howard University*

could help to improve working conditions or work to open new economic opportunities; and gaining the ear of sympathetic whites, especially in the South, persuading them that the poor Black women workers of their region needed the vote for their own protection.

The strategy to educate the Black public was used primarily by African American women in the North, women like Maria L. Baldwin, who responded to Du Bois's call for woman suffrage essays to be published in the *Crisis*. In making specific reference to the value of suffrage among school-teachers in Massachusetts, Baldwin noted from experience, "In several cases local schools have been kept, by the Women's Vote, from the control of persons who threatened all that was in them." Baldwin was one of the few African American women in the country to be administrators of predominantly white public schools. She was the principal of the noted Agassia School in Cambridge, a position she earned after working her way up from a teaching position. Women in the state of Massachusetts had won the right to vote in school elections in 1879, and Baldwin testified to her readers that even "so meagre a share of voting power" had given schoolteachers leverage in protecting their jobs and their schools.[39] Her argument for enfranchising African American women was aimed at Black voting men in the North, to whom she proved a practical justification for giving their women the power of the ballot.

Unlike Massachusetts, Rhode Island did not extend to women the right to vote before the passage of the Nineteenth Amendment, although Rhode Island women lobbied considerably for it. Mary E. Jackson, president of the Rhode Island Association of Colored Woman's Clubs, also justified Black women's quest for the vote in terms of their economic needs. As a civil service employee in the state, Jackson had access to data concerning the economic status of women in the United States. In 1912, she quoted statistics that indicated over eight million American females in the labor force. The majority of them, Jackson contended, worked because of necessity, and she asserted that "The laboring man had discovered beyond preadventure that his most effective weapon of defense is the ballot in his own hand. The self-supporting woman asks for and will accept nothing else."[40] As a club leader and a professional woman, Jackson directed her concerns about the plight of Black women workers, in particular, to African Americans throughout the nation, by writing periodically for the *Crisis*. Suffrage, she believed, was a means to elevate the economic plight of women of her race. In this sense, Jackson, a northerner, shared the concerns of many southern suffragists, such as Lucy Diggs Slowe.

Realizing Black women's precarious position in an expanding industrial economy, Slowe was an educated southern woman who dared to challenge the status quo. A suffragist and colleague of Angelina Weld Grimké, Slowe had also taught at Armstrong Manual Training School in Washington. Unlike Grimké, however, Slowe had been born into humble circumstances in Virginia and raised by an aunt in Baltimore. A scholarship brought her to Washington, where she graduated from Howard University, but not before she became in 1908 a founder and the first president of the Alpha Kappa Alpha Sorority. Women of this sorority of African Americans included Anna J. Cooper. This organization was the first of its kind for Black college women. From her undergraduate years, Slowe believed in the professional development of college-educated Black women. However, she observed that the teaching profession had become oversaturated with Black women. Optimistically looking to the day when woman suffrage would be a helpful reality, in 1918 she encouraged college-trained African American women to enter the fields of law, journalism, social work, and business. Black women, she believed, needed to be prepared to supervise other Black women, not only in educational positions, but also in the industrial jobs developing as a result of the First World War. They were needed to champion the rights of their less fortunate sisters, who, Slowe believed, had been wronged by society. A radical feminist, Slowe took at least part of her own advice to heart and by 1919 left the classroom to become an administrator, the dean of women at Howard

University.[41] Like Mary Jackson, Slowe looked to the ballot as a means to help expand opportunities for needy Black women's economic empowerment.

The less fortunate Black sisters of whom Slowe spoke were unable to make strides in higher education careers and seemed destined to perform menial tasks. The growing movement from rural to urban centers during the war accelerated the rising number of African American women in domestic services. Women such as Jeanette Carter, a Washington attorney, founded the Woman Wage Earners Association in the District of Columbia. Carter's aim was to organize Black women throughout the United States to better their economic conditions. The purpose of a March 1917 association convention was to assess the conditions and wages of working women and to determine ways that poor working conditions could be improved. In her speech, Carter said, "It is no longer considered wise or expedient for women to wait for men to do for them what women should do for women." In addition to this feminist position, Carter also sought a suffrage strategy to help better the working conditions of African American women, beginning in a southern city. The subsequent history of the organization is unknown, but by 1918, Jeanette Carter was appointed director of the Colored Bureau of Industrial Housing and Transportation in the U. S. Department of Labor.[42]

Carter's ideas for unionizing Black women were before their time, as were those of Slowe to prepare Black women for supervisory positions in industry. Yet they were reminiscent of Mary Ann Shadd Cary a generation before, as she attempted to mobilize African American women both politically and economically. These ideas revealed the continuing self-help and self-reliance themes as well as assertive feminism among Black Washington women. These Black women's voices revealed the nationalist feminist nature of their struggle.

North of Washington, other Black suffragists were more specific in emphasizing the need to protect Black women workers primarily through political party affiliation. Goals such as these were viewed favorably by S. Willie Layton, the secretary of the Philadelphia Association for the Protection of Colored Women as well as the president of the Black Baptist Woman's Convention. In a letter to Mary Church Terrell in 1916, Layton expressed her disillusionment with the Progressive Party, which she had supported in the past. Layton decided to move her support to the "Woman's Party," which she declared "affords our people one of the best chances since emancipation." Like other northern woman suffragists, Black disillusionment came with the realization that Progressives were satisfied with the status quo in race relations. The discussion of issues around racial conflict was believed to be a device in the Progressive Party. Consequently, white party members attempted to ignore debates about race. Little did Layton know that the

National Woman's Party leadership would also ignore race issues in developing their woman suffrage strategies.[43] Nonetheless, Layton was frustrated with her attempts to form political coalitions and was willing to try something new. Both Layton and Terrell soon after developed relationships with the National Woman's Party.

Wooing political support for Black women from liberal whites was also a strategy used by African American women leaders in the South. Lugenia Burns Hope made all efforts to make gains for Black women. She had the ears of the white southern female leadership during the early twentieth century because she was the wife of Atlanta University's first Black president, John Hope. Lugenia Hope became one of the first African American social workers in the South and the founder of the Neighborhood Union, a Black Atlanta settlement house. In 1919 she drafted a statement on behalf of the southern members of the NACW to the white women of the Women's Missionary Council of the American Missionary Association. Her statement contained a list of grievances Black women sustained in their relations with whites. Like Jeanette Carter, Hope was concerned about the plight of Black female domestic workers, who made up a sizable percentage of southern Black working-class women. Aside from unskilled agricultural labor, domestic or household labor was the dominant occupation among southern Black women. Hope's statement called for the protection of domestic workers in white homes where they were subjected to physical hardships, sexual abuse, and deplorable housing conditions. Taking a more conservative approach than that of Carter's wage-earners association, Hope recommended that whites agree to regulations for working hours and working conditions. She called for sanitary and wholesome housing facilities and provisions for recreation. As a result of the nature of domestic work, Black women were forced to be absent from their own children, and Hope recommended that white women help Blacks to establish day nurseries, playgrounds, and recreation centers.[44]

Moving from the plight of domestic workers to the indignities Black women suffered in the South, Hope noted the deplorable conditions under which they were forced to travel in segregated streetcars and train stations. In not only demanding equal accommodations for Black and white women in public transportation, Hope implored the white women of the Women's Missionary Council to support equal suffrage for all Blacks. The ballot, she reasoned, "is the safeguard of the nation."[45] Hope's statement combined three basic woman suffrage arguments propounded by Black suffragists of the times. One was that political pressure could be used to protect working women. Another was that women's lobbying could be used to assist Black men to regain their votes in the South. The final one was that Black women's political clout could be used to protect civil rights. Hope's biographer, historian Jacqueline Anne Rouse, found that for women like Hope, there were successes in their efforts to work with southern white women. Nonetheless, African American women learned that, more often than not, "white women could not completely divorce themselves from their belief in segregation and racial inferiority."[46]

Lugenia Hope represented the growing number of southern African American women who were in the public sphere due to their affiliation with Black church and educational institutions. Perhaps one of the most radical among them, she refused to compromise her position about racial discrimination when other African American women chose to avoid offending white benefactors, such as the women of the Missionary Council who were less sensitive to Black issues. Despite African American reluctance to take a public stand against racism, an outstanding representation of southern Black female leaders signed Hope's statement. They included Charlotte Hawkins Brown, founder of Palmer Institute, representing the North Carolina Federation of Colored Women; Marion B. Wilkinson, president of the South Carolina Federation of Colored Women; Lucy Laney, principal of Haines Institute and president of the City Federation of Colored Women's Clubs of Augusta, Georgia; Mary J. McCrorey, chairperson of the Committee of Management of the Charlotte, North Carolina, Branch of the Y.W.C.A.; Janie Porter Barret, president of the Virginia Federation of Colored Women's Clubs; Margaret Murray Washington, honorary president of the NACW; Mrs. Robert B. Moton, who represented the women of the Tuskegee Institute; Lugenia Hope herself, chairperson of the Department of Neighborhood Works, National Federation of Colored Women's Clubs; Minnie Lou Crosthwait, the registrar at Fisk University; and Mary McLeod Bethune, principal of the Daytona Normal and Industrial School for Negro Girls, representing the Southeastern Federation of Colored Women's Clubs.[47] For these women leaders of Black institutions dependent upon white philanthropy, signing the statement was taking a risk. Listing grievances that could easily be corrected by financial donations was one thing, but calling for political empowerment through enfranchisement was something else again.

All of these women were professionally trained African Americans representing thousands of their gender in southern Black institutions. Thus, Hope could not have selected a better group to endorse her plan. The Hope statement attempted to raise the consciousness of white women who were seeking interracial cooperation to solve pressing Black social ills. The statement espoused a political strategy, however, that most southern white women were not eager to face—the enfranchisement of Blacks. Despite the comprehensive list of important Black female signatories on the Hope statement, historian Cynthia Neverdon-Morton finds that the Missionary Council members made no substantive attempts to deal with the realities of the political issues raised.[48]

Explaining why whites in the South were reluctant to deal with political solutions to Black problems, African American women contemporary to the times, like Rosalie Jonas, made the connection between sexism, racism, the economy, and politics. Suffrage for Blacks would upset the status quo, as would suffrage for women. Jonas, who wrote for the *Crisis*, felt that universal suffrage threatened white oppressors, making it especially difficult in the South for African American women to lobby successfully for the ballot. Using Black southern dialect in a way similar to Harper's poetry, Jonas described the economic plight of Black women in the South, referring to the oppressor as "de Boss":

> When hit come ter de question er de female vote,
>   De ladies an' der cullud folk is in de same boat,
> Ef de Boss fellin' good an' we eats out his han',
>   All kin shout fur freedom, an foller de ban',
> We kin play at freedom, so long's we play,
>   But if we gits thinkin', an' comes out an' say:
> Case one's borned a female, an' one's borned Black,
>   Is day any reason fur sottin' way back?
> Is dat any reason fur sottin' da-put?
>   You kin betcher bottom dollar dat de Boss's fut
> Gwine ter sprout big claws, till day comes clar thoo,
>   An' he climps hit heavy on bote us two.
> Case de tears er de mudder, nur de sign er de cross,
>   Ain't shame all de debbil yit, outen de Boss![49]

Jonas published this poem in a 1912 issue of the *Crisis*, revealing her sophisticated level of political analysis, her literary talent, and her keen sense of how to capture the attention of the public via use of the popular culture of the times, use of slave dialect as a literary form. The political analysis is sophisticated because it treats racism and sexism as policies devised by the power structure in order to maintain control of the majority of the southern population. Few white women suffragists could acknowledge the reality of this analysis without disturbing the somewhat higher status they maintained in relationship to Blacks, whether they were male or female. The economic suffrage strategies African American women like Jonas offered during the first two decades of the twentieth century represent how far-reaching their ideologies had become, and their voices as nationalist feminists.

Conclusion

For over a forty-year period from the late 1870s through the First World War, the woman suffrage ideology among individual African American women evolved from the cry for universal suffrage to multifaceted arguments why Black women needed the ballot even more than others who were similarly disfranchised. The growth of the numbers of Black women in the public sphere and the vehicles of expression provided by Black institutions contributed to the spread of this ideology.

The period known among African Americanists as "the Nadir" is significant because these years spanned a low period in race relations in the United States, characterized by increased violence against Blacks and increased racial segregation. "The Nadir" ended with the new economic and political hope that urbanization and industrialization, stimulated by war, brought to Americans. At this point African Americans intended to reap the economic benefits that developed throughout the nation as a whole. The suffrage strategies developing among African American women at the end of this period reflected these rising expectations among feminists generally, radicalizing many of them by the end of "the Nadir." Black suffragists were influenced also by the politics and the economy of the changing times, which sent mixed messages of hope and despair.

Within this time perspective we see three generations of African American woman suffragists at work. Sojourner Truth and Mary Ann Shadd Cary were the last of the first generation, and both died before the century ended. Hattie Purvis, Frances Ellen Watkins Harper, and Charlotte Forten Grimké represented the second generation, women growing older and less active. None would live to see the success of the Nineteenth Amendment. For the most part, however, the new ideology came from the third generation of African American woman suffragists, many of whom had been born in the South. It is not surprising that the southern-born Black woman suffragists responded first to the growing racism apparent in the movement, which quickly spread nationwide.

In reviewing the most prominent African American suffrage spokeswomen in this chapter, I have recovered twenty-eight new names. Among this group, we hear the actual voices of fifteen who expressed ideas and strategies, arguing about why Americans should support the enfranchisement of Black women.

These women aspired to the same goal, but their tactics, ideas, and self-identity ranged from moderately conservative married women to radical single women, some of whom were lesbians. The Washington network of nine African American woman suffragists among them is important because it reveals the largest group of vocal Black women for whom records are available. The diversity of their views and in their level of feminist consciousness spans a twenty-year period, yet indicates that they held no monolithic position on the issues that concerned suffrage. Nonetheless, all of them argued that Black women needed the ballot in order to help themselves and their communities. Aside from four, the other twenty-five had been born in the former Confederate South. Washington, a city of opportunity for Blacks in the late nineteenth century, had been a drawing place for these highly motivated feminists. As the story continued to unfold, other places north and south of the District of Columbia witnessed the maturing of motivated Black feminists nationwide, putting the strategies and ideologies of their spokeswomen into action.

Chapter 5. Mobilizing to Win the Vote: African American Women's Organizations

> To arouse all women, especially colored women, to a sense of their responsibility, both in molding the life of the home and in shaping the principles of the nation; to secure the co-operation of all women in whatever is undertaken in the interest of justice, purity and liberty; to inspire in all women, but especially in colored women, a desire to be useful in whatever field of labor they can work to the best advantage.
>
> —National Association of Colored Women, 1898[1]

African American woman suffragists began to organize on local levels in the 1880s, and on the national level by 1895. However, as reformers, they had been developing their own associations in the North beginning in the antebellum period. During the Civil War, group mobilization spread into the South, primarily for educational and relief efforts. Although I have yet to find separate Black women's rights or woman suffrage organizations prior to the Civil War, politics informed by reform and protest movements was at the core of many of their early nineteenth-century organizations. Like their white counterparts, African American women joined to fight against slavery, and they organized to relieve the suffering of others who were abused. Organizations separated by race, like those separated by gender, appear to have been motivated similarly, by resistance to the hegemony of others or to discrimination. In addition Black women organized together because of similar cultural and life experiences, forging their own autonomy.

African American participation in suffrage-focused organizations during the period from 1865 to 1895, or the second generation of the movement, was similar to that of the first generation. Veteran campaigners joined with younger women to work for universal suffrage. In other ways, the nature and character of organizational activities changed. From the 1880s into the twentieth century, there was increased organized Black woman

National Association of Colored Women, founding meeting,
July 1896. The group met at the Nineteenth Street Baptist Church
in the District of Columbia. A New Negro for a New Century
(1900), Anacostia Museum, Smithsonian Institution

suffrage participation nationwide as Blacks living west of the Mississippi
River began to mobilize. Throughout the second generation and third
generation of suffragists—the women active from 1895 to 1920—organizations of African American women, at times working in concert with Black
men or with white women's associations, mobilized in all regions of the
nation.

On the national level, African American woman suffrage mobilization developed with the formation of a national Black women's club
movement. A response to the national reform era of the late nineteenth
century, the idea of unifying African American women who were searching
for ways to assist their communities germinated shortly after groups of white
women's clubs came together in a similar way. In many of the Black organizations that resulted from the coalition building, woman suffrage was an
agenda item. For some of these clubwomen, woman suffrage became the
primary goal of their organization, while for others, woman suffrage became
one of several departments in the association. By the first decade of the
twentieth century, the politicization intensified as a critical mass of African
American women's organizations developed to push for the enfranchisement of all Black women as a means to protect Black communities, and
for the reenfranchisement of Black men whose votes had been stolen from

them. These woman suffrage goals of African American clubwomen were clearly nationalist in character, demonstrating the significant differences in political awareness between Black and white suffragists. By the last decade of the woman suffrage struggle, Black clubwomen utilized multiple strategies to ensure reaching their goal for enfranchisement.

Organizing Strategies in the Late Nineteenth Century

As the interracial and mixed-gendered universal suffrage organizations of the middle nineteenth century began to disappear, Black, as well as white, women began to organize separately along gendered lines. As a result, groups like the American Equal Rights Association of the 1860s and the South Carolina Woman's Rights Association of the 1870s disappeared. Although African American women's groups began to take form, throughout the rest of the woman suffrage movement, Black men were often on the scene providing moral and physical support. As the century moved into the last decade, various all-Black female alliances formed around issues such as temperance, social and educational uplift, and church work. Many of the associations endorsed universal suffrage and votes for Black women among the strategies needed to accomplish the goals of their associations.

In 1880 when Mary Ann Shadd Cary formed the Colored Women's Progressive Franchise Association in the District of Columbia, the women met at the invitation of the Black minister of the Mount Pisgah Chapel on R Street, where several men participated in the deliberations with the women who were present. At the meeting, Cary submitted her statement of purpose, proposing that the members:

> demand equal rights
> reject the idea that only men conduct industrial and other enterprises
> obtain the ballot
> develop training programs for both Black girls and Black boys
> extend the number of occupations open to women
> propose cooperation among Blacks in the District of Columbia
> establish and support a newspaper operated by Black women, which
>   does not oppose equal rights for the sexes
> recommend a bank, a print shop, and cooperative stores for the
>   instruction of men and women
> develop a local labor bureau and employment directory
> inaugurate a local lecture bureau
> disseminate information on property investment
> aid both men and women to begin their own businesses.

In addition, Cary suggested the development of a joint stock company, in which women would have the "controlling official power."[2]

**Margaret Murray Wash-
ington** was the lady principal
of the Tuskegee Institute, vice
president of the National
Association of Colored
Women, and editor of the
association's official organ
National Association Notes.
Who's Who in Colored
America *(1927), Anacostia
Museum, Smithsonian Institu-
tion*

Although the organization met several times, with forty Black women
reported in attendance at the meeting of February 20, 1880, it does not
appear that this Black women's association was long-lived.[3] One reason may
have been the radical nature of Cary's ideas, predating the Black women's
club movement by more than a decade. The goals she set for the organization combined not only educational and political action but economic and
business development. The District of Columbia was a mecca for professional
African American life and business during this period, but even Howard
University—the center for much of this activity—was suffering monetary
exigencies at the time.[4] Perhaps Cary's goals were too overwhelming for the
group to accept. In addition, her nationalist feminist perspective proposed
revolutionary ideas destined to be controversial in her community, although
woman suffrage was an acceptable issue. It appears that among middle-class
African Americans in the District of Columbia, Cary's vision connecting
feminist goals to women's labor questions and toward facilitating Black
women's entrepreneurship just seemed to be before its time.

One issue Cary did not list, of universal concern throughout African

American as well as white communities, was alcohol abuse. Many people in Black communities blamed the substance-abuse problem for political corruption and family breakdown. One solution to the problem was legislation to control public drinking, a goal sought by supporters of the temperance movement. Black reformers soon recognized votes for women as a means to legislate against alcohol abuse, and woman suffrage which became a strategy of the temperance movement. Just as the members of the Women's Christian Temperance Union (WCTU) became some of the earliest to call for woman suffrage, African American temperance workers—women in segregated WCTU unions and both men and women affiliated with independent groups—argued for woman suffrage.

As "the Nadir" became a reality to African Americans throughout the nation by the 1880s, the return of Democratic Party control of southern state governments resulted in the return of white supremacy in the South, and the effect was felt in all regions of the nation. Politically, African Americans began to lose their influence in the Republican Party. In 1884, in calling upon Blacks to be more concerned about intemperance and less concerned about white Republican politicians, Frances Harper declared, "As a race, we have a right to be interested in the success of the temperance movement."[5] In character, Harper took action, working in both African American and racially integrated circles to solve the problems of substance abuse through moral and political means. By 1885, she was a director of the Woman's Congress, a group organized by white feminist Paulina Davis to discuss the moral and humanitarian activities of woman suffragists. Harper also continued her concern for the southern women of her race, who she believed needed to learn about the ill effects "of stimulants and narcotics on the human system." By 1887 she joined forces with the WCTU, becoming the Superintendent of Work among the Colored People of the North. Harper persuaded the white leadership of the need to include African American women in the WCTU and became the first Black female to serve on the executive board. Throughout the years of her affiliation with this first mass movement among American women, Harper traveled, lectured, and organized African American women into unions throughout the Northeast, using her home in Philadelphia as a base. She published her reports in the African Methodist Episcopal Church journal, the *AME Church Review*, spreading the propaganda of both temperance and woman suffrage beyond her own region.[6]

During the 1890s, other Black women like Harper and Mary Ann McCurdy acknowledged the correlation between suffrage and temperance movements. It appears that temperance work in small towns and communities motivated the beginning of African American women's organizational development in the post–Civil War years. The organizations that resulted took on the moral reform tone of African American organizations of both men and women in the antebellum period, when temperance was a major component of the reform platform. A generation later, however, the political component of women's temperance associations distinguished them from their antebellum predecessors.

In 1892 Mamie Dillard, a Black temperance organizer from Lawrence, Kansas, specifically connected the politics of reform to woman suffrage when she gave credit to the WCTU for influencing the passage of school suffrage legislation for women in several states. She noted, however, that although the WCTU was founded in 1874, its greatest work among Blacks had been since 1887, when Frances Harper had become a superintendent. Dillard encouraged the women of her race to join the segregated Black unions that were developing in her region. Such encouragement was fruitful, and by the turn of the century, there were several WCTU unions among Black women throughout the nation. For example, Emma J. Ray organized the Colored WCTU of Seattle, Washington. In addition, there were other unions of "colored women" in South Carolina, Tennessee, and Rhode Island.[7] Segregated unions allowed African American women the autonomy and leadership opportunities they would not have had if they were integrated into mainstream unions; nonetheless, segregation as a policy, nationwide, perpetuated the aura of Blacks as second-class citizens, which was how many white Americans perceived African American women.

Into the twentieth century, clubwomen such as Mary Church Terrell, often in writing or speaking about woman suffrage, viewed it as a strategy to remedy societal problems in need of reform. Speaking to a women's group at Howard University in 1910, Terrell argued that temperance workers were "engaged in a warfare which is as tremendous as the many battles that have been waged with the gun and sword." Terrell noted how the vote would aid women in winning the war against intemperance.[8] African American women's organizations saw woman suffrage as a strategy to fight intemperance until the Eighteenth Amendment, which prohibited the sale and manufacture of alcoholic beverages, was ratified in 1919.

Simultaneously, when African American women organized into broader, more encompassing associations during the late nineteenth century, woman suffrage was a dimension included in subcommittees and in meeting discussions. Initiating this trend, when the National Federation of Afro-American Women—probably the first national organization of Black women—met for the first time in 1895 in Boston, suffragist Josephine St. Pierre Ruffin was the convener, and hundreds of African American women answered the call she had made in the *Woman's Era*. As was still customary, several prominent men were invited to speak at the proceedings, including Blacks such as T. Thomas Fortune and Ruffin's son, Stanley. Other men included white reformers such as Henry Blackwell and William Lloyd Garrison, Jr., both of whom were invited with Fortune to speak on the topic, "Political Equality for Women." Afterward, among the lively discussions was one about woman suffrage for African American women. Writing for the *New York Sun*, Fortune described the group as "the new Afro-American women."[9]

Three years earlier, in 1892, Victoria Earle Matthews had become the president of the Women's Loyal Union. An African American social worker who moved from Georgia to New York City after the Civil War, Matthews had been born a slave in 1861. Her mother, Caroline Smith, had escaped to New York during the war, but returned to Fort Valley for her children in 1873. With very little formal education, Matthews worked as a domestic servant until she married. Her personal profile was similar to that of many other women in her organization. Writing under the pen name Victoria Earle, Matthews wrote creatively and became a journalist with T. Thomas Fortune's *New York Age*. It was through this association that Matthews met Ida B. Wells when Wells came to New York in 1892 to lecture against lynching. Matthews helped to organize the testimonial for Wells, and this fund-raising event led to the development of the Woman's Loyal Union of New York and Brooklyn. Three years later, Matthews was among the Black clubwomen attending the national conference that led to the founding of the National Federation of Afro-American Women.[10]

By 1895, there were four chapters of the Woman's Loyal Union in New York and Pennsylvania, and Matthews reported that members had collected over 10,000 signatures on petitions in support of Senator Henry Blair's Woman Suffrage Resolution in Congress. African American clubwomen such as these were continuing a long tradition of petitioning government for women's right to vote.[11]

Among the organized women in Black clubs during the late nineteenth century, petitioning appears to have been one of the major strategies, as it was among American clubwomen as a whole. The earliest of the Black clubs, founded between the 1880s and 1895, were not affiliated but, like the temperance unions, formed out of local needs for bettering African American communities. A survey of the Black woman suffrage clubs and the women's clubs with woman suffrage committees reveals nationwide group participation by the end of the century.

In the Middle West and Far West, five clubs represented Black women in cities—the Chicago Women's Club, the St. Louis Suffrage Club, the Jefferson City Frances Ellen Watkins Harper Club of Missouri, the Colored Women's Club of Los Angeles, and the Colored Woman's Republican Club of Denver. In addition, state suffrage societies among Black women existed in Idaho, Montana, North Dakota, Nevada, Arizona, Oklahoma, and

New Mexico. Western clubs clearly took the lead in the numbers organized. In the South, by the end of the century there were two more chapters of the Woman's Loyal Union, one in Charleston, South Carolina, and one in Memphis, Tennessee. Also founded were the Phillis Wheatley Club of New Orleans, the Colored Woman's League of Washington, D.C., and the Tuskegee Woman's Club. State societies among Black women in the South included organizations in Delaware and West Virginia. In the East, the groups included the Sojourner Truth Club of Providence, the New Era Club of Boston, and three chapters of the Woman's Loyal Union. Significantly, among this group of Black women's associations founded in the late nineteenth century, the first federated association developed, the Northeast Federation of Colored Women's Clubs, representing numerous organizations throughout New England and the Mid-Atlantic states.[12] As some of the club names indicated, honoring women important to African American history was consistent with Black community values. From the late nineteenth century into the twentieth century, common women's club names acknowledged the inspiration or leadership of Phillis Wheatley, Sojourner Truth, Harriet Tubman, and Frances Harper.

Three organizations appeared to be moving in the direction of unifying Black women's clubs nationally—the Woman's Loyal Union, the National League of Colored Women (formerly the Colored Woman's League of Washington), and the National Federation of Afro-American Women. When in 1896 both the League and the Federation met in the District of Columbia, the two groups convened at the invitation of the Reverend Walter H. Brooks, minister of the 19th Street Baptist Church, where representatives met to discuss bringing the two rival organizations together. A merger followed with the birth of a new organization, the National Association of Colored Women (NACW), with Mary Church Terrell as its first president. By the end of the century, the NACW was the largest federation of African American women's clubs in the nation. From the onset, woman suffrage was a notable department of the NACW and continued to be for the duration of the movement.[13]

The potential political impact of a national African American woman's club movement was quite significant and Black men in politics recognized it early as important. It was not surprising then to have Black Republican Party leader Richard T. Greener seeking party recognition for the women club leaders. In 1895 he succeeded in obtaining for the first time representation for Black women at a Republican National Convention. Although Greener and his supporters had quite a hard fight in their attempts to have the women equally recognized, they succeeded. As a result, Josephine St. Pierre Ruffin, Margaret Murray Washington, and Victoria Earle Matthews, all prominent leaders in the National Federation of Afro-American Women, were invited to participate in the convention held in Detroit, Michigan.[14]

National Strategies at the
Turn of the Century and Beyond

When in the late 1890s Susan B. Anthony invited representatives of national women's organizations to submit official statements to be published in the fourth volume of *The History of Woman Suffrage*, Margaret Murray Washington responded for the National Association of Colored Women. She was first vice president of the NACW and editor of its official organ *National Association Notes*. Washington's statement, probably written in about 1898, was the only one in the volume that represented African American women, because at the time the NACW was the sole national organization among Black women. Washington's remarks included the date of the founding of the NACW and its goals, which were veiled in subtle activist and feminist rhetoric. In addition she reported,

> The Convict Lease System, "Jim Crow" Car Laws, Lynching and other barbarities are thoroughly discussed, in the hope that some remedy for these evils may be discovered.... An organ is published called *Notes*, edited by Mrs. Booker T. Washington and an assistant in each State. The association has 125 branches in twenty-six states, with over 8,000 members.[15]

The statement was a political one in that it summarized many of the social issues African Americans sought to address through legislative means.

As the nation entered the twentieth century, there were two national organizations representing numerous state federations, chapters, or clubs of African American women, and both supported woman suffrage in various ways. Of the two, the NACW represented primarily lay groups of clubwomen, whereas the second organization, the Woman's Convention of the National Baptist Convention, represented what Evelyn Brooks Higginbotham calls "the coming of Age of the Black Baptist sisterhood."[16]

Founded in 1900 at the Richmond gathering of the National Baptist Convention, the Women's Convention (WC) was an auxiliary of the National Baptist Convention, which had been founded in 1895. The two bodies met together for annual meetings. The National Baptist Convention was an alternative place for African Americans denied a voice and a platform in the mainstream society which excluded them. The Convention offered men and women a place to elect representatives, to debate social and political issues, and to critique American politics. However, there were impediments to women's equal participation in the National Baptist Convention, which the women's auxiliary attempted to remove after a five-year struggle for a

Nannie Helen Burroughs (far left) and other members of the National Association of Colored Women. *National Museum of American History, Smithsonian Institution*

voice with the men. Nannie Helen Burroughs was the spearhead, the nationalist feminist, whose voice and position often appeared (from the point of view of mainstream society and some of the men in the Convention) to be too radical a voice. According to Higginbotham, the Women's Convention was a movement for self-representation and self-determination among female Black Baptists nationwide, which over a thirty-year period culminated in a membership of over a million women. From the moment of its inception, the WC became the largest body of African American women in the nation.[17]

By the first decade of the twentieth century, Chicago clubwoman Fannie Barrier Williams wrote a history of the "colored" women's club movement, which was first published in 1902. However, she made no mention of the WC. In the essay, she traced the development and status of the NACW, which by the turn of the century claimed 400 clubs of from 50 to 200 members in each. Barrier estimated that from 150,000 to 200,000 women were influenced through club activities, notably programs targeting poor women. In listing the first three presidents, she began with Margaret Murray Washington, who was the president of the National Federation of Afro-American Women, followed by Mary Church Terrell, who was the first president of the NACW, and finally Josephine Silome Yates from

Jefferson City, Missouri. The variations in regional location of the presidents—Alabama, Washington, D. C. and Missouri—revealed the national scope and activity of the membership. Williams included in her report the names of new organizations that had affiliated with the NACW since the turn of the century. These included 40 from the South, 35 from the Midwest, 25 from the Northeast, and 3 from the West, totaling 103 new clubs within two years, bringing in at least 5,000 more women. Apparently the centers for growth in club work among African American women had shifted from the West and the Northeast in the 1890s to the South a decade later.[18] The reason for this shift is not clear. Perhaps the growth in educational institutions founded by Black women such as Charlotte Hawkins Brown, Mary McLeod Bethune, and others accelerated club work in the South.

Many of the African American women of the times were involved with both the NACW and the WC, either as members or speakers at state, regional, or national conventions, or as workers in projects with women of both organizations. Higginbotham notes, however, that the WC criticized the NACW as being elitist and not welcoming membership from the "common toilers"— the working-class or poorer women of the race. The tone of Barrier Williams's history of the NACW revealed this elitism also. The WC, on the other hand, recruited a broader cross-section of African American women, targeting the working poor.[19] Because of this class dimension, we are able to view woman suffrage arguments and strategies directed to working-class as well as middle-class Black women. Often, however, race rather than class was the major issue confronting Black women's organizations seeking the vote for African American women.

For example, in 1903 Sylvanie Williams, president of the Phillis Wheatley Club of New Orleans and an active member of the NACW, wanted the issue of the racially segregated NAWSA convention in New Orleans to become known publicly. So Williams sent a copy of her report and a letter to the *Woman's Journal*, wherein she explained why racial segregation had prevented her from attending the New Orleans meetings. In addition, Williams wanted to state for the record "the fact that the NACW is represented in your distinguished body [NAWSA] and that the report be received and read. In justice to the 10,000 intelligent colored women comprising the National Association, I can do no less."[20]

Apparently Williams had been designated to represent the NACW at the woman suffrage convention being held in her own city of New Orleans, but she was not allowed to attend because of her racial identification. Adele Alexander interprets Williams's cryptic mention that the NACW was represented at this racially segregated convention to mean that other NACW members from out of town who could pass for white attended. Alexander suggests that Tuskegee's Adella Hunt Logan may have attended the NAWSA secretly. The NACW's immediate knowlege of what decisions had been discussed at the woman suffrage convention indicates that an NACW insider was in attendance.[21] In a photograph, Sylvanie Williams appears to be white. However, the leadership of the NAWSA and the local white suffragists knew that she identified as "colored." Consequently, Williams could not have attended the meeting secretly. Prejudice against African American club-women of all hues, Fannie Barrier Williams reported, had brought the women of the race closer together. In describing the work of Sylvanie Williams in particular, Barrier Williams wrote about "a fine example of the resource-fulness and noble influence that a cultivated woman can and will give to the uplift of her race."[22] Dealing with the politics of race and gender in a national arena required resourcefulness to be sure.

Throughout the two decades before the ratification of the Nineteenth Amendment, the NACW listed a "Suffrage Department," with a national representative as head. Creating a hierarchy for disseminating information to educate club members about the benefits of supporting the woman suffrage movement was a consistent strategy implemented by the NACW. During the earliest years, Adella Hunt Logan of the Tuskegee Woman's Club served in that capacity, addressing delegates at the national and state federation conventions, traveling on behalf of the organization to discuss woman suffrage strategies.[23] After Logan's suicide in 1915, Mary B. Jackson of Providence, Rhode Island, became the head of the Department of Suffrage. National department heads were assisted by local department representatives, who by the first decade of the twentieth century functioned through regional or state federations. They reported activities during the conventions, but also through the issues of *National Association Notes*. For example, in 1904, the Northeast Federation of Colored Women reported about the work of Marichita Lyons, a suffragist from the New York chapter of the Woman's Loyal Union. Described as "one of the most brilliant women in the North," Lyons lectured throughout the region, recruiting and spreading propaganda about the "Franchise." Another example came from the Florida State Federation of Colored Women's Clubs, which met in Jacksonville in 1916. There the head of the Suffrage Department was Mrs. I. J. Williams. Her responsibility was to coordinate the Suffrage Departments of the eighteen clubs that made up the federation.[24]

By 1915, when Margaret Murray Washington was president of the NACW, Josephine B. Bruce served as first vice president, and in that capacity she headed the national executive committee. During this period, Bruce was also the editor of *Notes*, although the journal continued to be published at Tuskegee. The wife of Blanche K. Bruce, Mississippi's first Black U.S. Senator, Josephine Bruce had chaired the executive committee in 1904, when she resided on the Bruce Plantation in Josephine, Mississippi. A political activist like her husband, who had supported woman suffrage when he served in Congress, Josephine Bruce lived again in the District of Columbia by 1915, bringing a new dimension to the pages of the NACW's official organ—editorials. Often her editorial comments carried a brief political statement that reflected the growing interest of the leadership and the membership in the woman suffrage cause. In the January-February 1915 issue, there were two editorials that made reference to Black women's votes. In the first editorial Bruce noted:

> Women are voting in some states; they probably will vote in more states. The questions that belonged a few years ago solely to men now belong jointly to men and women, and some of them more to women.

Again, when discussing Black women's efforts in the temperance movement, Bruce predicted, "There is a great on rushing wave for national prohibition on a purely practical efficiency basis. . . . Many women are destined to meet this question at the polls within the next year or two."[25]

References to woman suffrage increased, and the reasons why African American women should support the movement became issues of NACW deliberation. During this last decade before the passage of the Susan B. Anthony Amendment, Black women entered the discussion more actively than before, stimulated by gender-consciousness and political awareness often encouraged by their national organizations.

In 1916 the NACW held its convention in Baltimore, Maryland, and adopted there a "Declaration of Principles." Among the resolutions included in the declaration was support for the passage of the "Susan B. Anthony Amendment granting universal and equal suffrage to all women." The NACW printed a call for funds from the NAWSA, which pledged to raise a million dollars in 1917 to lobby for the "Anthony Amendment." Apparently the NACW intended to participate fully in the lobbying process and needed funding to do so. At that time, at least ten NACW state federations were in states where woman suffrage already existed, representing nearly one-fourth of the association's members. This potential voting, lobbying, and fund-raising force was essential to the white leaders of the NAWSA, who were courting African American clubwomen.[26]

In the meantime, issues concerning woman suffrage were heard prominently at the Baptist Woman's Convention, where resolutions were also made at national meetings. Leaders called for a united leadership that "would neither compromise nor sell out" support for Black women's votes. This call directly countered the prevailing prejudice Americans expressed about working-class Blacks, who were believed to be the descendants of freedmen who had sold their votes during Reconstruction elections. Black Baptist women soon learned to argue that woman suffrage could be used as a weapon to fight racial wrongs, and also to protect women. At the 1909 convention, women spoke about how votes could be used to influence state legislators and federal officials to improve the conditions under which Black women lived and worked. By 1912 they argued, "If women cannot vote, they should make it very uncomfortable for the men who have the ballot but do not know its value."[27] There was a greater apparent militancy among these primarily working-class women and their educated leaders than among their cohorts of the NACW.

Like the NACW, which organized national departments, the WC organized national committees, such as the Committee on the State of the Country, which was headed by Mrs. L. D. Pruitt of Texas. In 1912 she placed Black women and men on the same playing field, asserting that women were as capable as men in social reform activities. She predicted that reforms would not occur, however, until women had the vote. Similarly, Gertrude Rush, a prominent lawyer from Des Moines, Iowa, and a WC delegate, argued that the vote would allow Black women to fight for "better working conditions, higher wages, and greater opportunities in business." At the same time, she predicted that African American women voters could better regulate conditions for moral and sanitary reform, and work to end discrimination, lynching, and legal injustice.[28]

Unlike NACW members, who appeared to remain faithful to the Republican Party, WC members were more politically flexible. They refused to allow any party to assume their loyalty, urging members to support issues rather than parties. As a result, in 1912 Mrs. L. D. Pruitt and her committee endorsed Theodore Roosevelt for president on the Progressive Party ticket, because the party platform had supported woman suffrage, prohibition, and child labor legislation.[29]

In assessing the impact of the WC in molding woman suffrage strategies, Higginbotham finds that by the end of the First World War, leaders such as president S. Willie Layten posited that the church was the most logical institution to promote a voter education program. Layten envisioned the ratification of the woman suffrage amendment and believed that African Americans needed to prepare to make educated voting decisions.[30] Her assumption seems to have been that the majority of the membership were not well educated and would need training to become effective voters.

Lecturing and writing about the importance of Black women voters at conventions and in organizational journals was only one national strategy. Petitioning was another very important strategy with historic roots. The NACW vehicle for mobilizing direct suffrage action was the Equal Suffrage League, whose superintendent in 1908 was Sarah Garnet, an educator from Brooklyn, New York. She and her sister, physician Susan McKinney Steward, were born on the Shinnecock Indian reservation on Long Island, a community whose residents had long been of mixed African and Indian ancestry. The widow of the late abolitionist Henry Highland Garnet, Sarah Garnet was the leading activist of this organization of high-powered African American women. In 1908 the Equal Suffrage League mounted the task of obtaining thousands of signatures on petitions in support of the Bennet Bill, the pending woman suffrage legislation in Congress. The bill had been named for Sallie Clay Bennett of Kentucky, because she was the prime mover among the members of the NAWSA for a federal suffrage bill that would at least guarantee to women the right to vote for congressional representatives. A section of the petition read,

> Resolved:
> That we, the members of The Equal Suffrage League, representing the National Association of Colored Women through its Suffrage Department, in the interest of Enfranchisement, Taxation with Representation, ask to have enacted such legislation as will enforce the 14th and 15th Amendments of the Constitution of our country, the United States of America, throughout all its sections.[31]

The petition appears not to have been a generic one prepared by a national woman suffrage organization, because much of it focused on issues of concern to African Americans exclusively, issues the mainstream organizations would have avoided. It began with a letter to the members of the Congressional Committee on National Affairs, which reads in part, "In consequence of race discriminations made against us throughout the country as a class of American citizens, which deprive us of common opportunities and also subject us to all kinds of injustices. . . . "[32] This part of the statement alone revealed the autonomous position the NACW took in lobbying for support for the Bennet Bill. The political impact of this petition, which provided a long list of prominent African American women, was significant. The list included past NACW presidents Mary Church Terrell and Josephine Silome Yates, president Lucy Thurman, and executive committee chair Margaret Murray Washington. The list also included the names of the Equal Suffrage League officers, including president Dr. Verina Morton Jones, a Brooklyn physician who would later become a member of the NAACP executive board. This was certainly a message to the Republican Party members of Congress, especially in jurisdictions in the Northeast, where the large population of African American men voted the Republican ticket.[33]

Petitioning continued as a political strategy, along with sending letters and telegrams to specific congressional leaders and to the president of the United States. Even broader goals than woman suffrage were included in this politicization process, as Black clubwomen's fears about injustices increased.

Tensions emanating from World War I led to a marked increase in racial violence. White Americans seemed to have caught "lynch fever." Mobs murdered Blacks, especially men, for the slightest provocation. The apprehensions of Black clubwomen, who had argued that they needed the ballot to promote anti-lynching legislation and its implementation to protect themselves from moral and physical attacks, had been confirmed by a dastardly 1918 lynching. Mary Turner, a pregnant Black woman from Valdosta, Georgia, protested the lynching of her husband. Her punishment was brutal torture before being burned alive, her fetus cut from her abdomen. NACW leader Lucy Laney, founder of Haines Normal and Industrial Institutes in Savannah, Georgia, publicized the atrocity, sending letters urging African American women "to fast and pray to God and protest as well." Using the NACW and other women's organizations as vehicles for dissemination, Laney called for Blacks to petition authorities for an investigation and for prevention of such horrors against "defenseless Negro women." The Federation of Negro Women's Clubs of Georgia sent many telegrams, including one to President Wilson, who assured them that the matter would be taken up. However, their telegram to the president of the Georgia Federation of White Women resulted in rebuff. Nellie Peters Black, condoning the lynching of Mary Turner, told the group that "until you teach your people not to molest the whites, there could be no adjustment." On the other hand, the president of another white group, the Savannah Federated Women, sent a letter of sympathy and promised that "noble" white southern women would speak in defense of Black women.[34]

The incident and some of the adverse reactions to it convinced the Black women of Georgia that they could not count on whites for help. They needed to help themselves. Some argued that the solution to protecting Black women was the right to vote. The federation needed a viable woman suffrage association, they argued, to assure that Georgia's Black women obtained and maintained the ballot. Although the federation had a suffrage department, critics among the working-class members claimed it was controlled by the "elite" members, a middle-class minority, which critics believed considered themselves better than the working-class members. For that matter, critics felt the entire federation was controlled by the "elite" group that did not represent the masses of Black Georgia women.[35] Unfortunately, the Turner incident aggravated class polarization among the Georgia federation membership instead of uniting Black women in an effort to fight the true enemy—racism.

Class conflict did not appear to be a problem in the WC, as its members also spoke out and sent letters to federal officials and the president about lynchings. The strategy was initiated on a very hierarchic level, however, descending from the national leadership, as indicated by the convention in 1919. There the members voted to send Nannie Burroughs's report on lynching to President Wilson, to the members of Congress and to all state governors. In her report, Burroughs denounced the president for his silence on the lynching of Black people, on the one hand, while calling for a League of Nations to promote democracy on the other. Evelyn Higginbotham finds it not surprising that the War Department called for an investigation of Burroughs as a potentially dangerous radical.[36]

Although there appeared to be divisions among Black women on state and regional levels over class issues, on the national level, leaders understood the importance of unifying around the suffrage issue and used the media to spread their views. Mary B. Talbert, a Buffalo, New York, educator and the vice president of the NACW, realized that African American women needed to unite and to persuade other women of their race to struggle for the vote, mainly because white suffragists would not. In a 1915 article she wrote for the *Crisis* about woman suffrage, Talbert said, "It should not be necessary to struggle forever against popular prejudice, and with us as colored women, this struggle becomes two-fold, first because we are women and second because we are colored women."[37] To Talbert race and gender appeared to be the unifying factors by which issues of class should be disarmed. Like other nationalist feminists, she focused on political strategies to unify the women of her race.

As the struggle for an inclusive woman suffrage amendment began to come to closure, leaders of national African American women's associations appeared to put their disagreements aside. They closed ranks to reach their goal.

Black Women's Clubs Mobilize for the Vote

Hundreds of African American women's clubs mobilized for the vote during the years from 1900 to 1920. Some were independent clubs formed in churches and in neighborhoods to aid the community. Others were affiliated with national organizations such as the Baptist Women's Convention and the NACW, often through state federations. Still others were secret societies such as sororities of college women and their alumnae, or women's auxiliaries of Masonic orders. In addition there were a small number of organized trade union women and even some Black women's suffrage clubs. Collectively and singularly, each developed the appropriate strategies for gaining the ballot, or in states where women could vote, for electing the candidates of their choice.

For Black clubwomen who lived in the few states where woman suffrage had been legislated before 1920, the goals included working to support an all-inclusive woman suffrage amendment that would give all women the right to vote in any type of election. Colorado was such a state. In the summer of 1906, the Colorado State Federation of Colored Women's

Officers of the Rhode Island League of Colored Women. *National
Museum of American History, Smithsonian Institution*

Clubs met in Denver, where Mrs. J. P. Young of Pueblo chaired a session to
discuss the role of Black women voters. Women were encouraged to be
educated voters and to seek candidates who supported justice for Black
people. In addition, Elizabeth Piper Ensley, second vice president of the
federation, delivered an address, "Woman and the Ballot." It was obvious, not
only from the convention program but from the federation song, that these
Colorado clubwomen identified with their race and with politics. The
federation song was written by Eva Carter Buckner of Colorado Springs, to
the tune of the "Battle Hymn of the Republic." The first verse read as
follows:

> We're Colorado's colored women struggling for a place;
> We're loyal to our country and we're loyal to our race;
> We're holding high the banner, in the dust it must not trail,
> As we go marching on.
> > Onward, upward to the summit,
> > Onward, upward to the summit,
> > Onward, upward to the summit,
> > We're advancing step by step.[38]

Once Illinois women won local suffrage in 1914, Chicago's African
American clubwomen went to work immediately. During 1914 and 1915,

the members of the Alpha Suffrage Club published a newsletter, the *Alpha Suffrage Record*, which sought to educate the community about candidates and local issues that would appear on the ballot. Among the club officers were president Ida B. Wells-Barnett, first vice president Mary Jackson, second vice president Viola Hill, recording secretary Vera Wesley Green, corresponding secretary Sadie L. Adams, treasurer Laura Beasley, and *Alpha Suffrage Record* editor Mrs. K. J. Bills.[39]

Black community reactions to the Alpha Suffrage Club varied at first. Some Black women enthusiastically joined the club, founded in 1913, when Wells-Barnett explained how they could use their votes for their own advantage and the advantage of their race. As a result of her efforts, over sixty members of the club marched in the 1913 suffrage parade in front of the White House. On the other hand, some Black men in Chicago were suspicious of the club's efforts. According to Wells-Barnett, they jeered at the women as they canvassed African American neighborhoods to recruit Black voters and "told them they ought to be at home taking care of the babies." Other men accused the women of trying to take male places in politics. In this case, Wells-Barnett spoke to the sexism found among the men in her Black community. However, it appears that African American women in Chicago were able to disarm these men. The suffrage clubwomen responded to male fears by telling the men that they were registering to vote in order to put Black men into elective offices, and indeed this was their goal.[40]

Because most Black women did not live in places were women had earned the right to vote, throughout most of the first twenty years of the new century, African American women's clubs sought strategies for gaining enfranchisement rather than mobilizing their communities to vote. The reason for this reality was woman suffrage coming late to most states with large Black female populations. Voting appeared to be only a dream for clubwomen in the South, and even in other regions, Black clubwomen wondered if they would ever be included in a woman suffrage amendment. Faith appeared to be the basis for their struggle.

In New York State, African American women's clubs mobilized for suffrage along with white women's groups early in the century, mainly because New York had long been a site for the woman suffrage struggle. Club leaders like Mrs. R. Jerome Jeffrey of Rochester had been a cohort of Susan B. Anthony's since the late nineteenth century. As president of the New York Federation of Colored Women, Jeffrey was part of both the NACW and the NAWSA networks. She was visibly supportive of the movement, speaking at various gatherings, such as the third convention of the NACW, which met in Buffalo in 1902. There Jeffrey appeared on the program to lead the session where club representatives addressed the convention. By 1905 when the Black suffragists of New York State were represented at the annual convention of the New York State Woman Suffrage Association, Jeffrey brought greetings from the New York Federation of Colored Women. The same year the federation met in Rochester, where as president she gave the annual report.[41] Unfortunately, there appear to be no extant records of Jeffrey's voice in arguing for suffrage. Nonetheless, her presence and the presence of her organization in the club movement were often connected to woman suffrage activity.

Black woman suffragists mobilized in New York City boroughs in the 1890s, as indicated previously in the discussion of the Woman's Loyal Union. However the Black woman suffrage network in New York City broadened as white suffragists in the city realized the importance of African American men who voted and the political awareness of their women. As early as 1910, white women suffragists from several organizations worked with African American clubwomen, inviting them to form "colored" chapters of various suffrage associations. The suffragist Alva Belmont, a southern-born New York socialite who married and divorced a Vanderbilt before marrying the wealthy banker, Oliver Belmont, was one of the first to bring Black women into the New York City world of elite white suffragists. Approaching the members of the Negro Women's Business League, Belmont proposed funding a meeting room for African American suffragists, under the auspices of her organization, the Political Equality Association. When Belmont approached Mrs. I. L. Moorman, president of the Negro Women's Business League, with the idea, Moorman posed the question about the risks of African American women entering the woman suffrage movement. The *New York Times* reported Moorman to have said,

> I asked her if she really thought colored women would be allowed to vote if the ballot privilege was conferred on them, as it is to the colored men of the South. She assured me that if it were made the law that women might vote, the right would not be denied them. The Fourteenth and Fifteenth Amendments, she said, would be carried into effect. With this assurance I told her I felt that the colored women would be glad of the opportunity of joining the movement.[42]

Over 200 African American women met with Belmont and other white women, such as Ella Hawley Crossett, president of the New York State Woman Suffrage Association, and Mrs. Henry Villard, an NAACP member and the daughter of abolitionist William Lloyd Garrison. Among the prominent Black women there was Mrs. F. R. Keyser, president of the New York State Federation of Colored Women's Clubs. Gathering at a Black church in midtown Manhattan, the Mount Olivet Baptist Church, Moorman presided over the affair, where women of the Baptist Women's Convention were surely in attendance. Belmont promised to provide the women a suffrage headquarters if more than 100 joined her suffrage association. At the close of the meeting, the *Times* reported that about half of the Black women at the meeting indicated interest in joining. This appeared to be a significant meeting, perhaps the point wherein interracial woman suffrage cooperation in this New York voting district was initiated, for at the meeting Ella Crossett welcomed African American women to affiliate with her organization, the New York State Woman Suffrage Association. Crossett discussed efforts to have the word "male" stricken from the state constitution. A bill to that effect already was in the hands of the legislators, and she explained how the suffragists needed the support of Black voting men.[43]

Within six months of that meeting, over 100 African American women had joined the "colored" branch of the Political Equality Association. Alva Belmont was true to her promise and opened a permanent headquarters in Harlem. Moorman was placed in charge of the room, which was supplied with literature, lecture courses, and study classes. Belmont promised to provide the Black women larger accommodations as the membership increased in size. What African American women did not know was that Belmont would later secretly donate $10,000 to the Southern Woman Suffrage Conference, an organization that opposed a federal woman suffrage amendment because it would enfranchise southern Black women. This regional association was working to keep Black women from voting in the same way that Black men had been disenfranchised, a tactic Moorman had feared at the outset of her interaction with Belmont.[44]

As with the WCTU unions organized by Frances Harper in the 1880s, there were pros and cons to developing segregated organizations for Black women versus integrating them into chapters with white women. Separate chapters for Black women allowed for their continued autonomy, while segregated ones, as in the New York case, promoted white hegemony and patronizing relationships, wherein white women perceived Black women as lesser representatives of their gender, in constant need of aid.

By 1915 the *New York Times* reported that the "Woman Suffrage Party" was opening a suffrage headquarters for Black women, this time a house in midtown Manhattan on West Sixty-third Street. Belmont could very well have been influential in funding this center; however, I suspect that one of the competing woman suffrage organizations seeking a Black constituency provided the building. The *Times* reporter may have been making reference to the New York Woman Suffrage Party, which had been founded in 1910 by Carrie Catt, as the sponsoring organization. At any rate, the center opened with a large open-air meeting outside the building, and Black woman suffragists Dr. Mary Halton and Portia Willis were among the speakers. Lydia D. Newman was reported to be the person in charge of canvassing communities for Black support of the woman suffrage legislation pending in the state legislature. Her plan was to organize street meetings throughout the Thirteenth Assembly District from September through to election day. African American members of the suffrage association were invited to visit the center and watch their children's supervised play from the windows above the building's play area.[45]

The New York suffragists were working diligently for the woman suffrage legislation that year, and W. E. B. Du Bois used the pages of the *Crisis* to encourage African American men to support the pending referendum to strike the word "male" from the state constitution. Du Bois was serving as a member of the Elizabeth Cady Stanton centennial committee at the time, and was perhaps the most notable Black man to support the woman suffrage movement in the twentieth century. It was in the same August 1915 issue of the *Crisis* in which he wrote his plea to Black New Yorkers that Du Bois published his second symposium on woman suffrage. This symposium included articles written by prominent African Americans and leaders of the Black women's club movement, many of whom were presidents of state federations. For organized Black New York women, there were several organizational choices for cooperative strategy building in the movement—the white woman suffrage associations, and the men and women of the NAACP. In the case of the civil rights association, there were several white women members who were also woman suffragists. The most notable of them was NAACP lawyer and National Woman's Party organizer Inez Milholland.[46]

African American women of the state used both options. For example in 1915, New York state members of the Household of Ruth, the sister affiliate of the Grand United Order of Odd Fellows, a Black fraternal convention, met with the men of their organization at the statewide convention at Poughkeepsie, New York. The group had been founded in 1897, and each year both the men's and the women's groups met at the same time. In discussing suffrage resolutions, the members argued that "the women of our race are largely wage earners in industry and their labor needs the protection of the ballot." The women endorsed the woman suffrage referendum and authorized their District Grand Most Noble Governor, Lena M. Johnson, to send their resolution to the Woman Suffrage Party of New York, because one of the goals of the party was to eliminate all legal barriers against women, including inequities in pay and employment.[47] In this New York State case, African American women elected to form a loose coalition with a political organization of primarily white women in order to assure that working-class Black women were included in the state lobby for woman suffrage. The New York State referendum did not pass until 1917, the year that Du Bois had encouraged the Black men of the state to support the bill.

In other states outside of the South, more and more legislatures considered woman suffrage bills in some way or other, and African Americans urged their representatives to adopt woman suffrage bills. Such was the case in Ohio. In 1919, Black Republican women in the state reorganized and renamed their association when the Republican legislature defeated the equal rights bill. These clubwomen elected Rosa Moorman president of the Colored Women's Independent Political League. Before the vote on the equal rights bill, Moorman had taken a petition in support of it to the Ohio House of Delegates asking the Republicans to support the bill that would have provided for woman suffrage. She claimed that the men "whom we helped elect were utterly out of sympathy with the movement." As a result, women who formerly supported the Republican Party decided to organize independently, away from the party.[48]

As in Ohio and Illinois, African American men in Rhode Island had been voting since 1870 and their women, though disfranchised, remained actively involved in local politics. A good example of a Black women's suffrage network was the Colored Women's Civic and Political League of Rhode Island. The leaders were professional women and women married to professional men who supported their wives' political efforts. Among them was Mary E. Jackson, a state civil service employee who as early as 1904 worked prominently with the Northeast Federation of Colored Women and headed the Suffrage Department of the NACW. In addition, there was Susan E. Williams, a teacher; Maria Lawton, the wife of a government official; and Bertha G. Higgins, the wife of a physician. Of this group, Higgins was the prime mover on the local level. She had given up her dressmaking business after marriage to devote her time to homemaking and community service. Higgins was a founder and leader of several women's political organizations, mainly the League, and later, the Julia Ward Howe Republican Women's Club. In these associations, members fought for woman suffrage and black women's political patronage. During the struggle for women's votes, Black women like Higgins looked pragmatically at the Republican Party in Rhode Island, believing it could best facilitate their political goals, although a woman suffrage referendum never passed the state legislature. Nonetheless, these Black clubwomen joined a variety of organizations to foster the networking they felt was necessary for the survival of their community. In 1916, for example, the Julia Ward Howe Club members persuaded the Twentieth Century Art and Literary Club, a group of Black Providence women, to sponsor a suffrage minstrel show. The funds raised from this event benefited the Providence Woman Suffrage Party, which was primarily an organization of white women, yet an interracial association. Subsequently Howe Club members designed rallies and church affairs not only to support the woman suffrage campaign financially, but to recruit Black women into the movement.[49] Here we see Rhode Island suffragists using tactics similar to those New York suffragists adopted, coalescing with other like-minded women's groups.

The Julia Ward Howe Republican Women's Club was named for the nineteenth-century Massachusetts suffragist who had embraced African American women in the movement. Like the Alpha Suffrage Club of Chicago, the Howe Club in Providence provided significant Black female political mobilization for Republican Party candidates during political campaigns.

In 1920 Black woman suffragists in Rhode Island campaigned vigorously for the ratification of the Nineteenth Amendment, and for not only the Harding ticket, but for Rhode Island Congressman Clark Burdick also. The women were known for canvassing neighborhoods in efforts to get Black people out to vote the Republican ticket. When Harding, who was running for president, and Representative Burdick were successfully elected, both men sent Higgins letters of thanks for Black clubwomen's support during the elections. These personal citations revealed the political influence of African American women outside of the South and in the Republican Party.[50]

In the South, in contrast to the North, Black people had to be very careful about publicly supporting the Republican Party. In any event, most Black men could not vote in the southern states. Exceptions occurred in small communities like Tuskegee, Alabama, and perhaps even in Hampton, Virginia, where professional African American men were insulated in college towns and had maintained the privilege to vote granted by the Fifteenth Amendment. Woman suffrage, however, was not readily accepted by white women or white men in Alabama. Consequently, whites truly frowned on African American women who openly supported the cause. As Adele Alexander notes, a hostile environment awaited the women of the Tuskegee Woman's Club as they initiated their woman suffrage efforts at the turn of the century.[51]

The Tuskegee Woman's Club was the center for educational, social and political club work among the elite African American women connected with the Tuskegee Institute. The club had been founded with Margaret Murray Washington as president, in 1895. Shortly thereafter, she became founder and president of the Southern Federation of Colored Women's Clubs.[52] Adella Hunt Logan was one of the charter members of the Tuskegee Woman's Club and perhaps its most dynamic woman suffrage activist. She encouraged students and women faculty particularly to learn about and participate in the movement. Documented woman suffrage activities developed by the club at the Institute began in 1900. For example, Logan organized a political parade for her civics class at about the time for the kickoff of Republican President McKinley's reelection campaign. Logan also coached the debate team, which focused on the question of women voting. A decade later, the clubwomen were holding formal "suffrage nights," with "lantern shows," projecting images of famous suffragists such as Sojourner Truth, and convening suffrage lectures, often presented by Logan. In 1912, when the National Medical Association met at Tuskegee, Ruth Logan organized the opening ceremonies. Adella Logan's eldest daughter, Ruth taught physical education at Tuskegee, and like her mother was a suffragist and member of the Tuskegee Woman's Club. The opening featured a "suffragette parade," a suffrage sing-along, and women students wearing the yellow sashes with the phrase, "votes for women," symbolic of the iconography of the national movement.[53]

The suffrage activities of the club appear to have been primarily educational, for the idea of women voting in Alabama seemed merely a fantasy. However, after graduation many of the Tuskegee students returned to their homes or obtained employment outside of the South, where in another time and location Black women could dare to dream of actually voting. What is most significant about the Tuskegee clubwomen is their impact on the woman suffrage movement outside of their home communities. Adella Logan's words in particular graced the pages of the *Crisis* and the *Colored American Magazine*, where her voice reached a national African American audience.

By the end of the second decade of the twentieth century, many more African American women's suffrage and voters clubs emerged, primarily in states where women won the right to vote before the ratification of the Nineteenth Amendment, but also in states where voting was still just a dream for women. In Texas, where woman suffrage was enacted in 1918, there were the Colored Welfare League of Austin, the Negro Women's Voters League of Galveston, the Colored Women's Progressive Club of El Paso, and the Republican Voter's League of Texas, which was formed at the Texas State Republican Convention of 1918. In addition to Texas, Black women in California, another western state that enfranchised women before Nineteenth Amendment ratification, organized the Colored Woman's Republican Club of Los Angeles. In the South, there were the Washington Women's Republican League; Alpha Kappa Alpha and Delta Sigma Theta, two sororities founded at Howard University in the District of Columbia; and the Colored Women's Suffrage Club of Maryland, which was founded in a hostile environment by Estella Hall Young of Baltimore. In the East, clubs included the North East Woman's Suffrage Association of Boston, and in the woman suffrage state of New York, the Colored Women's Suffrage Club of New York City, four chapters of the Negro Women Voters in Queens, and the Woman's Non-Partisan League of New York City. The St. Louis Suffrage Club represented the Midwest.[54]

Conclusion

Mobilization for the right to vote appeared to have a snowballing effect among Black clubwomen, as more and more women's organizations joined the movement. Several reasons account for this phenomenon. As the Black women's club movement developed nationwide, there was greater exchange of ideas about common problems like intemperance, discrimination against African American women because of race and/or gender, and the disfranchisement of Black men. As other groups seeking redress of grievances through political means aligned with Black women, a critical mass of sentiments for enfranchising Black women developed. This illusion of strength promoted a sense of empowerment among women in clubs. For the most part, club leadership directed the strategy, and the leaders considered themselves to be the elite because they were educated and middle-class, although some of the clubs represented significant numbers of working-class and poorer women. As a result, when looking at club work, we tend to hear the voices of elite African American women who articulated the issues in need of attention. Nonetheless, as the drive to ensure the enfranchisement of all American women reached its apex, it appears that Black women closed ranks, putting aside internal differences and focusing on winning the prize.

Chapter 6. Anti–Black Woman Suffrage Tactics and African American Women's Responses

> If the Women of the dominant race had a broader and clearer vision of the
> Fatherhood of God and the brotherhood of man, and would exert that
> influence now in the legislative halls and criminal courts to correct some of
> the pernicious laws that discriminate so outrageously against a part of the
> citizens of this country because of their color, then I would say, God speed
> the day when all women might be given the franchise that their ballot
> might be thrown in the balance that justice, a fair chance, and equal oppor-
> tunity might be given to every man regardless of color or race.
> —Mrs. A. W. Blackwell (1917)[1]

Throughout the woman suffrage movement, African American spokeswomen countered the anti-woman suffrage arguments put forward by individual white males and females and by antisuffrage organizations. They also responded to the argument of those African Americans who questioned the motives of early twentieth-century white suffragists or who doubted how effective woman suffrage goals could be to Blacks.

Although the overwhelming majority of African Americans who commented upon woman suffrage supported it, a popular view evolved in the accounts of the woman suffrage movement that Blacks were "antis," or at best, indifferent to the cause of the enfranchisement of women. Moreover, the popular view, in generalizing about Black responses to the movement, made little distinction between the Blacks who chose universal suffrage over woman suffrage versus Blacks who chose to oppose women voting entirely.[2]

Woman suffrage, like all controversial issues, had its skeptics and its opponents. During the formative years of the movement, there was little organized antisuffrage activity; however, after the Civil War, the "antis" began actively to counteract suffrage ideas and their advocates. The antisuffrage argument was based upon the belief that women did not need or did not want or could not handle the responsibility of voting. By the 1890s, the "antis" had founded organizations throughout the nation, and their influence remained apparent for the duration of the struggle for woman's right to the vote.

As the antisuffrage forces mobilized nationally in the 1890s, "educated suffrage" became an important argument used to exclude Black women from the movement. Southern white women were taking greater interest in the woman suffrage movement. Simultaneously, anti–Black woman suffrage arguments developed, not only among those who basically opposed the movement, but among some white suffragists who had spoken on behalf of African American women in the past. Anti–Black suffrage sentiments came not only from southern white women who believed in white supremacy; some northern suffragists said that it was expedient to ignore Black women while wooing support for the movement from the South.

Exclusionary sentiments came from woman suffrage leaders outside of the South, revealing how for some their expressed fear of alienating white southern suffragists was merely a scheme for covering up the racism among women suffragists generally. Historian Marjorie Spruill Wheeler confirms that many white suffragists believed votes for white women could be used as a way of countering African American voters in the South.[3] Even the editors of a national journal, the *Suffragists*, published several news items aimed to show white southern suffragists how, even with a federal woman suffrage amendment, Black votes would be countered by white female votes in the South.[4]

Nevertheless, African American women persisted in their efforts not only to gain membership in the national woman suffrage organizations, but to assist all Black women in gaining the right to vote. It soon became evident to white politicians that African American women would resist any attempt to disfranchise Blacks. As a result, white Democratic Party southerners in particular feared the political clout that Republican Party African American females could develop not only for themselves and for their race as a whole, but against the southern Democrats.

It is not surprising that many feared the effect of African American female voters on the politics of the nation. Demographic data from the late nineteenth century to the decade of the woman suffrage blitz (1910–20) revealed the steady growth of the Black female population. In 1890 there were approximately 1.6 million Black females twenty-one or over in the nation. By 1910, in fifteen southern states alone, there were 4.4 million Black women of voting age, compared to the 10.6 million white women of voting age. Although the National Woman's Party reported that a federal suffrage amendment would not "complicate the race problem" in the South, since whites outnumbered Blacks, white supremacists maintained their misgivings, despite NWP attempts to calm their fears. On local levels, white suffragists responded similarly, as Suzanne Lebsock found among members of the Equal Suffrage League of Virginia.[5]

As Black women responded to antisuffrage arguments, Black men joined their women by reporting in the Black press about woman suffrage policies and activities that discriminated against African American women. Together they were determined to give racism a difficult time keeping Black women from the polls.

The Universal vs. the
Educated (Woman) Suffrage Strategies

Throughout much of the first generation of the woman suffrage movement, Blacks attempted to demonstrate that disfranchised African Americans and disfranchised women shared the common plight of oppression. In doing so, they aimed to unite the two groups for a greater drive toward universal suffrage. As Black suffrage advocates adopted this strategy, many woman suffrage advocates among whites moved further away from the universal suffrage cause and more toward the goal of enfranchising only white women. During the post–Civil War years, the cry from white women to enfranchise Black women lasted about ten years. For some this cry appeared to have been merely a ploy to gain sympathy from Republicans who supported the "Negro suffrage" cause. Once the argument seemed no longer expedient, some white women of the first generation ended their call for men to enfranchise Black women. Although African American women such as Sojourner Truth, Frances Harper, and Mary Ann Shadd Cary called for the ballot as a means of protecting themselves and the women of the race, the strongest outcry among Black men and Black women on behalf of the women of the race became evident during the last two decades of the nineteenth century, after white feminists ceased to call for the enfranchisement of Black women.[6]

Commenting upon the contradictions in the woman's movement as early as 1869, Harper knew that among most white suffrage leaders, gender took priority over race. As a result, she questioned the position Black women held among the priorities of white women. In response to Sarah F. Norton's appeal for feminist cooperation in establishing the Working Woman's Association in New York, Harper asked if the association "was broad enough to take colored women." Susan Anthony said "yes"; however, Harper retorted that when she was in Boston "there were sixty women who left work because one colored woman went to gain a livelihood in their midst."[7] In this context, when Frances Harper spoke of "women," she meant "white women."

As organized support for African American rights among reformers dissolved after Reconstruction, the white feminists' need to champion the rights of African American women evaporated and, as a result, the fight for Black female rights became low on the list of priorities. The white suffragists generally agreed with the prevailing views about race. As early as the 1870s, Black men and Black women became the scapegoats, and they were blamed for the failure of woman suffrage and Reconstruction. As northern and western suffragists allied with southern suffragists in accepting white supremacy, the alliance indicated that the feminists' fight, for the most part, was for white women to be included in the rights and privileges of a racist society. The common view among contemporary chroniclers of the woman suffrage movement is that the suffragists capitulated to racism by the turn of the century.[8] However, as early as 1878, at the Tenth Washington Convention of the NWSA, Frederick Douglass spoke of anti-Black prejudice among white suffragists. Furthermore, shortly afterward activities among Black women were written out of the *History of Woman Suffrage*. A late nineteenth-century example occurred in the South Carolina state history. Despite the fact that the South Carolina Woman's Rights Association was founded by Blacks in 1870, Virginia B. Young, in writing the history of the movement in that state, totally overlooked this group. She dated the beginning of the movement in her state as 1890, the year the organization over which she presided, the South Carolina Woman Suffrage Association, was founded. In the same way, Black women were nearly totally written out of the twentieth-century state histories compiled for the *History of Woman Suffrage,* despite previously noted evidence that Black suffragists were active during the early 1900s in Illinois, New York, and the District of Columbia. The one exception was the state history for Tennessee, which included Black women's activities.[9]

Overt discrimination against African Americans in the suffrage movement became most apparent in the 1890s. While stirring northern Black women to join the suffrage movement on one hand, Henry Blackwell (Lucy Stone's husband) publicly advocated "educated suffrage" as a means of eliminating the southern Black female voter on the other. In 1903 the NAWSA passed a resolution stating that there were more white native-born women who could read and write than all Black and foreign-born voters combined, so that "the enfranchisement of such women would settle the vexed question of rule by literacy, whether of home grown or foreign-born production."[10]

In spite of their personal opinions, suffragists like Susan Anthony were willing to sacrifice principle for the sake of expediency. In an 1894 meeting with Ida B. Wells-Barnett, Anthony explained why she had compromised her ideals against racial discrimination. Anthony had asked Frederick Douglass not to attend the forthcoming NAWSA convention scheduled for Atlanta, Georgia, which was to be the first southern-held convention. She did this to avoid embarrassment for Douglass as well as to avoid jeopardizing support of woman suffrage from southern white women. In recalling the incident in her journal, Wells-Barnett wrote what she remembered that Anthony said,

> Not only that, but when a group of colored women came and asked that I come to them and aid them in forming a branch of the suffrage association among the colored women, I declined to do so, on the ground of that same expediency.[11]

To Anthony, "expediency" appeared to mean sacrificing mobilizing Black women to join the national woman suffrage association in order to placate potential southern supporters. In response, Wells-Barnett criticized Anthony for sustaining the prejudice of white southern suffragists. Wells-Barnett felt that, although Anthony may have made gains for woman suffrage by her behavior, "she had also confirmed white women in their attitude of segregation."[12]

The same year, Elizabeth Cady Stanton attacked the concept of universal suffrage in the South and once again denounced the enfranchisement of illiterate people everywhere. During the NAWSA Convention held in Atlanta in 1895, she expressed her concern about the danger in enfranchising illiterate women, whose votes Stanton presumed would be manipulated by politicians. Her sentiment appealed to the southern audience because of its racist connotations; however, Harriet Stanton Blatch, Susan B. Anthony, and William Lloyd Garrison, Jr., opposed the idea. Needless to say, Stanton's view prevailed.[13]

Although Susan Anthony was not a proponent of "educated suffrage," she wanted to remove the race question from the suffrage campaign after the Fifteenth Amendment controversy. She was alleged to have dissuaded Helen Pitts, Frederick Douglass's second wife, from discussing the plight of Black women in southern prison camps at the NAWSA Convention in 1898. This meeting became a strategy session for southern whites, who, according to Louisiana suffragist Kate M. Gordon, seriously considered woman suffrage "as a means to the end of securing white supremacy in the state." Hence, Susan Anthony's motives may have been politically designed not to alienate these white suffragists. Carrie Catt of New York, who later became an NAWSA president, and Alabama suffragist Frances A. Griffin were invited to speak to a group of white men and women in New Orleans about how to use woman suffrage to that end. Adele Alexander found that by 1904 Catt wrote in the *Woman's Journal*, "It is little wonder that the North is beginning to question the wisdom of the indiscriminate enfranchisement of the Negro."[14] These sentiments do not make it clear whether Catt was merely rationalizing the expedient strategy of scapegoating African Americans in order to win southern support, or whether Catt truly believed Blacks to be unworthy of voting. Unlike Anthony, Catt used the race question frequently.

As for Frances Griffin, at the NAWSA meeting at Grand Rapids, Michigan in 1899, she addressed the national woman suffrage platform for the first time and set the tone for anti-Black sentiments when she spoke bitterly about her "Negro boy" gardener who, at twenty-three, was illiterate, but enfranchised.[15] It was at the same meeting that Anthony was alleged to have influenced white suffragists to oppose the motion by Lottie Wilson Jackson against Jim Crow accommodations for Black women in the South. Jackson was a Black delegate from Michigan, and she resolved "that colored women ought not be compelled to ride in smoking cars, and that suitable accommodations should be provided for them."[16] A bitter debate ensued. The resolution was ultimately tabled because it was considered irrelevant to the woman suffrage issues. Apparently embittered by the controversy and Anthony's rejection of Black women's concerns, Lottie Jackson voted against Anthony. According to reports published in the *Woman's Journal*, Jackson was the only delegate to oppose Anthony.[17]

The irony of this argument is that the so-called radical suffragists, Anthony and Stanton, had criticized the more conservative members of the woman suffrage movement prior to 1890 because they were unwilling to challenge all problems faced by women. After 1890, when the NWSA and the AWSA reunited, the woman's movement gained in popularity on a national level, the leadership became more conservative, and leaders did not require members to agree on anything other than woman suffrage. In an attempt to woo male support, as well as southern white female support, suffragists demonstrated that white women's views about race were the same as white males' views. Consequently, some suffragists were willing to argue that nonwhite women held no claim to suffrage.[18]

Opposition to the racism of individual suffragists or other reformers did not negate Black support for the ideals of the woman suffrage cause. As a result, African American women championed the suffrage movement in much the same way that Blacks generally supported the Populists and the Progressive movement—bypassing elements of the movements that deterred them, but defending basic and inclusive, democratic concepts. Similarly, Blacks accepted some, but rejected other sides of woman suffrage leaders like Susan B. Anthony, who had been an ardent abolitionist and one-time friend of universal suffrage. Like Wells-Barnett and Jackson, some African American suffragists admonished Anthony for what they perceived as racist behavior, but some also forgave her expedient course of action because of her past loyalty.[19]

African American Women Respond to the "Antis"

African American women responded, primarily in the Black press, to the general anti–woman suffrage rationale, which was not only illogical, but undemocratic. Josephine St. Pierre Ruffin challenged the woman suffrage opposition in Boston when "antis" attempted to sabotage municipal suffrage. In an editorial prepared for her Black women's newspaper, *Woman's Era*, coauthored with her daughter, Florida Ridley, Ruffin wrote sarcastically:

> The friends of equal rights owe a deep debt of gratitude to the Man Suffrage Association for the impetus their organized opposition to woman suffrage has given to the cause. Not for many years has so much interest and enthusiasm been shown in the annual meeting of the Massachusetts Woman Suffrage Association as in these held in Association Hall the week ending January [1896].[20]

By the early twentieth century, the opposition of Black females to the antisuffrage argument became even more pronounced. In 1900 Mary Church Terrell, then president of the NACW, addressed the NAWSA and opposed the anti–woman suffrage argument that it was "unnatural for women to vote." Proceedings chroniclers said that she called the discrimination against women as voters unjust and predicted that "the political disenfranchisement of woman shall be removed." In 1905 Ella Wheeler Wilcox, a prominent white feminist and poet from South Carolina, responding to an anti–woman suffrage editorial in the *Beaufort County News*, asserted, "Women's suffrage must and will come before another decade." Black journalist Grace Lucas-Thompson of the *(Indianapolis) Freeman* concurred with this view and published Wilcox's statement in her women's column of the *Freeman*.[21] In the case of both Ruffin and Lucas-Thompson, we hear the voices of Black women journalists specifically targeting African American women readers in their discussion about the politics of the "anti" debates.

The same year, Adella Hunt Logan wrote the most comprehensive attack upon the anti–woman suffrage argument from an African American woman of the time. In referring to the Fourteenth Amendment, she quoted the section on citizenship and argued that women should be included. She denounced those men who claimed to love the principles of the American Revolution, but failed to apply these ideals to women. In rejecting the argument that women were too modest to be seen in public at the polling booth, Logan declared that "every man who thinks knows that every woman who thinks just a little sees through this screen to her modesty."[22] In addition, she cited the success of woman suffrage in western states where the evils predicted by antisuffragists had not occurred. Like Blacks before her, such as Gertrude Mossell, Logan used the printed media to discredit the myth that women did not want to vote. Some did not, she claimed, but many more did. If that was a valid reason for disfranchising a group, then, she reasoned, the ballot should be taken from the men who did not choose to cast their votes. Logan resented being treated as a minor and challenged all the other excuses for denying women the ballot such as husbands represent wives; women could never understand politics; and women are not interested in politics. In this remarkable argument, we have an attack upon the "antis" expressed, in the Colored American Magazine, by an African American woman.[23]

A decade later, as the debate over suffrage intensified, Black women continued to offer rebuttals to critics. Many responded in 1915 when W. E. B. Du Bois called for essays to be published in the special woman suffrage issue of the Crisis. For example, Minnesota clubwoman Lillian A. Turner wrote facetiously, "I have ceased to tremble when I hear dire predictions of the ruin that is expected to follow the rapid approach of woman's franchise." In the same Crisis issue, Rhode Island clubwoman Mary E. Jackson wrote, "Looked at from a sane point of view, all objections to the ballot for women are but protests against progress, civilization and good sense."[24]

In their own words, these early twentieth-century African American spokeswomen expressed views quite similar to those that white women suffragists voiced against the "antis." Although all of these women were leaders in the NACW, they also affiliated with predominantly white suffrage groups such as the NAWSA and the Woman's Party. For the most part, these suffragists had to contend with conservative elements who were fearful of removing middle-class women from their "proper place"—the home.

As the suffrage campaign intensified, the antisuffrage argument became more entwined with other political considerations. In some states, a sizable liquor lobby supported the cause of the "antis," and these lobbyists attempted to sabotage the temperance wing of the woman suffrage forces. In the South the whole question of protecting white womanhood, as well as maintaining a disfranchised Black population, was another issue. In a vehement response to the southern position in 1919, the Black editors of the Messenger, A. Phillips Randolph and Chandler Owen, compared the southern Democratic Party leaders to the czar of Russia, calling them feudalistic opponents of democracy.[25]

As Congress debated the amendment in the summer of 1919, Black women whose men voted Republican in Ohio took action against the male elected officials who refused to support the Beatty Equal Rights Bill in the lower house of the state legislature. The bill failed by a vote of thirty-five to sixteen. As a result, the Colored Women's Republican Club in Columbus severed its party affiliation. This bold action was typical of woman suffragists throughout the nation, who organized politically without having the right to vote.[26]

Despite the evidence that Blacks opposed anti–woman suffrage arguments, national suffrage leaders needed to be reminded of that fact again and again. Du Bois, in editorializing in the *Crisis*, made it his business to do the reminding. In 1911, for example, he refuted a statement made by NAWSA president Anna Shaw indicting Blacks for opposing woman suffrage. Du Bois accused Shaw of a "barefaced falsehood." In addition, he chastised her for not attempting to enlighten those who she felt did not support woman suffrage. At the same time, Du Bois noted the hypocrisy among suffrage leaders who criticized Blacks for opposing woman suffrage, but not whites who opposed enfranchising Blacks.[27] The NAACP, like many institutions serving the African American community, understood the politics of the woman suffrage movement, part of which was to defame African Americans so that they would be excluded from the franchise entirely. As a result, the efforts African Americans had made since the Civil War to discredit the anti–woman suffrage arguments appeared to make little difference to those who refused to accept them.

African American Women Respond
to Anti–Black Woman Suffrage Strategies

Black women's responses to the gendered and racialized politics of the times varied. Many individual African Americans endorsed woman suffrage because it seemed a vehicle for helping the race. At the same time, others were discouraged from joining the national suffrage movement, suspicious of the leadership's position on enfranchising Black women. Nonetheless, African American women discussed the woman suffrage issues and usually resolved that they could accomplish more for the race by supporting the movement. As a result, they were obliged to counter the anti–Black woman suffrage strategies.

In 1899 Adella Hunt Logan wrote her concerns about the southern states' determination to disfranchise Black men and keep women from gaining the right to the ballot. In a letter to a white northern friend, Logan held little hope for white southern women's enfranchisement "and none for the black woman."[28] She clearly foresaw the bitter fight during the next two decades to include Black women in the woman suffrage amendment.

When the NAWSA convention met in New Orleans in 1903, the anti–Black woman suffrage strategy went into immediate effect. It was there that the executive board was forced to make a public statement about its attitude toward Black women as potential voters. At the time, the following women served on the board: Susan B. Anthony, Carrie Chapman Catt, Anna Howard Shaw, Kate M. Gordon, Alice Stone Blackwell, Harriet Taylor Upton, Laura Clay, and Mary J. Coggeshall. The statement contained the endorsement of these women as well as a strong states' rights position on the question of granting the ballot to Black women.[29]

During the convention week, Anthony visited the Phillis Wheatley Club, perhaps the largest group of African American women in the city. Sylvanie Williams, a suffragist and the club president, brought Anthony poignant greetings on behalf of the members. Her words seemed in direct response to the racial overtones of the policy statement of the NAWSA. In presenting a bouquet to Anthony, Williams stated,

> Flowers in their beauty and sweetness may represent the womanhood of the world. Some flowers are fragile and delicate, some strong and hardy, some are carefully guarded and cherished, others are rough treated and trodden under foot. These last are the colored women. They have a crown of thorns continually pressed upon their brow, yet they are advancing and sometimes you find them further on than you would have expected. When woman like you, Miss Anthony, come to see us and speak to us it helps us believe in the Fatherhood of God and the Brotherhood of man, and at least for the time being in the sympathy of women.[30]

Williams, who would have represented the NACW at the convention, could not attend the New Orleans gathering because Black women were not welcomed at the segregated affair. She was seriously offended by the policy.

The following year, Mary Church Terrell attended the NAWSA Convention held in the District of Columbia. During the proceedings, the white delegates spoke of the problems of child and animal abuse. In response to a call for federal legislation to protect children and animals, Terrell said:

> A resolution asks you to stand up for children and animals. I want you to stand up not only for children and animals but also for negroes [sic]. You will never get suffrage until the sense of justice has been so developed in men that they will give fair play to the colored race.[31]

Other African American women expressed similar sentiments when given the opportunity at NAWSA conventions. At the 1911 convention in Louisville, Kentucky, a Black female delegate attempted to formulate a resolution condemning disfranchisement on the grounds of both sex and race. Du Bois and Martha Gruening, a white NAACP leader and a suffragist, alleged that Anna Shaw aborted the resolution attempt. According to Gruening, Shaw gave two reasons for her actions. First, the suffragists did not want to offend their southern hostesses with a resolution that opposed the doctrine of white supremacy. Second, Shaw was quoted as having said,

I am in favor of colored people voting, but white women have no enemy in the world who does more to defeat our amendments, when submitted, than colored men, and until women are recognized and permitted to vote, I am opposed to introducing into our women suffrage convention a resolution on behalf of men who, if our resolution were carried, would go straight to the polls and defeat us every time.[32]

In response to Anna Shaw's allegation, which sounded quite similar to the ones made by suffragists during the Fifteenth Amendment controversy, Du Bois charged, "We have already shown that the statement that colored men opposed woman suffrage is false, and we have only to add that every effort was made to keep this resolution from being presented; and when it finally appeared it was incontinently side tracked in committee."[33]

Assessing the validity of the Shaw accusation is difficult because statistics are not available. Nonetheless, the Black male electorate could never have made the impact that she claimed that it could, because the majority of Black males lived in the South and their votes had been substantially reduced by the turn of the century. It appeared that African American men were being used as scapegoats, but then so were their women. In reply to accusations that Black women's clubs opposed woman suffrage, a Black suffragist from Vineland, New Jersey, stated, "It was the Labor Union, and the white women's clubs of New Jersey which defeated the Amendment." She claimed further that in her borough there were 722 votes for woman suffrage and that she personally secured 300 of them.[34]

Although white suffragists exaggerated the anti–woman suffrage activity among African Americans, there were a few Black men who voiced reservations, if not opposition to the movement. Often, what appeared to be anti–woman suffrage sentiments were really opposition to white women suffragists, whose racism Black men feared. Historian Glenda Gilmore suggests, in her dissertation about gender and Jim Crow politics in North Carolina, that some middle-class Black men were fearful that if their women attempted to vote they would face the same intimidation and indignities Black men had faced at the polls. For this reason, they expressed antisuffrage views.[35]

Perhaps the most vocal Black woman on this subject was Mary Church Terrell. In 1912 she wrote, "If I were a colored man, and were unfortunate enough not to grasp the absurdity of opposing suffrage because of the sex of a human being, I should at least be consistent enough never to raise my voice against those who have disfranchised my brothers and myself on account of race." However, Terrell observed in her travels that "the intelligent colored man who opposed woman suffrage is very rare indeed." In discussing woman suffrage, Terrell said that the majority of men whom she described as the "leading citizens" in their communities advocated it.[36]

Writing for the *Crisis* in 1915, Terrell compared the plight of Blacks and women. Her aim was to obtain support from Blacks who, because they distrusted white suffragists, failed to support the woman suffrage cause. She felt that the same antisuffrage argument used to withhold the ballot from women was used to prove that Black men should remain disfranchised. For this reason alone, she argued, African Americans should support woman suffrage. Likewise Coralie Cook, writing the same year in the *Crisis*, reminded skeptical Black men that "disenfranchisement because of sex is curiously like disenfranchisement because of color. It cripples the individual; it handicaps progress; it sets a limitation upon mental and spiritual development."[37]

Nonetheless, African American fears went beyond misgivings about white women, particularly in the South. There Black women resisted the idea that woman suffrage truly represented enfranchising all women, because they trusted the white power structure's promise to keep Blacks, both men and women, disfranchised. As the debates about enfranchising African American women intensified, southern suffragists such as Margaret Murray Washington became even more disillusioned by the movement. In 1912 she wrote a friend that most men and women of the race had other priorities. As for woman suffrage, she felt that Black women would "try hard to take our stand," but only when the nation reached the point of giving African American women equal rights with all other citizens.[38] Nationalist feminists, however, refused to be disillusioned and particularly sought to gain the vote, as whites feared, to establish universal suffrage for all Black adults.

Segregation and Exclusion among
Woman Suffrage Activists

Race consciousness was evident among African American women as growing numbers of race-specific civil rights associations, business groups, and self-help societies emerged at the end of the nineteenth century. White women did not have the severe problems of racial discrimination and segregation that compounded Black women's plight for education and employment as well as political equity. Segregation was the norm by the turn of the century, and white women, either consciously or unconsciously, accepted the vicious justification for it, just as did white men. As a result, Black women were not only discouraged from joining the suffrage organizations of white women, they were also segregated or excluded in their attempts to demonstrate on behalf of woman suffrage and from voting in areas where they had earned the right.

Despite the differences between the groups, there were some common causes and attempts at unity on local levels. Journalist Paula Giddings
refers to the women who made these attempts as "radical interracialists"—
Black women who were determined to enter the mainstream.[39] Nevertheless, doing so was not easy, for this was the era of Jim Crow nationwide,
especially in the South where most African Americans still lived. African
American women were involved in temperance work, suffrage groups, and
club work. The experiences of many of their leaders indicated the perva-
siveness of white female prejudice and discrimination against Black females
in women's groups, even among those who were part of the woman suffrage
coalition.[40]

Throughout the 1890s, Josephine St. Pierre Ruffin challenged white
women to unite with Blacks for the benefit of humanity, but her words went
virtually unheeded outside of Massachusetts. She was discriminated against
personally when attending the General Federation of Women's Clubs, which
met in Wisconsin in 1900. Disillusioned by the incident, the Black women's
club she represented, the Woman's Era Club, made an official statement that
included the view "that colored women should confine themselves to their
clubs and the large field of work open to them there."[41] In essence, they
voluntarily segregated themselves from the white club movement.

At the same convention of the General Federation of Women's Clubs,
Mary Church Terrell, representing the NACW, was refused permission to
bring the group greetings on behalf of her association because the southern
clubs objected, threatening resignation. Despite this rebuff, Terrell accepted
invitations to speak before other white groups during the early years of the
twentieth century. At the Minneapolis Convention of Women in 1900 she
addressed the group not only about the needs of Black women, but also
about the prejudice and lack of sympathy on the part of white women. Terrell indicted them for not extending a helping hand to African Americans
whose aims were similar to their own. The same year, she made a similar
speech at the NAWSA meeting in the District of Columbia.[42]

Ida B. Wells-Barnett reflected about how Fannie Barrier Williams, an
African American clubwoman in Chicago, attempted to join the Chicago
Woman's Club in 1894. The all-white group split over the controversy created by those who wanted a Black member and those who did not. After
fourteen months of controversy, Williams was admitted. At the turn of the
century, Wells-Barnett noted that the issue was still significant in Illinois
when the State Federation of Women's Clubs membership made it impossible for African American clubs to become members. Nonetheless, Black
women's clubs were so numerous that by the second decade of the twentieth
century a large federation of "colored" women's clubs was active in Black

communities throughout Illinois. By 1913, Wells-Barnett helped to organize the Alpha Suffrage Club of African American women, who were influential later in electing to Congress a Black Republican, Oscar De Priest.[43]

The experiences of Ruffin, Terrell, Williams, and Wells-Barnett were not unique. During the same period, the woman suffrage campaign gained momentum, but the national leadership emulated the racial attitudes of white women's clubs around the nation. Upholding segregation patterns sanctioned southern white mores as well as attitudes. As historian Aileen Kraditor observed, white supremacy was an influential factor in the strategy of the suffragists as the need developed for southern support for a woman suffrage amendment.[44]

In challenging Kraditor's assessment, historian Suzanne Lebsock used a case study of southern white suffragists, members of the Equal Suffrage League of Virginia. Lebsock feels that these women resisted race baiting about as much as could be expected of them, considering the "antis'" persistent position that woman suffrage was a threat to white supremacy. According to Lebsock, Kraditor's thesis was not sustainable in light of the Virginia suffragists whose desires to vote were not articulated to preserve white supremacy. I argue that they did not need to articulate the idea because the concept was a given—understood, if not accepted, by everyone in the South. In looking at the evidence Lebsock presents in defense of the Virginia suffragists, I interpret their motives differently than she does because I see that all of the kinds of prejudice Kraditor saw in assessing the national leadership—use of the expediency argument, and arguing that Black women's votes would not be a threat to white supremacy—were present in the case of the Equal Suffrage League of Virginia.[45]

These women may not have been overt in their racism; however, as Lebsock notes, they were socially prominent women, many of whom were of the wealthy elite. Southern women of this class came into being because of white hegemony, politically defined as white supremacy. They did not have to acknowledge consciously their desire to preserve white supremacy. Without it, the elite world would have dissolved. Their position was an unspoken presumption, that many suffragists outside of the South respected. It seems safe to say that as the woman suffrage campaign gained momentum, the national leadership emulated the racial attitudes of white women's clubs around the nation. Kraditor's findings seem to be substantiated.

Fear of offending southern white suffragists is one thing, but how can the prejudice against African American clubwomen in Wisconsin and in Chicago be explained? The Midwest was not alone. Similarly, there was prejudice against Black woman suffragists in the Northeast. The *New York Times* reported in 1911 the abortive efforts of the New York Woman Suffrage Party to hold a suffrage meeting with Black women from Harlem (the area the *Times* called "Little Africa"), at the apartment of Mrs. John Dewey. In recruiting the African American women in the Twenty-first Assembly District, meeting organizers had mobilized Black ministers to spread the word and invited Mary Church Terrell to speak. However, Dewey's white neighbors, in reading about the proposed meeting in the newspaper, sought an injunction to prohibit the gathering on the grounds that a "mixed" meeting of Black and white women violated the restrictive covenant laws that applied to the apartment building where Dewey resided. Consequently, the meeting was canceled, and the injunction against the gathering called off.[46]

New York City was not unique in citizen protest against mobilizing Black women politically. It appears that New Jersey citizens feared the potential of African American women also. In 1915 the *Times* reported the failure of a woman suffrage amendment to the New Jersey State Constitution. Citing Atlantic City, the newspaper noted, "Negro women as suffrage watchers at polling places are thought to have lost votes for the amendment here." White voters were heard to have said that they changed their minds about supporting the amendment when they saw so many Black women campaigning for it.[47] Clearly there was a nationwide, not just a southern, prejudice against African American women voting.

As for the woman suffrage leadership, it appears that white women outside of the South used southern white women's overt prejudice as an excuse for the NAWSA's discriminatory policies, while hiding their own similar feelings about Black women, although they shared many of the Black women's goals for reform and women's political equity. African American woman suffragists were quite aware of this position, and they were determined to move beyond the attempts to keep them disfranchised.

Black suffragists knew that, although those national suffrage leaders who courted Black support endorsed equal suffrage among the races while in African American circles, their public actions and statements to the mainstream society often contradicted their professed equalitarianism. An example is what happened at one of the most famous incidents of direct confrontation among the so-called radical woman suffragists of the early twentieth century—the famous suffrage parade in front of the White House. It was cosponsored in 1913 by the NAWSA and the Congressional Union for Woman Suffrage (National Woman's Party) of Washington, D.C. Alice Paul, founder of the NWP, was the parade organizer.

When Adella Hunt Logan read in the NAWSA newspaper, the *Woman's Journal*, that white women said they could not march in the parade if any African American women participated, she immediately went into action to subvert the exclusionary plan. Logan wrote Mary Church Terrell and other Black woman suffragists in the District of Columbia, encouraging them to march. News of the forthcoming Black participation must have forced the NAWSA to compromise its racial exclusionary strategy, deciding to segregate the Black suffragists at the back of the parade instead.[48] The *Crisis* reported the following:

> In spite of the apparent reluctance of the local suffrage committee to en-courage the colored women to participate, and in spite of the conflicting rumors that were circulated and which disheartened many of the colored women from taking part, they are to be congratulated that so many of them had the courage of their convictions and that they made such an admirable showing in the first great national parade.[49]

Du Bois was pleased about the way African American women per-sisted in their attempts to participate, because NAWSA officials had asked Ida B. Wells-Barnett, who was representing the Alpha Suffrage Club, not to march with the white Chicago delegation. The reason advanced was fear of offending "certain unnamed southern women" who had pledged not to march in a racially integrated parade. This request was made publicly of all the Black marchers. Nonetheless, Wells-Barnett integrated the Illinois del-egation despite this rebuff.[50]

Historian Wanda Hendricks has detailed the events and the signifi-cance of Wells-Barnett's leadership. In attending the march, Wells-Barnett marked one of her first official duties as president of the Alpha Suffrage Club. Describing the sixty-five Black Illinois women as enthusiastic delegates, Hendricks cites Grace Wilbur Trout, chair of the Illinois delegation, as the one who informed Wells-Barnett that the NAWSA "advised them to keep our delegation entirely white." Noting that the white delegates expected the Alpha Suffrage Club delegation to march with the Black contingent at the end of the procession, Hendricks concludes that the NAWSA acquiesced to the southern white suffragists to assure the public that African American suffrage was unconnected to white woman suffrage. Trout and others plead-ed with Wells-Barnett to march with the Black delegates, but she refused. Hendricks quotes Wells-Barnett as saying, "The southern women have tried to evade the question time and again by giving some excuse or other every time it has been brought up. If the Illinois women do not take a stand now in this great democratic parade then the colored women are lost."[51]

In the meantime, Virginia Brooks and Belle Squire were white suffragists who agreed with Wells-Barnett; however, other whites in the Illinois delegation admonished her for not being willing to march with the other women of her race. This disclosure about Illinois suffragists reveals that not only southern white suffragists, but some northern ones too, felt that Black women should be segregated in the march. Shortly after the admon-ishment Wells-Barnett disappeared from the parade, but as the delegates began marching down Pennsylvania Avenue, she stepped out of the crowd and joined Brooks and Squires in the parade. Hendricks believes that Wells-Barnett's refusal to be segregated in the march impeded the white "prerogative of discriminating against African American Women." Further, she argues that white women's endorsement of segregation blinded them to how they had forced African American women to separate their blackness from their femaleness.[52]

In the meantime, the rest of the Chicago delegation and the other Black women delegates were relegated to the end of the line. For example, Mary Church Terrell, who marched in the parade with African American Delta Sigma Theta Sorority women from Howard University, assembled in the area reserved for Black women. Several years later, Terrell confided her feelings about the NAWSA and about Alice Paul to Walter White of the NAACP. Terrell questioned, in particular, Paul's loyalty to Black women, concluding that, if she and other white suffragist leaders could get the Anthony amendment through without enfranchising African American women, they would do so.[53]

To put this discussion in context, it does not matter if contemporary historians debate whether or not white suffragists were racists. The point here is that Black leaders of the time believed that white suffragists were racists. African Americans did not trust the actions of the white suffragists, which Black leaders believed were exclusionary in terms of their race. Although northern suffragist leaders accepted the southern strategy in varying degrees, even those who did not personally endorse the idea could not announce from an NAWSA platform that Black women should be enfranchised equally with white women. The South was against a national policy of woman suffrage because it would include Black women. Northern suffragists realized that a national amendment needed some southern support in order to be successful. On the other hand, many white suffragists in the North hid behind the South in justifying racial prejudice. For example, although militant suffragist Alice Paul rejected both male and female Democrats, who were known for their anti-Black views, she did not publicly support Black female suffrage and, consequently has been charged with being prejudiced against Black women. On the other hand, New York suffrage leaders Alva Belmont, Mrs. John Dewey, and Harriet Blatch encouraged African American participation. These New York women appear, however, to have been in the minority.[54]

By 1914, the loose coalition between the NAWSA and the Congressional Union, led by Alice Paul, ended. Paul would not support the weak version of the Anthony Amendment fostered by the Democrats, whereas the NAWSA took the position of appeasing all those who had doubts about the Anthony Amendment. Thus, the cause of the African American woman suffered another blow. Kate Gordon, chairman of the Southern States Woman Suffrage conference, reiterated the woman suffrage policy of her organization—votes for women is a state right and not a federal right. Although southern militants opposed a national amendment, Gordon appealed to the southern white man by threatening to re-ally with those who supported a national amendment if white woman suffrage was not effected on a state level. The issue even reached national proportions. There was a congressional debate over granting white women (not all women) the suffrage. In testifying against the proposed amendment before the Senate Committee on Woman Suffrage, the National Association Opposed to Woman Suffrage asserted, "The first fruits of the Amendment would be to admit Negro women to the polls, when eleven states have successfully defied the Federal Government in any effort to admit Negro men to the polls."[55]

Although Gordon opposed a federal amendment if it did not include the word "white," other militant southern suffragists, like Mississippi's Belle Kearney, realized that opposing the amendment was not necessary to reaching their goal. On the eve of the Nineteenth Amendment's passage in Congress, Kearney attempted to change Gordon's mind, arguing that the South need not fear northern intervention on behalf of disfranchised Black women. Kearney had been convinced that northerners were sympathetic with the South's "negro problem."[56] Indeed, she was correct.

Not surprising, steps to disfranchise African American females who already had the vote was another anti-Black strategy observable in many localities across the country. As early as 1902, Kentucky had taken away the school vote from the women of the state in order to eliminate the Black female vote. In 1914 the Illinois legislature was considering the woman suffrage question, and according to the recollections of Ida B. Wells-Barnett, there was talk of limiting the legislation to include white women only. This threat led Black women, who in the past had been reluctant to join the Illinois Woman Suffrage Association, to join the Alpha Suffrage Club. The significance of this club's influence upon Chicago elections could be seen as far South as Alabama, where periodicals published pictures of Black Chicago women campaigning for African American candidates. Anti-suffrage fliers read, "Five Million of These Ladies Will Vote! How Many of These Will Your County and State Produce under Federal Suffrage?" Black woman suffragists of Chicago's second ward were said to have helped to defeat the candidate chosen by white suffragists. "Antis" predicted the advent of "Negro rule" throughout the South if a federal amendment enfranchised all women.[57]

Although in Virginia the legislative debates raised the issue of race infrequently between 1912 and 1920, outside of legislative halls the news media fanned the fears of "negro rule." "Antis" referred to the 1910 census,

Five Million of These Ladies Will Vote!

HOW MANY OF THESE WILL YOUR COUNTY AND STATE PRO-
DUCE, UNDER FEDERAL SUFFRAGE?
THE GRANDFATHER CLAUSE IN ALABAMA DIED AUTOMAT-
ICALLY IN JANUARY, 1903, SECTION 181.

MAJORITIES WIN AT THE POLLS

Suffragists of Ward 2, Chicago, advertised for a candidate for alderman. From several applicants they selected "Al Russell," saloon keeper, as
the best vote getter. This hand-picked suffragist candidate for alderman
was defeated on April 6, 1915, by a negro candidate, whose workers are
seen above.

The Anti–Woman Suffrage File, Political History Division, National Museum of American History, Smithsonian Institution

showing more Blacks than whites in twenty-nine Virginia counties. Virginia "antis" predicted that a woman suffrage amendment would bring an end
to the Democratic Party in Virginia, because the Black electorate would vote
the Republican Party. Lebsock notes how in 1915 the Equal Suffrage
League of Virginia responded to the "antis" by contending that white supremacy was in no danger. The suffragists argued that through poll taxes and literacy tests the Black women would be prevented from registering to vote,
just like their men.[58]

Nonetheless, African Americans stood ready for these impediments
to their enfranchisement. With such fears among white southern politicians,
it is not surprising how they reacted in 1918, the year Texas women won the
right to vote. The Black editor of the *Houston Observer* responded to fears on

the part of Black people about disfranchisement, when he called upon the men and women of the race to register to vote in spite of the poll tax, which, he felt, was designed especially to exclude Black voters. In urging African Americans to vote, the editor implored them to pay the poll tax so that they could "perform that sacred duty."[59]

As a result of these developments, Mrs. A. W. Blackwell, a Georgia woman missionary of the African Methodist Episcopal (AME) Church, predicted that white suffragists would institute a "grandmothers" clause once they obtained the vote in order to keep the more than three million Black women from voting. Blackwell, the corresponding secretary of the AME Church Women's Home and Foreign Mission Society in Atlanta, expressed views similar to those of Mary Church Terrell. Blackwell wrote that justice would not prevail, even with the ballot, until white women learned to teach their children respect for Black people and all other citizens. The leaders of the National Baptist Woman's Convention called not only for white women to cooperate with Black women, but for whites to teach their youth respect for all women. Moreover, they declared, "the longer and farther apart the women of the races remain, the greater will be the encroachment by white men."[60]

In the meantime, the NAWSA leaders vacillated between conciliating the whites in the South and courting the Blacks in the North. In 1911, NAWSA president Anna Howard Shaw endorsed Black suffrage. Carrie Catt, president of the NAWSA from 1916 to 1920, felt the South had to be placated, because a strong national organization was essential to the success of the national movement. Paradoxically, she appealed to both the Black male and female voters of New York in 1917, when she and Mary G. Hay, president of both the New York Equal Suffrage League and the New York City Woman Suffrage Party, wrote articles for the *Crisis*. In accepting the invitation, each woman wrote in support of universal suffrage. In the District of Columbia the same year, Congresswoman Jeanette Rankin of Montana addressed an enthusiastic group of Alpha Kappa Alpha sorority women at Howard University. There she assured the group of Black women that she wanted all women to be given the ballot regardless of race.[61]

Despite the overtures toward Black women by national suffrage leaders, cries of discrimination from African Americans continued. In 1911 Anna Shaw was accused of refusing to allow an African American delegate at the Louisville convention to propose an antidiscrimination resolution, making potential Black supporters of a woman suffrage amendment very suspicious of the movement leadership's motives. As president of the NAWSA from 1910 to 1915, Shaw avoided offending white southern suffragists and supported the states' rights position of the association, which further alienated Black voters.[62]

Carrie Catt believed in conciliation by any means, including urging southern white women not to attend the 1916 national convention in Chicago because the Chicago delegates would be mostly Black. In 1918, attempting to convince southern members of Congress to support the amendment, Catt wrote Representative Edwin Y. Webb,

> The women of New York are now the political equals of the men of New York, but the white women of the South are the political inferiors of the negroes [sic] who can qualify to vote. Upon the theory that every voter is a sovereign, the present condition in the South makes sovereigns of some negro [sic] men, while all white women are their subjects.[63]

Furthermore, when the New York State Woman's Suffrage referendum was pending in the legislature in 1917, Black female suffragists in the state complained of discrimination against their organizations by white suffragists at the statewide woman suffrage convention held at Saratoga. Mrs. John Humphrey Watkins, the white president of the Manhattan chapter of the New York Woman's Party, assured Black women that they were welcomed in the movement. Reportedly, the majority of the African American delegates were finally convinced that they shared equal status with white members; however, a vocal minority remained alienated from the whites. In the meantime, the Black women workers of the U.S. Printing Office in Washington, D.C., sought support from Congresswoman Jeanette Rankin when they called for equal pay with white women workers in their federal agency. Rankin refused to intervene on their behalf.[64]

By November 1918, African American men and women in the North, in particular, watched the press carefully for the congressional debates about the Anthony amendment, and they responded critically. An African American correspondent, whose letter was signed "J.K.L.," wrote to a Philadelphia newspaper and charged white Americans with political hypocrisy. The writer declared,

> Recently Mississippi's senior senator, John Sharpe Williams, proposed an amendment to the Anthony Suffrage Bill to the effect that only white women should be permitted to vote. Such an undemocratic measure belongs to the same class as the Prussian junker's three-class system. It is certainly out of place just now, when so-called Democrats are shouting the loudest about making the world safe for democracy.[65]

In this context JKL was referring to Woodrow Wilson's rhetoric about why Americans needed to support the country's entry into the World War. Although many African American men and women felt that supporting the war effort was not only patriotic but politically expedient, others questioned the contradiction in U.S. domestic and foreign policy. Amendments such as the one Senator Williams proposed further antagonized African Americans who were skeptical about how the woman suffrage amendment would benefit them. Williams's proposal read, "The right of white citizens to vote shall not be denied." The Senate vote was laid on the table; however, in 1919, Mississippi Senator Pat Harrison attempted unsuccessfully to have the word "white" placed in the original amendment, while Louisiana Senator Edward J. Gay called for an amendment providing the states instead of the Congress the power to endorse it. Fortunately, the politicians of the times did not submit to the states' rights ideology of the white supremacists. Through these closing years of the debate, however, the ideology remained unrelenting.[66]

The closer the woman suffrage legislation came to passage, the more white supremacists in the South resorted to tactics designed to sabotage it. In 1918 James Callaway wrote an article in the *Macon Telegraph* (reprinted in NWP literature), in which he attempted to discredit Susan B. Anthony. He recounted "some strange history" about the late suffrage hero and printed photographs of people he called "the three immediate women friends of the Anthony family." Two women were prominent, white suffragists in the nation's eye—Carrie Catt and Anna Howard Shaw. The third woman was Mrs. R. Jerome Jeffrey (the Black woman's club leader from Rochester), who was pictured with the caption "negro" below her name. Callaway indicted Anthony and other suffragists close to her because of their friendship with Jeffrey and other Blacks such as Frederick Douglass, Robert Purvis, and Booker T. Washington (all of whom were deceased). Callaway supported his claim that Anthony had betrayed the white women of the South by quoting excerpts from her biography to reveal her relationship with Black suffragists. Callaway ended his article with a plea to the Senate not to endorse woman suffrage, for to do so would be to affirm the beliefs of people like Anthony, whom he believed to be immoral. He wrote,

> All who have the interest of the white woman of the rural districts at heart pray that the Senate will have the wisdom to stand firm for the liberties of the women on the farm. It is a critical hour for the South—a crisis that involves her future civilization, her tranquility and her prosperity.[67]

Although Callaway published his attack in 1918, "antis" reprinted it for distribution for the duration of the struggle. In discussing this propaganda, Suzanne Lebsock looks at how it affected Virginia suffragists. She views the antisuffrage tactics as a way to smear NAWSA president Carrie Catt, who would address the Virginia General Assembly two years later. At the event, the House chamber was "blanketed" with these same Callaway leaflets. In Lebsock's view, Virginians connected the NAWSA with support for "social equality." Lebsock then contextualizes the 1919 Equal Suffrage

THE "THREE IMMEDIATE WOMEN FRIENDS" OF THE ANTHONY
FAMILY. SEE BIOGRAPHY OF SUSAN B. ANTHONY,
PAGE 1435, BY MRS. IDA HUSTED HARPER.

CARRIE CHAPMAN CATT   The Rev. ANNA HOWARD SHAW   "Mrs. R. JEROME JEFFREY"
(NEGRO)

From Left to Right: Carrie Chapman Catt; The Rev. Anna Howard Shaw; Mrs. R. Jerome Jeffery,
Negro woman of Rochester, N. Y. Often "Guest in Anthony Home" with Mrs. Shaw and Mrs. Carrie Chapman Catt, President of National Woman Suffrage Association, to which all Southern Suffragettes belong.

"Suffrage Democracy Knows no Bias of Race, Color, Creed or
Sex."—Carrie Chapman Catt.

**Look not to Greece or Rome for heroes,
nor to Jerusalem or Mecca for saints, but for
all the higher virtues of heroism, let us WOR-
SHIP the black man at our feet."**—*Susan B.
Anthony's Official History of Suffrage.*

*Anti–Woman Suffrage File, Political History Division, National Museum of
American History, Smithsonian Institution*

League decision to cooperate with the NAWSA in rejecting a membership
application from a federation of Black women's organizations, explaining
why this discriminatory judgment appeared to be expedient for the Virginia
suffragists.[68]

Nineteen nineteen was the year the Anthony bill was adopted by Congress, as anti–Black woman suffrage sentiments continued to plague the suffrage movement. Shortly before the legislation was adopted, several incidents occurred wherein suffrage leaders attempted to discourage activities by Black women. Mary Church Terrell reported to the NAACP that white suffragists in Florida discriminated against Black women in their attempts to recruit support for the campaign.[69] In response, the NAACP clashed with Alice Paul, who reportedly told Florida whites "that all this talk of Negro women voting in South Carolina was nonsense," and that the National Woman's Party leaders were organizing white, not Black, women in that state. Attempts by the NAACP to get Paul to repudiate the statement failed.[70] In a letter to Mary Church Terrell, Walter White noted a conversation he had with Alice Paul over the incident, wherein Paul denied making the statements. However, when White concluded his letter to Terrell, he wrote, "Just as you say, all of them are mortally afraid of the South."[71]

In March 1919, within a week of White's letter, Terrell received one from Ida Husted Harper, Susan B. Anthony's biographer and a NAWSA leader. Harper asked Terrell to use her influence to persuade the Northeastern Federation of Colored Women's Clubs, an organization of 6,000 Black women, to withdraw a request for cooperative membership in the NAWSA. In essence, Harper explained that Elizabeth Carter, president of the Federation, had sent Carrie Catt a request for NAWSA membership. After conferring with other NAWSA leaders such as Lila Meade Valentine of Virginia, Catt asked Harper to explain to the African American women that accepting the membership of a Black club was inexpedient for the NAWSA because the association was calling upon white southern support for the national amendment. Harper realized the sensitive nature of her request and asked Terrell and Carter not to make it public. In addition, Harper reminded Terrell of her prior loyalty to the "colored women," of her abolitionist background, and of her former association with the late Booker T. Washington, Alexander Walters, Ida B. Wells-Barnett, and other prominent Black woman suffrage supporters. In addition, Ida Harper asked the federation to withdraw "temporarily" the membership application to the NAWSA until the Nineteenth Amendment was ratified. She noted that the major obstacle to the amendment was fear among whites of the Black women's votes. Terrell communicated with Carter, but did not ask the Federation to withdraw.[72]

African American clubwomen were angered by NAWSA assumptions that they would bow out for the sake of the cause. They understood what white clubwomen did not. Blacks were seeking more than NAWSA membership; they were seeking NAWSA support for the enfranchisement of African American women. Elizabeth C. Carter admonished Harper for her arrogance and patronizing testimony, which presumed that African American women were not politically sophisticated enough to use NAWSA membership as a strategy to gain the vote. Fortunately, amendments seeking to enfranchise only white women failed with the close of the Sixty-fifth Congress. African Americans understood, however, how vulnerable their women were.[73]

During the same month, at the 1919 Jubilee Convention of the NAWSA in St. Louis, delegates discussed the question of race, and Black leaders directed their displeasure toward southern suffragists like Laura Clay of Kentucky. During the convention, Clay proposed changes in certain sections of the amendment "with particular reference to those parts that would permit the enfranchisement of Negro women in the South." It appears that as the success of a nonrestrictive woman suffrage amendment became apparent, some southern leaders feared the potential threat to the status quo that an active and fast-growing Black woman suffrage movement would have in states such as Tennessee and Kentucky. Convention delegates supported the Nineteenth Amendment, but some agreed that changes should be made in the wording to allow the South to determine its own position on the Black female electorate. In response to the NAWSA proposal, the NAACP board went on record as opposing any alteration of the amendment that would result in leaving its enforcement in the hands of the states.[74]

The substantial opposition to the adoption of the Nineteenth Amendment throughout the South was due to the perception of many whites that Black women were eager to win the right to vote in the entire region. The overwhelming majority of negative votes in Congress against the amendment in 1919 came from Mississippi, South Carolina, Alabama, Georgia, Louisiana, and North Carolina. Although there were several other reasons for southern opposition, it was widely believed that Black women wanted the ballot more than white women. Black women were expected to register and vote in larger numbers than white women; thus, the ballot would soon be returned to Black men. Opponents of Black female suffrage believed the result would be the return of the two-party system in the South, and if African Americans gained the vote, they would consistently vote Republican. These fears were realized in Florida after the passage of the Nineteenth Amendment. Black women in Jacksonville registered in greater numbers than white women. As a result, the Woman Suffrage League in Jacksonville was reorganized into the Duval County League of Democratic Women Voters. The members were dedicated to maintaining white supremacy and registering white women voters.[75]

Five months before ratification, white supremacists had circulated pro–Black woman suffrage articles from Black periodicals such as the *New York Age* and the *Crisis* in order to show whites how effective the woman suffrage amendment would be in strengthening the Black electorate. One report pictured Annie Simms Banks, a Black woman from Winchester, Kentucky, who became the "first Negro Woman delegate to a political convention." Another report came from the *Crisis*, which enumerated the Black women who were eligible to vote in the thirty-one states that had ratified the proposed woman suffrage amendment by March 1920. The *Crisis* report estimated that 750,000 Black women were eligible to vote in those states alone. Anti-Black propaganda accompanied these reprinted articles to fuel the "antis'" fire with predictions about Black women voters taking over the South.[76]

Even if African American women had united and flooded the polls as predicted, the enemy was overwhelming. In hindsight we know that the ballot could not have protected Black women for very long in most of the South. Yet in 1920, African American women continued to resist and were determined to get the vote.

Conclusion

Thus, Black women were virtually abandoned by most white female suffragists. Calls for interracial cooperation to assist Black women win the vote from African American women such as Josephine St. Pierre Ruffin, Mrs. A. W. Blackwell, Mary Church Terrell, and S. Willie Layton went unheeded. Frederick Douglass's and Frances Harper's words of 1869 were still valid fifty years later. Douglass said that in America, a Black woman is victimized "not because she is a woman, but because she is Black." Harper felt that for white women, the priorities in the struggle for human rights were "for sex, letting race occupy a minor position."[77]

The question remains, why did the majority of white women in the woman suffrage movement abandon or discriminate against African American women? Perhaps they lacked the multi-consciousness of working-class and poor women who were oppressed because of class, or of African American women of all classes who were oppressed because of race, if not class. The primarily elite and middle-class women of the NAWSA and later the Congressional Union and the National Woman's Party are good examples of this insensitivity. Of the extant issues of the NWP journal, the *Suffragist,* from 1914 through 1919, there are no pictures of African American women, although we know that professional Black women like Mary Church Terrell and S. Willie Layton were members. In fact, Terrell claims to have picketed the White House with her daughter Phyllis and NWP members, standing on hot bricks to keep from having cold feet during the winter months.[78] In addition, in the entire six-year period, there are only two news items referring to positive accomplishments of African Americans in

relationship to the woman suffrage movement. There are, however, numerous negative references to "negroes," such as the cover of a 1917 issue with a cartoon drawn by Congressman John M. Baer of a white woman jailed for picketing the White House. The caption reads, "Refined, intelligent, society women act as pickets and are thrown into the workhouse with negroes and criminals."

Is the journal cover an example of racism? Of course it is. Were the leaders of the NWP consciously anti-Black? Perhaps not. They reflected the mores, attitudes, and political views of middle-class and elite Americans of the times. Black women were either invisible or expendable because they, even more than poor white women, represented a lesser class, which created problems for many of the white women in the woman suffrage network.

As a result, it is not surprising to find that many white suffragists believed it was expedient to ignore their Black sisters. They realized that African American women were feared because whites, especially in the South, believed Black women would vote if given the opportunity. To many suffragists, Black women were not worthy of the right to vote. Hence, white suffragists attempted to keep Black women disfranchised, and African Americans protested. For the most part, the organized opposition to this form of racial discrimination came from Black men and Black women, not from the white female leaders of the suffrage movement.

Black political mobilization against discrimination as Congress debated Nineteenth Amendment legislation seemed strongest in New York state. By 1917 the New York state legislature had approved a woman suffrage bill that enfranchised over 75,000 African American women. The large majority of them voted the Republican ticket like their men. In addition, the NAACP national headquarters was located in New York City, where W. E. B. Du Bois launched his attack on racial discrimination and his campaign for Black woman suffrage. To the woman suffrage leadership, Black voters in New York state represented a formidable block they could not dismiss. Unlike the situation in other states, where white suffragists could ignore the potential influence of invisible Black women, white suffragists wooed Black New Yorkers and avoided provoking situations that could be identified as racially discriminatory. Besides New York, only in Illinois, where African American women also voted in large numbers before Nineteenth Amendment ratification, were Black women a visible political force not to be ignored.

Despite the racism in the movement, of the African Americans who responded to the woman suffrage arguments and activities, the vast majority supported the cause. Throughout the woman suffrage movement, only three out of eighty-three Black men were found to have publicly opposed woman suffrage. Not one of the Black women who spoke out about woman suffrage opposed it.[79] Although African American leaders expressed concern about the motives of white suffragists, they encouraged others to support the ideas of the woman suffrage argument. In recognizing that African Americans needed a political voice in order to bring about changes, some encouraged Blacks to put aside their fears about the racism apparent among many white woman suffragists and to support the movement for the good of the Black race.

As a consequence of the growing racism among whites on one hand and the increasing mobilization of Black women for the suffrage cause on the other, African American women turned more to themselves to find solutions for their own problems. The support Black women received from the men of their race seemed inversely proportional to the amount of backlash Black women received from white women. Male efforts to assist African American suffragists were especially notable in calling attention to white discrimination against Black women in the suffrage movement. For whatever reasons, African American men championed their women's struggle for the vote. The appearance of race solidarity, in the face of disunity among Black and white feminists, created a cleavage in the women's movement that would be difficult to mend once the Nineteenth Amendment was ratified.

Chapter 7. African American Women as Voters and Candidates

> By a miracle the 19th Amendment has been ratified. We women have now a weapon of defense which we have never possessed before. It will be a shame and reproach to us if we do not use it.
>
> —Mary Church Terrell, 1920[1]

A soon as it was conceivably possible, African American women registered, voted, and became candidates for elective office. Although the majority of Black women voted for the first time during the presidential election of 1920, African American women had voted since 1879 in school board elections in Massachusetts, where woman suffrage legislation provided limited participation. Not until the first decade of the twentieth century, however, was the effect of Black women's votes measurable in specific states, mainly in the West, where full suffrage had been legislated by the turn of the century. The African American population in woman suffrage states was low; hence, white concern about the effect of African American women voters there was negligible.

The major debate over the potential impact of Black women's votes developed in the decade before the Nineteenth Amendment was ratified, as states with larger Black populations—Illinois, New York, Texas—began to enact laws granting women the right to vote. Southern whites' fear of Black women voters increased, and once the Nineteenth Amendment was a fact, the white South mobilized to nullify African American women's votes, yet Black women struggled to vote and to keep the franchise.

In response to the southern strategy, political activities varied among Black women in different regions of the nation. In the North and the West, African American women organized to vote, campaigned for candidates, and ran for public office. In so doing, they put political pressure on Congress to curb southern tactics to disfranchise Black women. Thus, the increase in

Mary Church Terrell was the first president of the National Association of Colored Women and often represented the association as a suffragist at national woman suffrage conventions. *Moorland-Spingarn Research Center, Howard University*

various forms of Black female participation in the suffrage movement revealed Black women moving from woman suffrage arguments into active involvement in the political process. In the South, African American women mobilized to vote, campaigned for candidates, then faced rebuff when they attempted to register, or, if they succeeded in registering, when they attempted to vote. Southern Black suffragists moved from woman suffrage arguments into court, where they protested attempts to disfranchise them. In the meantime, Black organizations and Black male leaders came together to support the women's efforts. White women suffrage leaders remained on the sidelines refusing to become involved, while some southern white suffragists encouraged the disfranchisement of Black women.

In the years that followed the ratification of the Nineteenth Amendment, Black women in the North continued to participate in politics, but they too found that they had been abandoned by most white feminists and the Republican Party as a group. In addition, they became disillusioned by national politics, after struggling so hard to support woman suffrage and the Republican Party for over two generations.

African American Women as Voters before
the Nineteenth Amendment

During the last quarter of the nineteenth century, Black women voted when woman suffrage became a reality in selected states. Editorials in the *Woman's Era* noted the struggle for municipal suffrage for women in the 1890s, and by 1915, the former editor, Josephine St. Pierre Ruffin, noted that she had voted forty-one times under Massachusetts's school suffrage law. Ruffin saw African American women's votes as a positive force for their people, which she articulated in her own voice. She had witnessed this fact in her own state: "We are justified in believing that the success of this movement for equality of the sexes means more progress toward equality of the races."[2]

Testimony such as this was difficult to come by since few Blacks lived in areas where women had achieved suffrage before the turn of the century. Although the African American population was minimal in the western states with woman suffrage laws, Black women in Colorado were reported to have participated in the political activities of the state. According to woman suffrage chronicler Helen Woodbury, a contemporary observer, Blacks living in Colorado in 1900 made up 1.6 percent of the population. The African American population in the state was largest in Denver, where 2.9 percent of the adult population was Black, and one-half of the Blacks were female. Woodbury found that distinguishing the Black vote from the white vote was virtually impossible except in the city of Denver, where, in 1901 "a colored woman's Republican club" was organized. From her statistical findings, Woodbury concluded that a larger percentage of Black women voted in the Denver election of 1906 than did white women, and that 620 Black women, or 45.2 percent of the 1,373 eligible Black voters in Denver, voted in 1906.[3]

Apparently, Woodbury had not been aware of the woman suffrage activities of the Colorado State Federation of Colored Women's Clubs, whose members met the summer before the 1906 election. The federation met in Denver, where one of the honored speakers at the convention was Judge Ben B. Lindsay of Denver, whom Black women voters had helped to elect on the Progressive ticket. Lindsay must have been aware of the influence of African American women voters in the state because of his willingness to address them during an election year.[4] Here it is important to note that the Black women who voted in Colorado did so on the basis of the issues and the candidates' commitment to them, rather than the party.

Historian Beverly Beeton notes, however, that in Colorado suffrage for women was a matter of race as early as the territorial politics of the 1870s. For more than twenty years thereafter lawmakers resisted women's petitions for the vote, arguing about the unidentified "problems" that would accompany the enfranchisement of "Negro wenches" and Chinese women. The successful referendum did not come until 1893, when a coalition of Republican, Prohibitionist, and Populist parties endorsed equal suffrage. Beeton credits Carrie Catt, with the help of organizational and financial support from eastern suffragists, for developing the strategy that converted Colorado men to supporting the referendum.[5]

In the Midwest, suffragists successfully lobbied state legislatures in Ohio and Illinois for woman suffrage referendums, and by the 1910s, Illinois women had gained partial suffrage. In 1910, when the general assembly of Illinois granted women the right to vote for trustee of the University of Illinois, Ida B. Wells-Barnett was among the first to urge Black women to register. Wells-Barnett noted the following in her journal:

> When I saw that there might be granted a restricted suffrage, and the white women of the organization [Illinois Woman Suffrage Association] were working like beavers to bring it about, I made another effort to get our women interested.[6]

Wells-Barnett, like Josephine St. Pierre Ruffin before her, witnessed discriminatory practices among white suffragists in the North. Wells-Barnett's testimony reveals another authentic voice of an African American woman addressing the racism in the woman suffrage movement.

By 1914 Wells-Barnett and a few of her Black suffrage friends set out to encourage Black women to take advantage of expanded woman suffrage rights, which allowed them to vote in municipal elections. As a result, they mobilized the Alpha Suffrage Club during the political campaigns of 1914 and 1915. The work of the Alpha Suffrage Club became quite effective thereafter. Members participated in several campaigns in which Black men attempted to run as independent candidates for alderman. Ida B. Wells-Barnett felt that the effectiveness of the Black suffragists in recruiting African Americans to register to vote, including the Black men who resisted them, was demonstrated when registration in the second ward ranked sixth out of the thirty-five wards of the city. Ironically, she noted that the men had stopped resisting the women but that no male leader had encouraged Black women to vote until politician Oscar De Priest sought their help. He praised the women for their work, and when a vacancy occurred for alderman in 1914, he began to campaign for the seat with the help of the Alpha Suffrage Club.[7]

News of the female support of De Priest's candidacy traveled within Black circles. In March 1915, Grace Lucas-Thompson, writer of the Woman's Column in the (Indianapolis) *Freeman*, reported that "woman's vote played no small part in the recent nomination of a Negro for alderman at Chicago, Illinois. Their vote aggregated 1,093."[8]

As a result of his experience with the Black suffragists of Chicago, De Priest became an outspoken advocate of woman suffrage. In 1915 he acknowledged that,

> When colored men were primary candidates for alderman, the women of the race seemed to realize fully what was expected of them and, with the men, rolled up a very large and significant vote for the colored candidates, and they were consistent at the election, contributing to a plurality of over 3,000 votes for the successful colored candidates in a field of five.[9]

De Priest concluded that the women of his race were as qualified as men to play an active role in politics. The following November, he ran against two white candidates for the seat of alderman in his district and won.[10]

Measuring the effect of Black women's votes in California is more difficult than for Illinois and Colorado. Los Angeles, like Chicago and Denver, was the largest urban center in its state and contained the greatest number of Black voters. As a result, the available California data come from Los Angeles, where Black women had been lobbying for suffrage since the 1890s. California women won the right to the ballot in 1911. During the 1912 campaign, African American women worked diligently throughout the state. The Woman's Suffrage Advocate was a statewide organization of Blacks and whites that appointed several special workers among Black communities in California. Workers reported that "the Negroes generally supported the suffrage movement."[11]

During the 1914 primary campaign, Los Angeles editors Charlotta Spears and J. B. Bass used the *California Eagle* to remind readers that the African American Council had endorsed woman suffrage, and had urged all eligible men and women to register and to vote "in every city, county, and state election." Like the African American voters of Chicago, the Black women of California were encouraged by the Council to come together around race issues, not gender issues. The *Eagle* editors emphasized that only those candidates who were in sympathy with civil rights and equal rights for Blacks in the courts and in public accommodations would be endorsed. However, Spears and Bass were equally concerned about gender issues. The same year, the *Eagle* had endorsed in the primary election Helen K. Williams, the white Democratic Party candidate for lieutenant governor of California. Williams was disqualified because of her gender, and the *Eagle* decried the act because it was discriminatory and politically unsound.[12]

Though located in Los Angeles, the *Eagle* was the only Black newspaper in the state, and it had a national reputation in Black circles. Hence, it is not surprising that its plea to voters was not limited to Los Angeles. In 1915, an *Eagle* editorial predicted that Black women voters were essential to the success of their race and encouraged them to participate in the political process.[13] Furthermore, in 1916, the *Eagle* reported the enthusiasm of Los Angeles suffragists, both Blacks and whites, who rallied to support the Republican candidate for the presidency, Charles Evans Hughes. Revealing the faith the editors had in Los Angeles Black women voters, the *Eagle* editorialized, "Their effort was a highly commendable one and reflects signal credit upon both the race and the hosts that are battling for emancipation of the people from conditions as they now exist."[14]

In this context, the editors referred to the plight of women as well as Blacks. It is difficult to tell whether both Spears and Bass were equally dedicated to women's political participation. However, we can speculate. Spears, a South Carolina native who moved to California in 1910 to work on the *Eagle* staff, had taken over the paper by 1912. As managing editor, she made Joseph Bass the editor, and they appear to have shared political views. Shortly thereafter they married, and she continued to work diligently in California and then in national politics. Bass left the Republican Party in the 1940s to become a founding member of the Progressive Party, and in 1950 ran unsuccessfully for California's fourteenth legislative district seat in Congress. Charlotta Bass became nationally known, when in 1952 she became the first woman in United States history to run for the vice presidency on a national ticket—that of the Progressive Party.[15]

Nonetheless, in 1916 Charlotta Bass, like many other African American woman suffragists supported Hughes, the Republican presidential candidate. It seems the issues, rather than the party, determined her endorsement. Apparently Hughes was campaigning heavily among Blacks and among women, because the same year, the National Association of Colored Women endorsed his bid for the presidency, unlike Du Bois, who was among the few prominent African Americans to declare for Wilson. The National Woman's Party endorsed Hughes also, but not because of their members' long allegiance to the Republican Party, as was the case with many African Americans. The NWP was frustrated by Wilson's inability to free himself from the Democratic Party strategy that refused to support the Anthony bill. This created conflict between the NWP and the NAWSA, which attempted to stay neutral in party politics.

By 1917 the male voters of New York were asked to decide on another woman suffrage referendum. In the November issue of the *Crisis,* Du Bois wrote a strong editorial urging African American men in New York to support the referendum. Furthermore, he advised those who wanted to help in the campaign to communicate with the "colored" New York City chapter of the New York Woman Suffrage Party.[16]

Black women in New York City participated in a number of political activities during the 1917 campaign. They organized their own chapters of the Woman Suffrage Party and sent delegates to state conventions. Annie

K. Lewis, for example, was the president of the Colored Woman's Suffrage Club of New York City. In September of 1917, the delegates at the State Woman Suffrage Party Convention held in Saratoga elected her vice president of the New York Woman Suffrage Party.[17] This was a significant event, for rarely did Black women gain leadership positions when they participated in interracial women's organizations.

Throughout the campaign for woman suffrage in New York, white suffragists sought the important Black vote and cooperated with African American suffragists in planning strategies, despite the occasional cries of discrimination from Black suffragists. In October 1917, both Black and white opposed the use of militant tactics, such as picketing the White House, because they felt more male votes would be lost than won as a result of such efforts. One of the antisuffrage arguments in New York was the claim that political activity stimulated militancy among women. The suffragists did not want to feed this argument. During the last weeks of the campaign, Black women canvassed for male voters and encouraged them to support the amendment to the state constitution.[18]

New York voters conferred full suffrage upon all women of the state on November 6, 1917; the state thereby became the first east of the Mississippi River to do so. African American women played a prominent role in obtaining the victory. Not only were 75,000 Black women enfranchised, but the first Black representative to the New York State Assembly, Edward A. Johnson, and the first Black representative on the board of aldermen, James C. Thomas, Jr., of New York City, were also elected.[19]

By 1918 African American women's enthusiasm was quite apparent, with voting initiatives encouraged by New York City women across class lines. In Harlem, Black women organized the Women's Non-Partisan League, and four branches of the Negro Women Voters were organized in the Jamaica, Corona, Flushing, and Richmond Hill communities of Queens County.[20]

The success of the New York City campaign seemed more significant for Black women voters than did the Chicago victory. More New York African American women appeared to have been involved in several precincts and in various political organizations. The result was greater political gains for New York Blacks than for those in Chicago. Among the African Americans, two women delegates to the Republican state convention were elected.

By 1918 it was apparent that northern and western Black women voters seriously supported candidates not only by campaigning but by voting. Ohio had finally granted women the right to vote and in Dayton, more than fifty African American women pledged themselves to the independent candidates during the 1918 election. The same year, Black women in Chicago and New York City organized again around the candidates of their choice.[21]

On the eve of the ratification of the Nineteenth Amendment, a critical mass of African American women were voting in Massachusetts, New York, Ohio, Illinois, Texas, Colorado, and California. As a result of their growing visibility, two things became apparent. First, Black women participated actively in politics—primarily supporting the Republican Party—despite barriers placed before them. Second, forces in the Democratic Party and others who saw Black women voters as a threat to the racial status quo realized the potential impact of enfranchising African American women nationwide.

Nineteenth Amendment Victory
and African American Women Voters

The Nineteenth Amendment was ratified in August 1920. As a result, first-time women voters nationwide were eligible to participate in the November presidential election. African American women had been mobilized in various states in the nation. To the dismay of some and the pleasure of others, Black women nationwide eagerly registered to vote.

In Rhode Island, Bertha Higgins noted how very proud she was of the Black women in Providence, who were represented at City Hall that day in July 1919 when Rhode Island women first registered to vote. She noted that "Mrs. Parker, one of our race, was the second to register."[22]

The 1920 Republican presidential candidate, Warren G. Harding, was quite aware of the potential Black female vote and consciously sought support from northern Black women's groups and from national Black women's organizations. Among African American women, there were conflicting reports about Harding, who was believed by many Blacks in the Midwest to be of African American descent. Black females who supported him did so not just because they thought he was African American, but because of his willingness to work with women, Blacks, and grassroots people when he was an Ohio senator as well as while campaigning for the presidency. One of the biggest attacks from his critics was about the very thing that attracted Black women to his campaign. Harding was criticized because the newspaper office that he and his wife owned in Marion, Ohio, was staffed by women and African Americans.[23]

Several Black women became involved in the Harding-Coolidge campaign on national, regional, and local levels. Lethia C. Fleming, for one, was the national director assigned to the organization of colored women for the Republican Party. In an open letter to all African American women, written in October 1920, Fleming noted the importance of the Nineteenth

Mary B. Talbert, suffragist and vice president of the NACW during the 1920 presidential campaign. *Twentieth Century Negro Literature (1902), Anacostia Museum, Smithsonian Institution*

Amendment to Black women. She urged them to vote for the Harding-Coolidge ticket and to put Republicans in Congress. She stated,

> The Nineteenth Amendment was nothing less than a miracle. It was impossible to enfranchise the white woman without drawing us up to the same standards. We as Colored women have prayed for a better day, a day when we would be in a position to demand fair play and an equal chance. We must not now neglect the opportunity given us to serve the Party of Lincoln, McKinley and Roosevelt....
>
> So my dear fellow citizens, we must elect Warren G. Harding and Calvin Coolidge, and with them a Republican Congress; then we can feel that we as Race women have real friends at the head of our great Nation.[24]

Fleming was based in Chicago, at the Midwest headquarters of the Republican National Committee. Aside from this information, I have been able to learn little else about her. Nonetheless, political organizing and networking among African American women like Fleming and others underlines the partisan dimensions of anxiety among the Democrats over Black women's votes. In addition to Fleming, Mary Church Terrell was an avid supporter of the ticket, mainly because she was a Republican, but also because she was impressed by Harding's speech to feminists during a Washington rally, in which he offered his support for the "Anthony Amendment."[25] Like Terrell, Bertha Higgins supported Harding in the 1920 campaign. In fact the two women corresponded, as Terrell was the director of the Committee for Eastern District Work among Colored Women, and Higgins directed the Providence committee for work among Black women. Terrell wrote, "We want to reach each and every woman in your state, so that she will register and vote for Warren G. Harding as president and Calvin Coolidge as vice-president."[26]

Mary Church Terrell was stationed in the national Republican headquarters in New York City. There she reported how difficult it was to find a space to work, and how ambivalent she was about meeting with the Black Republican women, many of whom were captains of their respective electoral districts. Terrell had heard rumors that efforts had been made by some to prejudice the women against her. Here she was, a southern woman from a jurisdiction where she could not vote, attempting to lead the experienced Black New York suffragists. Fortunately, the rumors were not true, because "each and every one of them," she wrote in her journal, promised to cooperate with her, and they did. All the politically active women gave Terrell the support she needed to build an organization of Black women to campaign for the Harding-Coolidge ticket. In her words of encouragement, Terrell repeated a recurring theme used by many African American suffragists before her: "However much the white women of the country need suffrage, for many reasons which will immediately occur to you, colored women need it more."[27]

Republicans in the North recognized the power of African American women voters. The women of the Julia Ward Howe State Republican Club, for instance, received letters of thanks from both Harding and Burdick for campaigning so effectively.[28] The women of the Northeastern Federation of Women's Clubs supported the Harding ticket as well. The federation, representing over 6,000 women, held its annual convention in Brooklyn during August 1920. The delegates sang an original song, "Votes for Women," and pledged their support to Harding, "the Republican nominee for president."[29]

On the other hand, members of the national organization—the NACW—were displeased by a plank in the Republican Party platform and questioned whether they should endorse the ticket. At the time the largest organization of African American women in the nation, the NACW met in Tuskegee, Alabama, in July 1920, where suffragist Hallie Q. Brown, the first vice president, charged that "the Republican Party is that party that has stood by us, [but] it was noticeable at the Chicago convention that the platform committee reported not a plank, but a splinter against lynching."[30] During the session, the group received a telegram from Harding. After it was read, some delegates called for the NACW to go on record endorsing the Republican Party, but the motion was defeated after a heated debate. Instead, NACW president Mary B. Talbert was instructed to send a telegram to Senator Harding that acknowledged his greetings and promised Black women's dedication to racial uplift, but included no endorsement.[31]

Perhaps it was the large southern delegation at Tuskegee that rejected the Harding-Coolidge endorsement at the convention, for northern women like Talbert, who lived in New York state, had been courted politically and won over by the ticket. This was not the case for Southern women. They may have been more sensitive about the lynching issue than northern women, but then Hallie Quinn Brown was from Ohio and she was incensed by the failure of the Republican platform to condemn lynching, a crime against Black people that African American clubwomen had fought since the 1890s.[32] I suspect that the southern restraint reflected the lukewarm position Republicans took against the way African Americans were impeded by Jim Crow policies.

Perhaps it was Harding's campaign strategy that made the difference. He felt that he could afford to woo northern Blacks and not alienate white Republicans in the process, whereas his southern campaign took on a totally different approach. Christia Adair, a schoolteacher from Kingsville, Texas, testified to that reality when Harding campaigned in Houston, Texas. Adair took a group of schoolchildren to the train station to greet Harding on his whistle-stop tour of Texas. White teachers were there also with their students. Because Adair's husband worked for the train company, he told her the best place to stand so that she and the children would be the first to greet the senator. When the train stopped, Harding found himself in front of a group of Black children, at which time he reached over their heads to shake the hands of the white boys and girls behind them, ignoring the Blacks. Adair was so incensed by this rebuff that she changed her political affiliation and became a Democrat.[33]

Texas was the first southern state to provide full woman suffrage before the ratification of the Nineteenth Amendment. With the need for an intelligent female electorate in mind, Black women organized voter leagues there in 1917, the year Texas women won the right to vote. At least two leagues were cited in the *Negro Year Book*; they were the Colored Welfare League of Austin and the Negro Women Voter's League of Galveston. The women of Austin held voter education classes, and the women of Galveston held mass meetings to arouse interest in voter registration.[34]

Fear of Black female voters resulted in immediate discrimination against them. Six African American women were refused the right to register at Fort Worth on the ground that the primaries were open to white Democrats only. However, attempts to disfranchise Black female voters failed

Christia Adair of Kingsville, Texas, was a suffragist who attempted to register during the 1918 primaries. *Schlesinger Library, Black Women's Oral History Project, Radcliffe College*

in Houston in 1918. When the women attempted to register, they were informed that the law specifically stated that only white women were eligible to register. The local branch of the NAACP had a legal document drawn that quoted the Texas bill granting woman suffrage in the state. The bill said "any" woman, and it provided for the elective franchise at any and all primaries, nominating conventions, and general elections. Following the NAACP threat to sue, Black women were allowed to register. A similar attempt to disqualify Black females from registering failed in Waxahachie, Texas.[35] In hindsight, it would have been better had the NAACP sued, because women in other areas of Texas who were being turned away from the polls had no idea that they were illegally being denied the right to register or to vote.

In Kingsville, Texas, Black women succeeded in registering, but when they attempted to vote in the primary, white officials prevented them. According to the recollections of Christia Adair, Black women were told they could not vote, although their white suffragist companions had been allowed to cast their ballots. When the Black women asked for an explanation, they were given vague answers that did not satisfy them. Finally, Mrs. Simmons asked if the reason they were being denied the right to vote was because they were Black. The registrar then informed her that Blacks could not vote in the Texas primaries. Adair and the other Black women felt that there was nothing they could do about the situation and left the polling place. She said they were hurt because many of them had worked so hard in the woman suffrage movement. Adair did not note the reaction of the white women suffragists who had campaigned with them and had gone with them to the polls.[36]

Incidents such as those occurring in Texas were unheard of in the Northeast. Consequently, northern African American women were fooled by what in their region appeared to be the fading of racial prejudice on the political party level. On the eve of the ratification of the Nineteenth Amendment, there appeared to be a division in the strategies Black clubwomen used to better their conditions and those of their people. Southern African American women responded cautiously to the enfranchisement of women, while northern Black women responded enthusiastically to the call of political party politics.

African American Women as Political Candidates

In the northern states, Black women felt they could make significant contributions to the political process. Some remembered a generation earlier, when as children and young women they had viewed the political roles African American women assumed in the South during the Reconstruction years. In addition, some women lived in communities where their men voted and sought political support from the women of the race. This was true for New York State, where African American women candidates for political offices emerged in 1918, the year after the state legislature approved woman suffrage.

New York State was a Republican stronghold, and a large majority of African American men voted Republican. It should not be surprising then that Gertrude E. Curtis of the ninth district and Laura B. Fisher of the twentieth district were chosen as delegates to the New York State Republican convention. Two unnamed Black women were selected as alternates.[37]

In 1920, for many African American women living in the North, the highlight of their participation came when women ran for elected offices. As noted, a significant number of identifiable African American female candidates ran for office in 1918. In 1920 Mrs. Edward Washington ran for the Haddenfield, New Jersey, school board, and Mrs. W. L. Presto ran for the

Kentucky Is First to Reap Result of Susan B. Anthony Amendment

MRS. ANNIE SIMMS BANKS

First Negro Woman-Delegate to a Political Convention

Negro Woman Sits as Delegate In Republican Convention

Anti–Woman Suffrage File,
Political History Division,
National Museum of American
History, Smithsonian Institution

state senate from Seattle, Washington. Although Presto was defeated, she was believed to be the first Black female candidate for a state legislature. Her feminist platform included an attack on discrimination in any form, support for equal pay for equal service regardless of gender, revisions of the state's child labor law, an increase in the widow's pension to meet the high cost of living, support of free tuition in the state institutions of education for tax-payers' children, and several other policies that appear to have been "progressive." Finally, Grace Campbell, a probation officer from New York City, ran from the nineteenth district for the New York State Assembly in 1920 as a Socialist Party candidate.[38]

The emergence of candidates such as Presto and Campbell, in particular, reveals the political sophistication of Black female voters. They not only sought to become elected officials, but campaigned on tickets not traditionally espoused by Black voters or, for that matter, female voters. Their concerns went beyond the problems of Black communities and the issues urged by social feminists, reflecting the growing socialist movement among intellectuals and professionals of the times.

Although they were cautious, many Black women in the South attempted to exercise their right to vote. The experiences of Southern African American women as voters began in a manner similar to those of north-ern Black women. However, the southern white strategy, which aimed to keep all Blacks disfranchised, created barriers against African American women at the ballot box.

Unlike the situation in Texas, Black women voters in Kentucky met little resistance immediately following women's enfranchisement in that state. The fact that white women outnumbered Black women by nine to one may have been a factor. Segregationists in Kentucky could not realistically fear a Black voter takeover and made no real effort to prevent Black women from voting. As a result, African American women in Kentucky quickly became involved in Republican politics. By March 1920, Annie Simms Banks was appointed a delegate to the state Republican Party convention, repre-senting the seventh district. Her position was a first for southern Black wom-en, and Banks participated actively as a member of the rules committee. During the convention, this Clark County teacher was reported to have said,

> We are just beginning to open our eyes in politics, but before long we are going to make ourselves felt, and you can depend on Annie Simms Banks of Winchester to do her part for the grand old party.[39]

The Banks testimony may have been alarming to some whites who moni-tored the Black political response to woman suffrage. However, nationally, the average American did not see Black women as political beings.

Once the Nineteenth Amendment was ratified, African American women throughout the nation surprised those who doubted whether they would register to vote during the 1920 presidential election. Nationwide, Black women had mobilized into "women's citizenship classes," in anticipa-tion of voting. The statewide NAACP branches in Alabama, Georgia, Vir-ginia, West Virginia, Illinois, Kansas, Kentucky, Missouri, Ohio, Oklahoma, and New York organized classes aimed to provide "the political education and training of the newly enfranchised colored woman voter." However, political education was not enough in the South. Colored Women Voters' Leagues were organized with the special task of instructing Black women seeking to qualify to register to vote in areas where they faced white oppo-sition: Alabama, Georgia, Maryland, Florida, Tennessee, and Texas. Leagues were also significant because the members actively sought to qualify Black men as voters as well.[40]

As a result of the work of the leagues, heavy registration was report-ed in Baltimore, Savannah, Atlanta, Jacksonville, and throughout the state of Tennessee. Monroe Work, editor of the *Negro Year Book*, credited Black woman suffrage clubs with much of the work needed to register the women of their race. An NAWSA account noted similar conclusions about the Black women of Nashville, Tennessee, who were said to have registered 2,500 strong. They had organized into suffrage associations to instruct Black women how to register, and as a result, almost all were said to have voted.[41]

By 1921 in Virginia, Maggie Walker, banker and executive head of the Independent Order of St. Luke, ran for office on the all-Black ticket of dissident Virginia Republicans. She ran as a candidate for superintendent of public instruction, but of course lost.[42] This Republican ticket was a symbolic one; however, it was essential to show the white Democratic Party in the South that what they feared was true. Woman suffrage did open the door, though only for a short time, to African Americans who challenged white supremacy.

The Disfranchisement Process in the Post–Nineteenth Amendment Years

African Americans' hopes for political equity were dashed as the majority of black women who still lived in the South were quickly disfranchised. In addition, the black Republican women and men outside the South began to lose their political influence within a decade after the passage of the Nineteenth Amendment.

Disfranchisement had been predicted by several white southern suffragists. Kentucky's Madeline McDowell Breckenridge, for one, considered herself a liberal on racial issues, but did not believe African American women should be voters until they could be properly educated. Breckenridge advocated educational requirements at the state level that would eliminate most potential Black voters. Nonetheless, Marjorie Spruill Wheeler notes that Breckenridge opposed the blatantly racist statements made by other white suffrage leaders like Louisiana's Kate Gordon and Mississippi's Belle Kearney.[43]

Despite optimism among Black leaders, African American women met considerable resistance throughout the southern states. By November 1920, the *Messenger* declared that "in the South Black women have the vote in name only." Editors Randolph and Owen reported the subterfuge and trickery used in the attempt to disfranchise Black women. They were not surprised, however, and they called upon Black women in other sections of the nation to help their southern sisters. They urged "Negro women to stand-up and fight as the political, economic and social equals of their white sisters."[44]

As though in response to the *Messenger*, Black female participation in the elective process during 1920 was extensive enough to occasion a prediction from Georgia State Representative Thomas M. Bell that the Nineteenth Amendment would destroy white supremacy in Georgia since the

Nannie Helen Burroughs and students at the National Training School for Women and Girls. In 1920 Burroughs served as the president of the National League of Republican Colored Women in the District of Columbia. *National Museum of American History, Smithsonian Institution*

amendment had enfranchised Black women. His observations of the registration patterns of Black women in Virginia caused him to fear for Georgia. He urged white women of the state to register to vote to counteract the Black vote before it was too late.[45]

In North Carolina, the fears of Mrs. A. W. Blackwell came true when the legislature introduced a bill known as the "grandmother clause" for women voters. The bill attempted to protect illiterate white women from disfranchisement, but the legislators had not taken into account that "grandfather clauses" had been nullified by the U.S. Supreme Court. The southern strategy was to prevent African American women from voting in much the same way that the South had disfranchised Black male voters.[46] As a result of the 1920 election, however, Du Bois noted that Black women had registered in large numbers throughout the South, especially in Georgia and Louisiana, despite deliberate attempts to discourage them. Du Bois warned that the white South was preparing to disfranchise Black women. Hence, he believed Blacks had to prepare themselves to resist. He exclaimed,

> There is already some open discussion among newspapers and a feverish discussion in secret societies and behind closed doors after the servants retire. The South proposes to keep colored women from voting in exactly the same

way in which it had disfranchised colored men. Can it do it? Are we going to let it do it?[47]

African American women attempted to resist registration practices that discriminated against them. One of the major avenues of protest was through the NAACP. Nearly three million Black women were enfranchised by the Nineteenth Amendment, and three-fourths of them lived in the South. William Pickens, NAACP field secretary, recorded several incidents that he either witnessed personally or about which he received reports. In South Carolina, for example, Pickens noted that Black women constituted the largest group in the state; thus, they posed a major threat to white supremacy. During the first day of registration, Black women in Columbia, South Carolina, apparently took the white male registrars by surprise, and no plan to disqualify them was in effect. Many Black women reported to the registrar's office, but the only discrimination was in that whites were registered first. As a result, some African Americans were kept standing for hours. Pickens reported that at times registrars would stop in the midst of registering a Black woman to wait on a white one. Some Black women waited in line nearly twelve hours, such was their determination. The following day, property tax requirements were declared mandatory for Black women, and the minimum tax receipt was set at 300 dollars' worth of property. (Whether these requirements were on the books, but just not implemented, is not clear.) If the women could prove they had paid the required taxes, the next test was to require Blacks to read from the state or federal constitution and to interpret the document. None of these tests was required of white women. Furthermore, white lawyers were on hand to quiz and harass Black women. Although the *Columbia State,* a local newspaper, reported that few Black women were interested in registering, Pickens testified that, to the contrary, South Carolina's Black women were very much interested. However, they were insulted and often disqualified. By the end of the registration period, Pickens reported that twenty of these women had signed an affidavit against the registrars. A month later, thirty-two women hired a lawyer in Columbia to appeal the discriminatory action of the registrars, and the suit was filed with the attorney general of the state. African American women in Richland County, South Carolina, also planned to appeal their disqualifications by the state registrars. The local NAACP asked readers of the *Crisis* to contact the national office if they knew of any similar cases. It should not be surprising that substantial woman suffrage activity was evident in Columbia and Richland County, because during the post–Civil War years, Black leaders from these areas had openly supported the woman suffrage movement.[48] Nonetheless, court action in 1920 failed. Black support of woman suffrage in South Carolina was not enough to prevent the disfranchisement of the large majority of African American women by the early 1920s.

Press reports from Richmond, Virginia, noted similar attempts to deny the right of voter registration to African American women. According to Suzanne Lebsock's findings about Black women in Virginia, their voter registration response overwhelmed the registrars, who were not prepared for so many women voters. Both Black and white women's groups had mobilized. However, the white registrars did not make it easy for the Black women. Nonetheless, Maggie Walker chaired the committee of activist women in Richmond, which held mass meetings to get out the Black women's votes. As a result of the large female participation in Richmond, three white women deputies were hired to process the white female applicants, but the Black women were left in long lines still waiting to be registered at the close of each day. Although Maggie Walker and Ora Brown Stokes, an African American social worker, complained and petitioned the registrar to appoint Black deputies, none was appointed. Lebsock notes that, because the Black women's lines moved so slowly, and because Black women were likely to be challenged, more often than not they were left in line and not registered. Despite the barriers, 2,410 Black women registered in Richmond, but many more were not able to do so.[49]

Attempts to stop African American women from registering were also reported in North Carolina. A Black woman of Newburn signed an affidavit testifying to the difficulty she had in attempting to register to vote. She was asked to read and to write the entire state constitution. Upon completion of the reading, she attempted to begin the writing. At that point she was informed that, no matter what she did, the registrars would disqualify her because she "belonged to the Negro race."[50]

The NAACP presented evidence of discrimination against Black female voters to Congress in 1920. Several African Americans on the NAACP board of directors joined in the fight to end discrimination against the women. They were vice presidents Archibald Grimké, Mary B. Talbert, and executive officers James Weldon Johnson, Walter White, Addie Hunton, and William Pickens. They gave testimony at the congressional hearing in connection with the proposed enactment of the Tinkham Bill to reduce representation in Congress from states where women were restricted from voting. In a successful attempt to defeat the bill, white southern congressmen claimed that Black women were not disfranchised, just not interested in voting. Despite the massive evidence to the contrary produced by the NAACP, the bill failed. This was not a new strategy among disfranchised Blacks, for the Force Bill, which had been proposed to reduce congressional representation in districts where Black men were restricted from voting, had failed to pass Congress in 1890.[51]

The effect of attempts by whites to disfranchise Black women was reflected also in literature. A Black female poet from Seattle, with the pen name "Anise," wrote a poem at the end of 1920 in which she described the problems experienced by Black women voters at southern polls. On the first day, she declared, they were humiliated and kept in line many hours, "but still the colored women kept on coming!" She noted that, on the second day, Black women were given difficult examination questions and were disqualified on technicalities, "but still the colored women kept on coming!" Finally, on the third day, the sheriff threatened them with violence, "but still the colored women kept on coming!" Anise ended her poem with the following lines:

> But I hear some judge is going
> To throw the ballots OUT,
> For fear those colored women
> Might really come
> To believe
> That representative government
> Exists
> In America![52]

The situation led William Pickens to raise the following question: "Will the women of the United States who know something at least of disenfranchisement tolerate such methods to prevent intelligent colored women from voting?"[53]

The inability of Congress and the NAACP to protect the rights of Black women voters led the women to seek help from national white woman suffrage leaders. Not surprisingly, these attempts also failed. In 1920 the NAWSA had changed its name to the League of Women Voters (LWV), a nonpartisan organization designed to maintain women's political participation on national and local levels. At the 1921 national convention held in Cleveland, African American women brought their complaints about disfranchisement before the LWV. Although some of the white southern suffrage leaders had refused to join the LWV, those southern delegates at the convention threatened to walk out if the "negro problem" was debated. In typical League fashion, a compromise resulted, wherein African American women were allowed to speak before the body, but no action was taken by the organization.[54]

When the African American women suffragists sought assistance from the National Woman's Party, they were totally rebuffed. The NWP leadership position was that, since Black women were discriminated against in the same ways as Black men, their problems were not women's rights issues, but race issues. Therefore, the NWP felt no obligation to defend the right of African American women as voters.[55]

In this case, Wanda Henderick's analysis holds true: the white feminists attempted to require African American women to separate their blackness from their femaleness. Later, when NWP officials attempted to gain Black support for the Equal Rights Amendment during the early 1920s, leaders disclaimed prejudice against Black suffragists. In order to prove their case, the NWP submitted a letter to NAACP field secretary Walter White, which included a transcribed interview with Mary Church Terrell. Although Terrell said she was "distressed" because the NWP had been criticized for "unfriendliness to our race," Terrell diplomatically affirmed the belief among many Blacks that NWP workers discriminated against African American women's concerns and cries for assistance. She noted,

> The only disappointment I suffered was at the time a colored deputation visited Miss Paul on the question of the passage of a resolution affecting the vote of colored women. I was the spokesman of that deputation and I will confess that I was grievously disappointed that the Woman's Party could not see its way to do what we asked, which was that they take up as their next work after the winning of the suffrage a campaign to see that no colored women were debarred from voting on account of their race. But still I could see their point—that they wanted to continue to work on discriminations that were common to all women, and not on discriminations that were based on race only, rather than on sex.[56]

Although the NWP felt that Terrell's statement repudiated any charges of racial discrimination on the organization's part, in reality, Terrell affirmed Alice Paul's position against assisting women voters who were suffering because of racial discrimination.

Abandonment by white women suffragists in 1920 really came as no surprise to most Black women leaders. The preceding decade of woman suffrage politics had reminded them of the assertions of African American woman suffrage supporters of the past. By 1920 the situation had changed very little, and many African American suffragists had been thoroughly disillusioned by the racism of the white feminists they had encountered.[57]

Within a few years, white supremacy was victorious throughout the South. Unlike Black men, who had been disfranchised within twenty years after the ratification of the Fifteenth Amendment, Black women had lost the vote within less than a decade. Nonetheless, African American women continued to be involved in local and national politics for as long as they could during the 1920s. In Baltimore alone, the Black electorate increased from 16,800 to over 37,400 in 1921, indicating that the number of Black women voters surpassed the number of Black men registered to vote. This was a unique situation, nonetheless. By 1922, attempts to thwart the remaining influence of Black women voters were spreading across the South. As a result, the NACW recommended that all of its clubs lobby for the enforcement of the Nineteenth Amendment.[58]

By 1924 Nannie Burroughs had assessed the status of Black women of voting age and their relationship to white feminists. Burroughs felt that white women continued to overlook or to undervalue the worth of African American women as a political force in the nation. She advised white women politicians to tap the potential Black female electorate before white men exploited it. With the exception of Ruth Hanna McCormick, who recruited Mary Church Terrell to head her 1929 Illinois campaign for the United States Senate, warnings such as Burroughs gave did not seem to influence white female leaders. For example, disillusioned members of the Republican Colored Women State Committee of Wilmington, Delaware, protested unsuccessfully when they lost their representation on the state Republican committee. A merger of the Women's Advisory Committee, a white group, with the State Central Committee had caused the elimination of Black women representatives. White female Republicans had not worked to solve the problem, which further alienated the Black women. The decline in Black women's participation in Republican Party politics was evident by 1928, when only 8 out of 104 Black delegates to the Republican National Convention were women, a sizable reduction from previous years. The same year, the NACW program did not even bother to include suffrage among its priorities for women of their race, since the majority of Black women—those living in the South—had been disfranchised.[59] As for Black women living in the North, many of them were disillusioned by political party politics and either did not participate or became independents.

By the 1930s, even Bertha Higgins, a hard-working Republican for over thirty years, was expressing her disillusionment with the party. In forming the Colored Independent Political Association of Rhode Island in 1932, she drafted a resolution stating reasons why the members had abandoned the Republican Party. One resolution read as follows:

> We proclaim our independence as citizens and resolve to act with any party no matter what its name, in seeking better conditions for our people through the instrumentality of better laws and a liberalized constitution of our state.[60]

Conclusion

As the woman suffrage era ended in the 1920s, few organized, mainstream feminist activities were apparent among the disillusioned Black suffragists of the period. African American women leaders and their organizations began to focus more on issues that continued to plague both the men and the women of their race, rather than on issues that concerned white feminists. The economic plight of African American women kept most of them in poverty and among the lowest of the working classes. So-called middle-class Black women were still relatively few in number. They were more concerned about uplifting the downtrodden of their race or in representing people of color throughout the world than in issues that were limited to middle-class feminists. As a result, during the 1920s there was little concern among African American women over the Equal Rights Amendment debate between the more conservative League of Women Voters and the more radical NWP. Although the economic roles of many white American women were expanding, the status of Black women remained basically static between the world wars. Hence, African American feminists identified more with the plight of people of color, who found themselves in similar oppressed situations. Former Black suffragists were more likely to participate in the Women's International League for Peace and Freedom (WILPF) or the International Council of Women of the Darker Races than in the LWV or the NWP.[61]

Mary Church Terrell, for one, was a member of all four organizations. Twenty years after the ratification of the woman suffrage amendment, she wrote her autobiography. At the age of seventy-seven, she was one of the few living links with three generations of Black feminists. In her introduction she made a revealing statement:

> This is a story of a colored woman living in a white world. It cannot possibly be like a story written by a white woman. A white woman has only one handicap to overcome—that of sex. I have two—both sex and race. I belong to the only group in this country which has two such huge obstacles to surmount. Colored men have only one—that of race.[62]

Terrell's reference to her status as an African American woman applied throughout U.S. history to most Black women, regardless of class. In view of this, it is not surprising that African American women struggled, often in vain, to keep the right to vote, believing that the franchise could in some way improve their position in American society.

Chapter 8. The Nineteenth Amendment and Its Meaning for African American Women

The Right to Vote: Its Ideological Meaning

The history of suffrage movements in the United States involves the quest of disfranchised men and women for the right to make political choices. Their hope has been that making the choices will give them a voice in the governmental decision-making process. Throughout suffrage history in the United States, the desire for the ballot box has pitted the power brokers against the powerless. More often than not, the powerless have had to be awakened to the potential of their voting power.

Historically, once awakened, the desire of the powerless for political equity is stimulated. This awakening process connected African American women suffragists to the same path that other groups had followed and would later follow—propertyless white men, African American men, persons without education, white women, Native Americans, and young people. The process varied from group to group, determined by the effort needed to awaken members from their political lethargy and the barriers placed in the way of their enfranchisement. In the case of the majority of Black women, slavery, illiteracy, poverty, and gender proscription provided significant barriers to thwart group political awakening. Such a combination of barriers and multiple forms of oppression rarely limited the development of political acumen among other groups seeking suffrage.

As a result of the many barriers, it should not be surprising that the majority of African American women who argued in behalf of woman suffrage were educated women from the so-called middle class. However, the first known Black female suffragist, Sojourner Truth, was illiterate and from the working class. We may never know how many working-class African American women struggled for the right to vote during the years of the woman suffrage movement. We do know that with time, more and more working-class Black women advocated woman suffrage and actively participated in the movement.

Once African American women became politically aware of the vote as a prize worth seeking, they began to move down the path to suffrage. However, for them, there were two major forks in the path that other groups did not encounter. One was the branch all women took, a protracted road to the ballot box. Women, more so than men, have had to struggle longer on the suffrage path to reach the prize. In this sense, all women shared the same historical experience. Nonetheless, white women, even those of the working class, did not have to contend with the double burden of racial and gender discrimination as a barrier to their right to vote. The second fork appeared when, once the franchise had been achieved, some women kept it but others could not. Black men and Black women shared the sojourn on this path. Only African American people in the United States gained the right to vote by federal constitutional amendments, but then generally lost it through state constitutional loopholes. Black women lost the vote even faster than Black men had lost it before them, because the legal loopholes were in place by the time African American women gained the ballot.

Yet African American men who were fortunate enough to live in areas where state constitutions were not changed to challenge their rights to the political process had different experiences from their women. Struggling not only against the anti–woman suffrage arguments aimed at all women, African American women encountered the anti–Black woman suffrage voices of white men and white women. In addition mainstream suffragists often included African American women in the movement on gendered grounds, but rejected them on racial ones. As a result of these forks in the path, the story of Black women suffragists in the United States is different in many respects from other suffrage histories and deserves to be analyzed from a perspective of its own. It is not surprising that Black women's reasons for joining the movement were sometimes the same as, but also different from those of white suffrage advocates. African American women's reasons for becoming suffragists reflected their multiple consciousness, which was based on generations of experiences resisting multiple forms of oppression. In arguing their reasons for seeking the right to vote, many of them revealed their feminism, which can be contextualized as being Black nationalist feminist in character.

Although woman suffrage meant different things to different African American women, most believed that the ballot was essential to the growth of democracy and to the advancement of human rights in the United States. They believed that Black women were victims of both racial and sexual oppression, and that women, both Black and white, were second-class citizens because they lacked the right to choose those who determined the laws and policies of the nation. African American women argued also that, in a democratic society, such a denial of political rights was a mockery of justice. In addition, they claimed that women were intelligent enough to make sound political decisions. These arguments, based upon the ideals of "justice," characterized the beliefs of African American women throughout the duration of the suffrage campaign.

During both the nineteenth and the twentieth centuries, the woman suffrage supporters advanced the belief that women were more moral beings than men; therefore, women would make more effective reformers if armed with the ballot. Black and white suffrage advocates supported this view, which originated with female abolitionists in the antebellum period, and continued again with the progressive movement during the first two decades of the twentieth century. However, justification for woman suffrage went beyond the ideas of justice and female moral superiority for the majority of African American female suffrage advocates. By the late nineteenth century, their rationale had grown to include the argument that African American women needed the vote in order to help uplift the Black race and to obtain their own rights. During the final two decades of the movement, leading up to the passage of the Nineteenth Amendment, Black women continued to voice the self-help rationale. In the South, they added the argument that as voters they could help to reenfranchise Black men, who in the thirty years following their national enfranchisement, had virtually lost the vote in the South through legalized racial discrimination. While racism intensified as a national theme, African American women suffragists nationwide foresaw their potential exclusion from the woman suffrage amendment and lobbied even harder to preserve the idea that they too deserved political equity.

In reality, anti-Black attitudes among whites permeated the woman suffrage movement from the post–Civil War years through the successful twentieth century campaign for the Nineteenth Amendment. Despite arguments that national suffrage leaders were not really racists when they ignored or rebuffed Black women who sought inclusion, there is evidence that northern woman suffrage leaders used southern suffragists as foils for racist behavior among white women nationwide. Then again, the first major conflict within the national woman suffrage movement was over the question of race. Over time, Blacks became suspicious of the white suffragists and criticized early attempts by whites to jeopardize the success of "Negro suffrage" and then later efforts by whites to jeopardize the inclusion of Black women under the woman suffrage amendment to the federal Constitution. Nonetheless, African Americans rejected attempts to exclude them from the movement and Black women found a variety of ways to participate.[1]

As participants, Black women attended meetings of the national woman suffrage associations and served as officers of national and local woman suffrage organizations. For example, during the 1860s, approximately 9 percent of the American Equal Rights Association leadership was Black, and observers noted that a sizable number of African American women attended the proceedings. As group members, Blacks engaged in the petitioning of federal and state governments on behalf of woman suffrage and actively campaigned for woman suffrage referendums and amendments. In addition, African Americans joined dozens of groups that were either woman suffrage associations or women's clubs with woman suffrage goals. Although the majority of these organizations were local ones, some represented federations of women's clubs with large memberships. Of those on a national level, the Equal Suffrage League of the NACW represented over 40,000 African American women in 1908, and the Baptist Women's Convention represented over 50,000 Black women in 1912. Moreover, the participants in these organizations and other African American women's groups often formed coalitions with white suffrage leaders or associations. Black women used oratory and literary skills, in prose and in poetry, to express their desire to vote, or their opposition to the various ways whites attempted to keep them disfranchised.[2]

Black women suffragists came from a variety of backgrounds, from the relatively affluent, who were well educated, to the working class, some of whom were illiterate. Basically, however, their arguments were the same, with the more privileged African American women speaking on behalf of the more downtrodden women of their race. Differences of region, rather than economic and educational status, influenced the varied reasons why Black women believed voting women could better address Black community problems than disfranchised women. For example, prior to the ratification of the Nineteenth Amendment, southern women were more concerned about the disfranchisement of Black men than were northern women. However, northern women were sensitive to the needs and specific problems of southern women. Strategies often differed more because of region than because of class. Northern Black women seemed more convinced that working for the Republican Party would insure their enfranchisement than southern Black women, who were suspicious of all white politicians.

Nonetheless, once African American women received the right to vote, they participated actively in the political process. Reports indicated that 620 Black females voted in Denver's 1906 city election. In 1915 Black women in Chicago were responsible for over 1,000 votes, which helped to elect alderman Oscar De Priest. In 1916 in Vineland, New Jersey, 300 Black women voted to approve the state woman suffrage referendum, and in Nashville, Tennessee, 2,500 voted in the elections of 1920. Campaigning for the candidates of their choice was another method of participation. This was evident in 1914 in Chicago, in 1916 in Los Angeles, and in 1918 in Dayton, Chicago, and New York City. After the passage of the Nineteenth Amendment in 1920, Black women formed and participated in voter education leagues throughout the country and especially in the South, where opposition to African American women voters was greatest.

The highlight of Black female participation in the movement came when they ran for elective offices. Reports indicated that two African American females were elected delegates and two were elected alternates to the New York Republican convention in 1918. In addition, an unreported number were elected to the Texas Republican convention the same year, and one Black woman was elected to the Kentucky Republican convention in 1920. Black female candidates ran in 1918 for the school board in New Jersey and for the state senate in Washington, and in 1920 for the state assembly in New York.

However, the mere winning of the ballot by women, both Black and white, could not solve the problems social feminists hoped it could and would. Intemperance, crime and prison abuse, consumer abuse, and discrimination against women in education and in the marketplace remained problems. Although Black women did not gain protection of their civil rights immediately and although Black males were not restored to the franchise rolls for some time, woman suffrage did extend the ballot to all women, not just those of the educated, white middle-class. Unfortunately for three-fourths of the nation's African American women, it was suffrage in name only.

During the years that followed the passage of the Nineteenth Amendment, southern Blacks, both male and female, remained virtually disfranchised, as southern governments circumvented the amendment. Northern Blacks, for a time, made some inroads into politics on the local level. However, the immediate success in the realization of woman suffrage was not the solution to societal problems but the triumph of democratic principles. The right of all women to vote was acknowledged in the Constitution. It was this principle that motivated the early African American suffragists to struggle on behalf of woman suffrage initially. The need to complete the goals of the early woman suffrage advocates—to bring all women into a position of first-class citizenship—remained a challenge to Americans long after the Nineteenth Amendment was ratified.

The question still remains among students and scholars of the woman suffrage movement: whose are the authentic voices to tell African American women's story in the movement and to tell about the meaning of the movement for their communities? The answer is, the voices of the Black women suffragists themselves. Although for much of the nearly 150 years since Black women arrived on the woman suffrage scene, they have remained nearly invisible as active players, the words and views of some have survived. Nonetheless, the white women leaders of the movement constructed the history and determined the value of Black women to the movement. For the most part, white women's voices are heard and believed. Even Susan B. Anthony, more sensitive about race than many white women leaders, determined which of the many African American spokespersons, male and female, were notable, and whether the woman suffrage movement was broad enough to be inclusive of Black suffragists.

In the fourth volume of *The History of Woman Suffrage,* Anthony and coauthor Ida Husted Harper included a chapter on national women's organizations. They included one African American women's group, the NACW, with a description written by Margaret Murray Washington (Mrs. Booker T. Washington), who was vice president and the editor of the official organ of the association. They also included a section called "Eminent Advocates of Woman Suffrage," in which only two African American women were listed: Mary Church Terrell and Ida B. Wells. Significantly, such noted African American women leaders as Margaret Murray Washington, of Tuskegee, Alabama, and Sylvanie Williams of New Orleans, Louisiana, were missing. Both women were notable clubwomen who should have been listed among the prominent suffragists. However, they resided in the lower South. Perhaps Anthony felt it was expedient not to list them. Whatever the reason, omitting their names made them invisible to woman suffrage history, because students and scholars over the years have listened to Anthony's voice without seeking the voices of the African American women themselves.[3]

Similarly, contemporary researchers find it difficult to see or to hear the voices that discriminated against Black women in the movement, despite the extant accounts of prejudice from suffragists such as Josephine St. Pierre Ruffin, Ida B. Wells, Mary Church Terrell, and Sylvanie Williams. They prefer to listen to Anthony, who believed that white women would end racism and discrimination against Blacks once women had the right to vote. This would happen, she argued, because women had higher moral values than men.[4] We know that Anthony presumed in error. There is a lesson, however: students of movements that involve questions about race must look for the authentic voices.

Postscript to Winning the Vote

When the over seventy-year struggle for woman suffrage ended in 1920, African American suffragists realized their dilemma as forces throughout the nation organized to deprive them of their hard-won prize and, it seemed, to keep them at the bottom of the economic ladder. In 1920 Howard University professor Benjamin Brawley examined the economic status of African American women in the United States. He found that there were over one million Black females in the work force in 1910. Fifty-two percent of them worked as farmers or farm laborers, and 28 percent worked as cooks or washerwomen. In essence, 80 percent of Black women workers were doing arduous, menial work. Brawley speculated that conditions had not improved by 1920. In 1922 Elizabeth Ross Haynes, an African American social worker, found that two million Black women in the nation worked in three types of occupations: domestic and personal service, agriculture, and manufacturing. Of the two million, 50 percent were in domestic service. Only 20,000 held semiskilled jobs in manufacturing industries. Haynes's findings in 1922 were in keeping with Brawley's speculations.[5]

Unfortunately, the position of Black women in the work force had not changed significantly by 1935. African American women ranked lowest on the economic scale among men and women, Black and white. The average weekly wage for a Black domestic worker was three dollars and washerwomen received a mere seventy-five cents a week. Working conditions, as well as wages, were substandard, and African American women were exploited by white women as well as by white men. Woman suffrage had not helped the majority of Black women as Anthony had predicted.[6]

Simultaneously, Black women leaders in the United States observed the connection between racism and gender proscription worldwide. As a result, they made attempts to foster cultural and political awareness among women of color cross-culturally. African American women began to call for coalitions of women of color all over the globe. Among the organizations that fostered such ideas were the NACW, the International Council of Women of the Darker Races, and the women's arm of the Universal Negro Improvement Association.[7]

For example, the NACW was the only national organization to help fund the Third and Fourth Pan African Congresses, held in London in 1923 and in New York City in 1927. When Du Bois and other organizers struggled to keep this international group afloat, African American women maintained the vision. The conferences brought Black delegates from all over the world together in international venues. Several African American women attended these conferences, including poet Jessie Fauset, who had represented the NACW at the first Congress, which was held in London in 1919. The goal of the body was to develop strategies for cooperation among African diaspora people worldwide. Here we see another level of political awakening among educated Black women and men.[8]

It should be apparent that the significance of African American women's struggle for suffrage goes beyond winning the right to vote. The struggle was instrumental in their development of strategies for other battles for which race and gender intersect, battles where they refused to separate their identification by both race and gender. The significance also involves the continuous interplay of race and gender on the political awakening and beliefs of Black women in the United States. Because of racism, Black women's experiences and goals were different from those of white suffragists. Racism stimulates multiple levels of consciousness and survival strategies among African American women—past and present. Feminist history must face the reality: although most suffragists were feminists, many of the white ones were also racists. Institutionalized racism in the United States was and continues to be a national phenomenon, rooted deeply in the history of the nation. Race prejudice was not limited to just southern suffragists.

Racism aside, many white women suffragists sought the vote only for themselves. Conversely, African American women were universal suffragists in the sense that their voices called for the vote for all citizens, not just for themselves.

NOTES

1. Revisiting the Question of Race
in the Woman Suffrage Movement

1. See Rosalyn Terborg-Penn, "Afro-Americans in the Struggle for Woman Suffrage" (unpublished dissertation, Howard University, 1977), appendices.

2. For example, see the review of *The Afro-American Woman: Struggles and Images,* by Bess Beatty, *Journal of Southern History* vol. 45, no. 2 (May 1979): 304–305.

3. See, for example, Nettie Rogers Shuler and Carrie Chapman Catt, *Woman Suffrage and Politics* (New York: Scribner's, 1926); Alma Lutz, *Created Equal: Elizabeth Cady Stanton, 1815–1902* (New York: John Day, 1940).

4. Eleanor Flexner, *Century of Struggle: The Woman's Rights Movement in the United States* (New York: Atheneum, 1973); Aileen Kraditor, *The Ideas of the Woman Suffrage Movement, 1890–1920* (Garden City, NY: Anchor Books, 1971).

5. Benjamin Quarles, "Frederick Douglass and the Woman's Rights Movement," *Journal of Negro History* vol. 25 (January 1940): 35–44.

6. Elizabeth Cady Stanton et al., eds., *The History of Woman Suffrage, 1848–1920,* 6 vols. (New York: Arno Press and the New York Times, 1969), hereinafter cited as HWS; the Susan B. Anthony Papers, Manuscript Division, Library of Congress, Washington, DC, hereinafter cited as Anthony Papers; Ida Husted Harper, ed., *The Life and Work of Susan B. Anthony,* 3 vols. (Indianapolis: Hollenbeck Press, 1908).

7. Helen Laura Sumner Woodbury, *Equal Suffrage: The Results of an Investigation in Colorado, Made for the Collective Equal Suffrage League of New York State* (New York: Harper and Brothers, 1909), 70.

8. Elinor Lerner, "Immigrant and Working Class Involvement in the New York City Woman Suffrage Movement, 1905–1917: A Study in Progressive Era Politics" (unpublished dissertation, University of California–Berkeley, 1981), 172, 391.

9. Ellen Carol DuBois, *Feminism and Suffrage: The Emergence of an Independent Women's Movement in America, 1848–1869* (Ithaca: Cornell University Press, 1978); Bettina Aptheker *Woman's Legacy: Essays on Race, Sex, and Class in American History* (Amherst: University of Massachusetts Press, 1982); Elisabeth Griffith, *In Her Own Right: The Life of Elizabeth Cady Stanton* (New York: Oxford University Press, 1984).

10. See Angela Y. Davis, *Women, Race and Class* (New York: Random House, 1981); Paula Giddings, *When and Where I Enter: The Impact of Black Women on Race and Sex in America* (New York: William Morrow and Co., 1984).

11. Marjorie Spruill Wheeler, *New Women of the New South: The Leaders of the Woman Suffrage Movement in the Southern States* (New York: Oxford University Press, 1993).

12. See Adele Logan Alexander, *Ambiguous Lives: Free Women of Color in Rural Georgia, 1789–1879* (Fayetteville: University of Arkansas Press, 1991); Elsa Barkley Brown, "Negotiating and Transforming the Public Sphere: African American Political Life in the Transition from Slavery to Freedom," *Public Culture* vol. 7, no. 1 (Fall 1994);

Sharon Harley, "For the Good of Family and Race: Gender, Work and Domestic Roles in the Black Community, 1880–1930," *Signs* vol. 15, no. 2 (Winter 1990); Wanda Hendricks, "Ida B. Wells-Barnett and the Alpha Suffrage Club of Chicago," in *One Woman, One Vote: Rediscovering the Woman Suffrage Movement*, ed. Marjorie Spruill Wheeler (Troutdale, OR: NewSage Press, 1995); Evelyn Brooks Higginbotham, *Righteous Discontent: The Woman's Movement in the Black Baptist Church, 1880–1920* (Cambridge: Harvard University Press, 1993); Darlene Clark Hine, "Rape and the Culture of Dissemblance: Preliminary Thoughts on the Inner Lives of Black Midwestern Women," *Signs* vol. 14, no. 4 (Summer 1989); Nell Irvin Painter, "Sojourner Truth in Feminist Abolitionism: Difference, Slavery, and Memory," in *An Untrodden Path: Antislavery and Women's Political Culture*, ed. Jean Fagan Yellin and John C. Van Horne (Ithaca: Cornell University Press, 1992).

13. Brown, 126–35.

14. For primary evidence of free Black women's political and reform activities see, Dorothy Sterling, ed., *We Too Are Your Sisters: Black Women in the 19th Century* (New York: W. W. Norton, 1984).

15. Rosalyn Terborg-Penn, "Discrimination against Afro-American Women in the Woman's Movement, 1830–1920," in *The Afro-American Woman: Struggles and Images*, ed. Sharon Harley and Rosalyn Terborg-Penn (Port Washington, NY: Kennikat Press, 1978), 17–27.

16. William L. O'Neill, *Everybody Was Brave* (New York: Quadrangle Press, 1969), 71–72, 74–75; Kraditor, 126–28; Sherna Gluck, ed., *From Parlor to Prison: Five American Suffragists Talk about Their Lives* (New York: Vintage Books, 1976), 16.

17. For a New York City case, see S. Sara Monoson, "The Lady and the Tiger: Women's Electoral Activism in New York City before Suffrage," *Journal of Women's History* vol. 2, no. 2 (Fall 1990); 100–35.

18. Limited or full woman suffrage states by 1918 included: Wyoming, Massachusetts, Colorado, Idaho, Utah, Washington, California, Oregon, Kansas, Arizona, Illinois, Montana, Nevada, North Dakota, Nebraska, Rhode Island, New York, Arkansas, Michigan, Texas, South Dakota, and Oklahoma.

19. Wheeler, *New Women,* chapter 4.

20. Paula Baker, "The Domestication of Politics: Women and American Political Society, 1780–1920," *American Historical Review*, vol. 89, no. 3 (June 1984): 639.

21. Rosalyn Terborg-Penn, "Discontented Black Feminists: Prelude and Postscript to the Passage of the Nineteenth Amendment," in *Decades of Discontent: The Women's Movement, 1920–1940*, ed. Lois Scharf and Joan M. Jensen (Westport, CT: Greenwood Press, 1983), 264–67.

2. African American Women in the First Generation of Woman Suffragists

1. *Weekly Anglo-African*, 29 October 1859. The correspondent used the pen name "Laura."

2. HWS 1: 73–74.

3. Griffith, 63.

4. Ibid., 58; Quarles, "Frederick Douglass and Woman's Rights," 35.

5. HWS 1: 824; for an explanation about why Truth attracted so much attention from middle-class white women, see Painter, "Sojourner Truth in Feminist Abolitionism."

6. HWS 1: 115–17; Sojourner Truth, *Narrative of Sojourner Truth: A Bondwoman of Olden Times* (Chicago: Johnson Publishing Co., Ebony Classics, 1970), 103–105.

7. HWS 1: 567–68.

8. Margaret Washington, ed., *Narrative of Sojourner Truth* (New York: Vintage Books, 1993), xviii.

9. HWS 1: 376, 386.

10. HWS 1: 375, 384.

11. *A Narrative of the Life and Travels of Mrs. Nancy Prince,* in *Collected Black Women's Narratives,* introduction by Anthony G. Barthelemy (New York: Oxford University Press, 1988), 47.

12. Observe Frederick Douglass's words when he debated a white woman during the 1868 American Equal Rights Association meeting: "The government of this country loves **women**. They are the sisters, mothers, wives and daughters of our rulers; but the Negro is loathed." HWS 2: 311.

13. HWS 1: 384.

14. Ibid.

15. Nell Irvin Painter, "Sojourner Truth's Defense of the Rights of Women (as reported in 1851; rewritten in 1863)," in *Women's America: Refocusing the Past,* 4th ed., ed. Linda K. Kerber and Jane Sherron DeHart (New York: Oxford University Press, 1995), 215–17.

16. HWS 1: 668; HWS 3: 72–73; Diary of Charlotte Forten Grimké, 1: 45, 52, 180, Moorland-Spingarn Research Center, Howard University, Washington, D.C.

17. Benjamin Quarles, *Black Abolitionists* (New York: Oxford University Press, 1969), chapters 9 and 10.

18. Baker, 632, 634.

19. Jim Bearden and Linda Jean Butler, *Shadd: The Life and Times of Mary Shadd Cary* (Toronto: NC Press, 1977), 13, 139.

20. Ibid., 160–62.

21. Ibid., 162–63.

22. (New York) *Weekly Anglo-African,* 6 August 1859.

23. Quarles, *Black Abolitionists,* 199–201.

24. HWS 1: 254–55.

25. Quarles, *Black Abolitionists,* 208.

26. Aptheker, 13.

27. Ibid., 31–32.

28. Griffith, 111.

29. Brown, 124–25.

30. Quarles, "Frederick Douglass," 35.

31. See Miriam Gurko, *The Ladies of Seneca Falls* (New York: MacMillan, 1974), 220–26; Robert L. Allen and Pamela Allen, *Reluctant Reformers* (Washington: Howard University Press, 1974), 141–49; Flexner, 142–45; David Morgan, *Suffragists and Democrats* (East Lansing: Michigan State University Press, 1972), 187; DuBois, *Feminism and Suffrage,* chapter 6; Aptheker, chapter 2; Anne F. and Andrew M. Scott, *One Half the People* (Philadelphia: J. B. Lippincott, 1975), 16; Griffith, chapter 8; Andrea Moore Kerr, "White Women's Rights, Black Men's Wrongs . . . ," in Wheeler, *One Woman, One Vote,* 64–70.

32. HWS 2: 183, 191, 379.

33. HWS 2: 182; HWS 3: 457.

34. HWS 2: 220.

35. HWS 2: 222, 309, 381.

36. Ida Husted Harper, 1: 270.

37. DuBois, *Feminism and Suffrage,* 164.

38. Aptheker, 12.

39. Griffith, 111.

40. HWS 2: 94–95.

41. Harper, 1: 287, 290.

42. HWS 2: 233, 235–36, 238.

43. Frank R. Levstik, "Charles Langston," in *Dictionary of American Negro Biography*, ed. Rayford W. Logan and Michael R. Winston (New York: W. W. Norton, 1982), 381.

44. HWS 2: 259–61; DuBois, *Feminism and Suffrage*, 89; HWS 2: 237–38, 241.

45. Eugene H. Berwanger, "Hardin and Langston: Western Black Spokesmen of the Reconstruction Era," *Journal of Negro History* vol. 65 (Spring 1979), 105–106.

46. HWS 2: 236; Berwanger, 106.

47. Berwanger, 110–11; Kerr, 66.

48. HWS 2: 233, 237, 265.

49. Ibid., 193, 197–98.

50. HWS 2: 927–28.

51. Ibid., 226–27, 245; Kerr, 67–68.

52. Griffith, 118; HWS 2: 378–91.

53. HWS 2: 347, 383–85.

54. HWS 2: 391–92.

55. Aptheker, 49.

56. Nell Irvin Painter, *Sojourner Truth: A Life, A Symbol* (New York: W. W. Norton, 1996), 224–25.

57. DuBois, *Feminism and Suffrage*, 166–67; Kerr, 71–72.

58. Rosalyn Terborg-Penn, "Nineteenth Century Black Women and Woman Suffrage," *Potomac Review* vol. 7 (Spring-Summer 1977), 14–15.

3. African American Woman Suffragists
Finding Their Own Voices

1. France E. Harper, *Sketches of Southern Life* (Philadelphia: Ferguson Brothers, 1896), 16.

2. Ellen Carol DuBois, "Taking the Law into Our Own Hands," in Wheeler, *One Woman One Vote*, 84–86; Griffith, 119.

3. *Revolution*, vol. 2, no. 20, 19 November 1868, 307.

4. Griffith, 148.

5. *(Washington) New National Era*, 10 August 1871, 23 April 1874.

6. Bearden and Butler, 211–14.

7. Mary Ann Shadd Cary Speech to Judiciary Committee, folder 6, box 2, Mary Ann Shadd Cary Papers, Moorland-Spingarn Research Center, Howard University, Washington, DC, hereinafter cited as MASC Papers.

8. Cary Speech to Judiciary Committee, MASC Papers. In her biography of Oregon suffragist Abigail Scott Duniway, Ruth Barnes Moynihan quotes from the Oregon Herald, "Mrs. A. J. Duniway, a colored , and two white women" tried to vote in Portland. Moynihan notes that Duniway's grandson, David, a retired state archivist, identified the "colored" woman as Mrs. Beatty. Apparently no sources on this woman reveal her first name. Ruth Barnes Moynihan, *Rebel for Rights: Abigail Scott Duniway* (New Haven: Yale University Press, 1983), 85, 238 n. 4.

9. HWS 2: 626–27, 689.

10. Quarles, "Frederick Douglass," 35.

11. Terborg-Penn, "Nineteenth Century," 17.

12. DuBois, *Feminism and Suffrage*, 201–202.

13. DuBois, "Taking the Law into Our Own Hands," 97.

14. HWS 3: 31, 72–73, 955.

15. Both Dorothy Sterling, *We Too Are Your Sisters*, 411, 416, and Dorothy Salem, *To Better Our World: Black Women in Organized Reform, 1890–1920* (Brooklyn: Carlson Publishing, 1990), 38, state that more Black women, including Sojourner Truth, affiliated with the NWSA than the AWSA. On the other hand, Nell Painter says that Truth tried

to straddle the two organizations, but "came finally to rest with the AWSA." Painter, *Sojourner Truth: A Life, A Symbol,* 232. Similarly, Adele Logan Alexander concludes that more African Americans supported the AWSA than the NWSA. Alexander, "Adella Hunt Logan, the Tuskegee Woman's Club, and African Americans in the Suffrage Movement," in *Votes for Women: The Woman Suffrage Movement in Tennessee, the South and the Nation,* ed. Marjorie Spruill Wheeler (Knoxville: University of Tennessee Press, 1995), 75. My research findings disagree with both Sterling and Salem.

16. Terborg-Penn, "Afro-Americans in the Struggle for Woman Suffrage," 46–49.

17. HWS 3: 268–69; Sterling, 96, 180.

18. *Crisis* vol. 10 (August 1915); 188.

19. Terborg-Penn, "Nineteenth Century Black Women," 16; HWS 3: 821, 827–28; for a history of the Rollin family women, see Carole Ione, *Pride of Family: Four Generations of American Women of Color* (New York: Summit Books, 1991).

20. HWS 3: 827–28.

21. HWS 3: 827–28.

22. Ibid., 828.

23. HWS 2: 803.

24. Petition for Woman Suffrage, House of Representatives, RG 233, HR 45th Congress, 1877–79, 45A. H11, folder 14, National Archives, Washington, DC.

25. HWS 3: 828; HWS 2: 833–34, 842.

26. Truth, *Narrative,* 151.

27. Ibid; 176, 177, 189.

28. *Revolution,* vol. 3 (4 March 1869): 139.

29. Monroe A. Majors, *Noted Negro Women: Their Triumphs and Activities* (Chicago: Donohue and Henneberry, 1893), 84; *(Chicago) Tribune,* 6 March 1869.

30. Majors, 84–85.

31. Scope Notes, MASC Papers; HWS 3: 19, 61, 72–73.

32. HWS 3: 773.

33. M. A. McCurdy, "Duty of the State to the Negro," *Afro-American Encyclopedia,* edited by James T. Haley (Nashville: Haley and Florida, 1895), 137–41, 144–45.

34. *(New York) Freeman,* 26 December 1885.

35. HWS 4: 898, 1104.

4. Suffrage Strategies and Ideas

1. Adella Hunt Logan, "Colored Women as Voters," *Crisis* vol. 4 (September 1912): 245.

2. See Rayford W. Logan, *The Betrayal of the Negro: From Rutherford B. Hayes to Woodrow Wilson* (London: Collier-Macmillan, 1965). Logan is best known for developing "the Nadir" concept, which he introduced in the first edition of his book, originally published in 1954 as *The Negro in American Life and Thought: The Nadir, 1877–1901.*

3. HWS 4: 117, 123.

4. Logan, *The Betrayal of the Negro,* 11; Brown, 120–21.

5. See for example: Adele Logan Alexander, "Adella Hunt Logan," in *Black Women in America: An Historical Encyclopedia,* ed. Darlene Clark Hine et al. (Brooklyn: Carlson Publishing, 1993), 729.

6. *Atchison Blade,* 10 September 1892, 10 December 1892.

7. Ida B. Wells-Barnett, *Crusade for Justice: The Autobiography of Ida B. Wells,* ed. Alfreda M. Duster (Chicago: The University of Chicago Press, 1970), 61–67, 77–86, 107–13, 121–22.

8. McCurdy, 141–45.

9. HWS 4: 1100; Louis R. Harlan, *Booker T. Washington: The Making of a Black*

Leader: 1856–1901 (New York: Oxford University Press, 1972); Adele Logan Alexander, "How I Discovered My Grandmother . . . and the Truth about Black Women and the Suffrage Movement," MS (November 1983): 29–37.

10. Alexander, "How I Discovered My Grandmother," 30.

11. Adella Hunt Logan, "Woman Suffrage," *Colored American Magazine* vol. 9 (September 1905): 487.

12. Ibid., 489.

13. See Melton A. McLaurin, *Celia, A Slave: A True Story of Violence and Retribution in Antebellum Missouri* (Athens: University of Georgia Press, 1991), chapter 8; Darlene Clark Hine, "Rape and the Culture of Dissemblance: Preliminary Thoughts on the Inner Lives of Black Midwestern Women," *Signs* vol. 14, no. 4 (Summer 1989): 912–14.

14. Logan, "Woman Suffrage," 487.

15. Penelope L. Bullock, *The Afro-American Periodical Press, 1838–1909* (Baton Rouge: Louisiana State University Press, 1981), 107–10.

16. Logan and Winston, 233–34, 273–74; Janice Sumler-Edmond, "Charlotte L. Forten Grimke," in *Black Women in America*, 505–506.

17. Logan and Winston, 271–73; Elizabeth Bown-Guillory, "Angelina Weld Grimke," in *Black Women in America*, 504–505.

18. *Who's Who in Colored America, 1928–1929*, ed. Joseph J. Boris (New York: Who's Who in Colored America Corp., 1929), 86, 357; Gwendolyn Etter-Lewis, "Baha'i Faith," in *Black Women in America*, 63.

19. Louise Daniel Hutchinson, "Anna Julia Haywood Cooper," in *Black Women in America*, 275–78.

20. Evelyn Brooks Higginbotham, "Nannie Helen Burroughs," in *Black Women in America*, 201–203.

21. HWS 4: 358–59.

22. *(Washington) Post*, 10 February 1900, box 39, Mary Church Terrell Papers, Manuscript Division, Library of Congress, Washington, DC, hereinafter cited as MCT Papers.

23. HWS 5: 105–106.

24. HWS 2: 233, 391–92; HWS 5: 83, 746; Kraditor, 213.

25. McCurdy, "Duty of the State to the Negro," 142–45.

26. Harper, *Sketches of Southern Life*, 16.

27. Anna J. Cooper, *A Voice From the South, by a Black Woman of the South* (Xenia, OH: Aldine Printing House, 1892), 139.

28. N. H. Burroughs, "Black Women and Reform," *Crisis* vol. 10 (August 1915): 187.

29. HWS 4: 298; Mary Church Terrell, "Susan B. Anthony, The Abolitionist," *Voice of the Negro* vol. 3 (June 1906): 411–16; *Syracuse Herald*, 28 May 1908, MCT Papers.

30. HWS 4: 268–69.

31. HWS 4: 393–99; Harper, *Susan B. Anthony* 3: 1257.

32. Scope Notes, Angelina Weld Grimké, "The Social Emancipation of Women," box 12, Angelina Weld Grimké Papers, Moorland-Spingarn Research Center, Howard University, Washington, DC.

33. Winnifred Harper Cooley, "The Younger Suffragist," in *The New Feminism in Twentieth Century America*, ed. June Sochen (Lexington, MA: D. C. Heath and Co., 1971), 17–23.

34. Kathy A. Perkins, ed., *Black Female Playwrights* (Bloomington: Indiana University Press, 1990), 6–9; Kathy A. Perkins, "Mary P. Burrill," in *Black Women in America*, 198.

35. Carolivia Herron, "Introduction," in *Selected Works of Angelina Weld Grimke*, ed. Carolivia Herron (New York: Oxford University Press, 1991), 6–7; Linda M. Perkins, "Lucy Diggs Slowe," in *Notable Black Women*, ed. Jessie Carney Smith (Detroit: Glendale Research, 1992), 1032.

36. Ibid.

37. See Sharon Harley, "For the Good of Family and Race: Gender, Work and Domestic Roles in the Black Community, 1880–1930," *Signs* vol. 15, no. 2 (Winter 1990).

38. Bearden and Butler, 222–23.

39. Maria L. Baldwin, "Votes for Teachers," *Crisis* vol. 10 (August 1915): 189.

40. Mary E. Jackson, "The Self Supporting Woman and the Ballot," *Crisis* vol. 10 (August 1915): 187–88.

41. Lucy D. Slowe, "After Commencement What?" *Howard University Record* vol. 12 (December 1918): 19–21; Gloria Harper Dickinson and Anita Williams McMiller, eds., *The Alpha Kappa Alpha Ivy Leaf, v1, n1 and The Ivy, v1, n1,* 75th Anniversary edition (Chicago: Alpha Kappa Alpha Sorority, 1996), 57–58, 61, 64.

42. *(New York) Age,* 29 March 1917; *Crisis* vol. 17 (December 1918): 90.

43. "Willie" to Mary Church Terrell, 19 June 1916, box 2, MCT Papers.

44. Lugenia Burns Hope, "The Colored Women's Statement to the Women's Missionary Council, American Missionary Association," box 6, Neighborhood Union Papers, Trevor Arnett Library, Atlanta University, Atlanta, GA, hereinafter cited as Neighborhood Union Papers.

45. Ibid.

46. Jacqueline Anne Rouse, *Lugenia Burns Hope: Black Southern Reformer* (Athens: University of Georgia Press, 1989), 91.

47. Ibid.

48. Cynthia Neverdon-Morton, *Afro-American Women of the South and the Advancement of the Race, 1895–1925* (Knoxville: University of Tennessee Press, 1989), 226–30.

49. *Crisis* vol. 4 (September 1912): 247.

5. Mobilizing to Win the Vote

1. HWS 4: 1051. This organizational statement opened the listing for the NACW in chapter 75, "National Organizations of Women." Margaret Murray Washington was listed as the contact person: "An organ is published called *Notes,* edited by Mrs. Booker T. Washington and an assistant in each state."

2. "Statement of Purpose, Colored Woman's Progressive Franchise Association," folder 5, box 1, MASC Papers.

3. *(Washington) People's Advocate,* 21 February 1880; Bearden and Butler, 222–23.

4. Thomas Holt, Cassandra Smith-Parker, and Rosalyn Terborg-Penn, *A Special Mission: The Story of Freedmen's Hospital, 1862–1962* (Washington: Academic Affairs Division, Howard University, 1975), 15–17.

5. France E. W. Harper, "The Democratic Return to Power," *AME Church Review* vol. 1 (1884): 225.

6. F. E. W. Harper, "A Factor in Human Progress," *AME Church Review* vol. 2 (1885): 18; Mrs. F. E. W. Harper, "The Woman's Christian Temperance Union and the Colored Woman," *AME Church Review* vol. 4 (1888): 314; HWS 4: 136.

7. Mamie Dillard, "The Work of the W.C.T.U.," *Atchison Blade,* 5 November 1892; Emma J. Ray, *Twice Sold and Twice Ransomed: The Autobiography of Mr. and Mrs. L. P. Ray* (New York: Books for Libraries Press, 1971; reprinted from a copy in the Fisk University Library Negro Collection, 1926), 66; J. W. Gibson and W. H. Crogman, eds., *Progress of a Race* (Napersville, IL: J. L. Nichols and Company, 1902, 1912), 210–14.

8. Terrell, "Citizenship," 5.

9. *Woman's Era* vol. 2 (August 1895): 1, 19; T. Thomas Fortune, "The New Afro-American Woman," *New York Sun,* 7 August 1895.

10. Floris Barnett Cash, "Victoria Earle Matthews," in *Black Women in America,* 759–61; Rosalyn Terborg-Penn, "African-American Women's Networks in the Anti-Lynching Crusade," in *Gender, Class, Race and Reform in the Progressive Era,* ed. Noralee Frankel and Nancy S. Dye (Lexington: University of Kentucky Press, 1991), 150–51.

11. *Woman's Era* vol. 2 (August 1895), 5.

12. HWS 4: 499; Woodbury, 70; *Woman's Era* vol. 3 (August 1895): 5; vol. 3 (July 1896): 1–2; vol. 5 (January 1897): 3–4; vol. 3 (June 1896): 3; vol. 1 (July 1894): 5; Fannie Barrier Williams, "Club Movement among Negro Women," in *Progress of a Race*, ed. Gibson and Crogman, 206, 209.

13. Fannie Barrier Williams, 205–206; Dorothy Salem, "National Association of Colored Women," in *Black Women in America*, 842–46.

14. Richard T. Greener to John Bruce, 12 December 1985, box 1, folder A, John E. Bruce Papers, Schomburg Center for Research in Black Culture, New York, NY.

15. HWS 4: 1051.

16. Higginbotham, 150.

17. Ibid., 12, 150–51.

18. Fannie Barrier Williams, 209.

19. Ibid., 206–207.

20. *Woman's Journal*, 18 April 1903.

21. Alexander, "Adella Hunt Logan, Tuskegee Institute," 102, n. 37.

22. Fannie Barrier Williams, 207.

23. Fourth Annual Convention of the Southern Federation of Colored Women's Clubs, New Orleans, LA, 29–30 December 1902, National Association Notes folder, Margaret Murray Washington Papers, Tuskegee University Archives, Tuskegee, AL, hereafter cited as M. Washington Papers; Program, Fourth Convention of the National Association of Colored Women, St. Louis, MO, 11–16 July 1904, 5, M. Washington Papers.

24. *National Association Notes* vol. 7, no. 11 (July 1904): 22–23; Program, State Federation, Guest of City Federation of Colored Women's Clubs, Jacksonville, FL, 28–30 June 1916, Women's Clubs—Proceedings and Programs folder, M. Washington Papers.

25. "Editorials," *National Association Notes* vol. 17, no. 3 (January-February 1915): 13, 14.

26. *National Notes*, October 1916, 11–12, Tuskegee Archives.

27. National Baptist Convention, *Twelfth Annual Report of the Executive Board and Corresponding Secretary of the Woman's Convention, 1912* (National Baptist Convention, 1912), 39, hereinafter cited as *Woman's Convention*, with the year. Among the leaders of the WC, there were several suffragists. The most prominent in leadership positions were president S. Willie Layten of Philadelphia and corresponding secretary Nannie Helen Burroughs.

28. Higginbotham, 226–27.

29. Ibid., 226.

30. Ibid., 227.

31. The Equal Suffrage League Petition, box 1, MCT Papers.

32. Ibid.

33. Terborg-Penn, "Afro-Americans in the Struggle for Woman Suffrage," 145–46.

34. Monroe Work clipping file, Black Women, 1911–20, *Savannah Journal*, 12 June 1920, Tuskegee Archives, Tuskegee Institute, Tuskegee, AL, hereinafter cited as Work File, with citation.

35. Ibid.

36. Higginbotham, 225.

37. Mary B. Talbert, "Women and Colored Women," *Crisis* vol. 10 (August 1915): 184.

38. Program, Third Annual Convention of the Colorado State Federation of Colored Women's Clubs, 13–14 June 1906, Tuskegee Archives.

39. Wells-Barnett, *Crusade*, 346; *Alpha Suffrage Record* vol. 1 (March 1914): 1, Ida B. Wells Papers, Regenstein Library, University of Chicago, Chicago, IL, hereinafter cited as IBW Papers.

40. Ibid.

41. Program, Third Convention of NACW, Buffalo, New York, 9–12 July 1902, M. Washington Papers; box 6, Anthony Papers.

42. "Negro Women Join the Suffrage Fight," *New York Times,* 7 February 1910, 4.

43. Ibid.

44. "Aids Colored Suffragettes," *New York Times,* 28 September 1910, 6. Christopher Lasch, "Alva Erskine Smith Vanderbilt Belmont," in *Notable American Women, 1607–1950,* ed. Edward T. James et al. (Cambridge, MA.: Belknap Press of Harvard University Press, 1971), 1: 127.

45. "Suffrage Center for Negroes," *New York Times,* 29 August 1915, 6; "Negro Suffrage Headquarters," *New York Times,* 2 September 1915, 5.

46. *Suffragist,* 23 December 1916, 3. Milholland died suddenly in 1916.

47. *(Indianapolis) Freeman,* 28 August 1915.

48. *Crisis* vol. 18 (July 1919): 17.

49. Rosalyn Terborg-Penn, "African Feminism: A Theoretical Approach to the History of Women in the African Diaspora," in *Women in Africa and the African Diaspora,* ed. Rosalyn Terborg-Penn et al. (Washington: Howard University Press, 1987), 56–57.

50. Clark Burdick to Bertha G. Higgins, 5 November 1920, box 86; Charles E. Harding to Bertha G. Higgins, 21 February 1921, box 87, Bertha G. Higgins Papers, Rhode Island Black Heritage Center, Providence, RI, hereinafter cited as BGH Papers.

51. Alexander, "Adella Hunt Logan," 82.

52. Program, Fourth Annual Convention of the Southern Federation of Colored Women's Clubs, 29–30 December 1902, Women's Clubs Proceedings and Programs folder, M. Washington Papers.

53. Alexander, "Adella Hunt Logan Tuskegee Institute," 83–86, 91–92.

54. Terborg-Penn, "Afro-Americans in the Struggle for Woman Suffrage," 178–80.

6. Anti–Black Woman Suffrage Tactics and African American Women's Responses

1. Blackwell was identified only by her picture and her organizational title. Her undated pamphlet is located in the Trevor Arnett Library at Atlanta University and was originally contained in the Slaughter Collection; Mrs. A. W. Blackwell, 3–4.

2. See Miriam Gurko, *The Ladies of Seneca Falls: The Birth of the Woman's Rights Movement* (New York: MacMillian Publishing Co., 1974), 215; Carrie Chapmen Catt and Nettie Rogers Shuler, *Woman Suffrage and Politics: The Inner Story of the Suffrage Movement* (New York: Charles Scribner's Sons, 1926), 54–60; Allen, 142, 145. For details on the black male response to those who accused them of opposing woman suffrage, and for an analysis of the myth of anti–woman suffrage sentiments among black men, see chapters 3 and 6, Terborg-Penn, "Afro-Americans in the Struggle for Woman Suffrage."

3. Wheeler, "New Women" 101–102.

4. "The Southern States Woman Suffrage Conference," *Suffragists* vol. 14 (November 1914): 2; "Chief Justice Clark on Woman Suffrage and the Race Problem," *Suffragists* vol. 16 (October 1915): 2; "Southern Chivalry," *Suffragists* vol. 1 (January 1916): 2.

5. U.S. Department of the Interior, *Eleventh Census,* 1890, 1: 3, 166; "Will the Federal Suffrage Amendment Complicate the Race Problem," flier, National Woman's Party, National Literature, Anti–Woman Suffrage folder, Political History Division, Smithsonian Institution. For a good analysis of anti–black woman suffrage activities in the South, see Bettina Aptheker, chapter 3; Suzanne Lebsock, "Woman Suffrage and White Supremacy: A Virginia Case Study," in *Visible Women,* ed. Nancy A. Hewitt and Suzanne Lebsock (Urbana: University of Illinois Press, 1993), 75–76.

6. HWS 2: 94–95, 216, 396, 443–44; *New York Tribune*, 13 January 1869; *New National Era*, 24 October 1872.

7. HWS 2: 390–92.

8. Allen, 128, 151; Kraditor, 138–39; David Morgan, *Suffragists and Democrats: The Politics of Woman Suffrage in America* (East Lansing: Michigan State University Press, 1972), 187.

9. HWS 3: 74. See HWS 6; Rosalyn Terborg-Penn, "The Historical Treatment of Afro-Americans in the Woman's Movement, 1900–1920: A Bibliographical Essay," *A Current Bibliography on African Affairs* vol. 7 (Summer 1974): 249–50.

10. *Woman's Era* vol. 2 (August 1985): 19; HWS 4: 216, 246; James M. McPherson, *Abolitionist Legacy: From Reconstruction to the NAACP* (Princeton, NJ: Princeton University Press, 1975), 320–21.

11. Wells-Barnett, *Crusade*, 230.

12. Ibid.

13. McPherson, 319–20. "Educated suffrage" continued to be popular among white suffragists in the twentieth century. See for example, Margaret Deland, "The Third Way in Woman Suffrage," *Ladies Home Journal* 30 (January 1913): 11–12.

14. Alexander, "Adella Hunt Logan, Tuskegee Institute," 102, n. 34.

15. McPherson, 321; HWS 4: 341, 678, 680–81.

16. HWS 4: 348.

17. *Woman's Journal*, 13 May 1899.

18. Allen, 155–56.

19. See *Negro Year Book*, 1918–21, and *Woman's Era*, 1894–97; Kraditor, 213.

20. *Woman's Era* vol. 2 (January 1896): 12.

21. HWS 4: 359; *(Indianapolis) Freeman*, July 1905; National Baptist Convention, *Women's Convention*, 1913, 33.

22. Logan, "Woman Suffrage," 487.

23. Ibid., 487–88.

24. Turner, 192; Jackson, 187.

25. Editorial, *Messenger*, March 1919, 5.

26. *Crisis* vol. 18 (July 1919): 17.

27. Editorial, *Crisis* vol. 3 (October 1911): 243–44.

28. Alexander, "Adella Hunt Logan, Tuskegee Institute," 73.

29. HWS 5: 55, 59–60.

30. Ibid., 60, n. 1.

31. HWS 5: 105–106.

32. *Crisis* vol. 4 (June 1912): 76–77.

33. Ibid.

34. *Negro Year Book*, 1916, 37–38.

35. Quoted in Alexander, "Adella Hunt Logan, Tuskegee Institute," 103, n. 47.

36. Mary Church Terrell, "The Justice of Women Suffrage," *Crisis* vol. 4 (September 1912): 191.

37. Ibid.; Cook, 185.

38. Quoted in Alexander, "Adella Hunt Logan, Tuskegee Institute," 101–102, n. 29.

39. Paula Giddings, *When and Where I Enter*, 154.

40. Terborg-Penn, "Discrimination against Afro-American Women," 21.

41. Gibson and Crogman, *Progress of a Race*, 216–20.

42. *Minneapolis Journal*, November 1900, MCT Papers; HWS 1883–1900: 358–59.

43. Wells-Barnett, *Crusade for Justice*, 345–47.

44. Kraditor, 213–14; Wells-Barnett, *Crusade for Justice*, 229–30.

45. Lebsock, 67, 71, 76.

46. *New York Times*, 22 February 1911, 6; 26 February 1911, 5.

47. Ibid., 20 October 1915, 2.

48. Alexander, "Adella Hunt Logan, Tuskegee Institute," 78.

49. *Crisis* vol. 5 (April 1913): 298.

50. Kraditor, 167–68.

51. Hendricks, 268–69.

52. Ibid., 270.

53. Walter White to Mary Church Terrell, 14 March 1919, MCT Papers.

54. Morgan, 92; conversation with Edith Mayo, Curator, Woman's Collection, Division of Political History, Smithsonian Institution, 30 June 1976, Washington, DC.

55. Morgan, 93–94; quoted in *Negro Year Book*, 1914, 43.

56. Wheeler, 100–105, 143.

57. HWS 4: xxvii; Wells-Barnett, *Crusade*, 345; "Five Million of These Ladies Will Vote," flier, Anti–Woman Suffrage folder, Political History Division, Smithsonian Institution.

58. Lebsock, 70–71.

59. Quoted in the *Negro Year Book*, 1918, 60.

60. Blackwell, 3–4; National Baptist Convention, *Woman's Convention*, 1916, 31–33.

61. Morgan, 106–107; *Crisis* vol. 15 (November 1917): 19–20; *New York Age*, 10 May 1917.

62. Terborg-Penn, "Discrimination against Afro-American Women," 25.

63. Catt letter to Webb, 5 January 1918, box 340, National Archives, House of Representatives RG 233 HR 65 A-H8-14.

64. *New York Age*, 20 September 1917, 13.

65. *Crisis* vol. 17 (November 1918): 25.

66. HWS 5: 645–46; Terborg-Penn, "African American Women and the Woman Suffrage Movement," 149–50.

67. James Callaway, "Some Strange History," *Macon Telegraph,* 26 May 1918, reprinted in National Woman's Party literature, Anti-Woman Suffrage folder, Political History Division, Smithsonian Institution.

68. Lebsock, 75–76.

69. Walter White to Mary Church Terrell, 14 March 1919, box 3, MCT Papers.

70. Kellogg, 208.

71. Walter White to Mary Church Terrell, 14 March 1919, Box 3, MCT Papers.

72. Ida Husted Harper to Mary Church Terrell, 18 March 1919; Ida Husted Harper to Elizabeth Carter, 18 March 1919, box 3, MCT Papers; Lebsock 76–79.

73. Elizabeth C. Carter to Ida Husted Harper, 10 April 1919, Suffrage file, NAACP Papers, Manuscript Division, Library of Congress, Washington, DC.

74. Kraditor, 168–69; *Crisis* vol. 17 (June 1919): 103; HWS 5: 580–81; Kellogg, 208.

75. Kenneth R. Johnson, "White Racial Attitudes as a Factor in the Arguments against the Nineteenth Amendment," *Phylon* vol. 31 (Spring 1970): 31–32, 35–37.

76. *New York Age*, 31 March 1920; *Crisis* (March 1920), reprinted in National Woman's Party literature, Anti–Woman Suffrage folder, Political History Division, Smithsonian Institution.

77. HWS 2: 383, 385.

78. Mary Church Terrell, *A Colored Woman in a White World* (Washington: National Association of Colored Women's Clubs, 1968), 316–17.

79. See Rosalyn Terborg-Penn, "Afro-Americans in the Struggle for Woman Suffrage," appendices.

7. African American Woman as Voters and Candidates

1. Terrell, *A Colored Woman,* 308. Terrell was Director of Work among [Republican] Colored Women of the East.

2. Josephine St. Pierre Ruffin, "Trust the Women!" *Crisis* vol. 10 (August 1915): 188.

3. Helen Laura Sumner Woodbury, *Equal Suffrage: The Results of an Investigation in Colorado, Made for the Collective Equal Suffrage League of New York State* (New York: Harper and Brothers, 1909), 70, 114, 117. According to William O'Neill, the Woodbury study was the only contemporary analysis of the effects of woman suffrage in any state prior to the ratification of the Nineteenth Amendment. O'Neill, 64–65.

4. Program, Third Annual Convention of the Colorado State Federation of Colored Women's Clubs, 13–14 June 1906, Tuskegee Archives.

5. Beverly Beeton, "How the West Was Won for Woman Suffrage," in Wheeler, *One Woman One Vote,* 109–10.

6. IBW *Journal,* chapter 11, 1, IBW Papers; Wells-Barnett, *Crusade,* xxviii, 346.

7. Wells-Barnett, Crusade, 346.

8. *(Indianapolis) Freeman,* 13 March 1915, February–July 1915.

9. Oscar De Priest, "Chicago and Woman's Suffrage," *Crisis* vol. 10 (August 1915): 179.

10. Ibid., Wells-Barnett, *Crusade,* 347.

11. *Negro Year Book 1912,* 31.

12. *California Eagle,* 26 September 1914, 22 August 1914.

13. Ibid., 3 April 1915.

14. Ibid., 21 October 1916.

15. See Gerald Gill, "'Win or Lose—We Win': The 1952 Vice Presidential Campaign of Charlotta A. Bass," in Harley and Terborg-Penn, *The Afro-American Woman;* Kathleen Thompson, "Charlotta Spear Bass," in *The Black Woman in America,* 93.

16. Editorial, *Crisis* vol. 15 (November 1917): 43.

17. *(New York) Age,* 27 September 1917.

18. *(New York) Age,* 4 October, 1 November 1917.

19. *Crisis* vol. 15 (December 1917): 26.

20. *Crisis* vol. 13 (September 1918): 240; *Negro Year Book,* 1918–19, 56.

21. *Negro Year Book,* 1918–19, 56.

22. "History of Black Women in the Suffrage Movement in Rhode Island," Item 264, BGH Papers.

23. William Estabrook Chancellor, *Warren Gamaliel Harding: President of the United States* (Worcester, OH: Sentinel Press, 1921), 7–10, 22, 80–81. This underground book was virtually destroyed by the Republican Party. A surviving copy is located in the New York City Public Library; interview with Jeanne Terborg, June 1980, Jamaica, New York.

24. Letter from Lethia C. Fleming, Republican National Committee Mid-West Headquarters, 22 October 1920, reel 18, MCT Papers.

25. Newspaper clipping, 1 October 1920, reel 18, MCT Papers.

26. Mary Church Terrell to Bertha G. Higgins, October 1920, Item 17, BGH Papers.

27. Terrell, *A Colored Woman,* 308–10.

28. Clark Burdick to Bertha G. Higgins, 5 November 1920, 86; Charles E. Harding to Bertha G. Higgins, 21 February 1921, 87, BGH Papers.

29. Work File, *(Brooklyn) Standard Union,* 9 August 1920, Tuskegee Archives.

30. Work File, *(Tampa) Times,* 15 July 1920, Tuskegee Archives.

31. Ibid.

32. See Rosalyn Terborg-Penn, "African-American Women's Networks in the Anti-Lynching Crusade," 148–61.

33. Ruth Edmonds Hill, ed., *The Black Women Oral History Project* (Westport, CT: Meckler, 1991), 1: 60–61; Chancellor, 15–16.

34. *Negro Year Book,* 1918–19, 57–59.

35. *Crisis* vol. 16 (September 1918): 240; *Negro Year Book,* 1918–19, 57–58.

36. Hill, 1: 60–61.

37. *Crisis* vol. 13 (September 1918): 240.

38. *Crisis* vol. 13 (September 1918): 240; *Negro Year Book*, 1918–19, pp. 56–58; *Messenger* vol. 2 (November 1920): 138–39.

39. *New York Age*, 31 March 1920.

40. *Crisis* vol. 19 (November 1920): 23–25; *Negro Year Book*, 1921, 40.

41. *Negro Year Book*, 1921, 40; HWS 6: 606.

42. Lebsock, 90.

43. Wheeler, *New Women,* 100–105, 143.

44. Editorial, *Messenger* vol. 2 (November 1920): 131, 147.

45. *Negro Year Book*, 1921, 41.

46. Ibid., 40–41.

47. *Crisis* vol. 21 (February 1921): 200; *Crisis* vol. 20 (May 1920): 5.

48. *Crisis* vol. 21 (November 1920): 23-24; William Pickens, "The Woman Voter Hits the Color Line," *Nation* vol. 3 (6 October, 1920): 372–73; HWS 3: 828–29.

49. Lebsock, 83–84.

50. NAACP, *Eleventh Annual Report*, 15; Pickens, 373.

51. NAACP, *Eleventh Annual Report*, 25–30; *Negro Year Book*, 1921, 42–43.

52. *Crisis* vol. 21 (January 1921):122–23.

53. Pickens, 372–73.

54. Giddings, 166; Wheeler, *New Women*, 189–90, 194–95.

55. Rosalyn Terborg-Penn, "Discontented Black Feminists," 267.

56. NWP letter to Walter White, 2 September [1924], reel 15, MCT Papers.

57. Ibid., 261, 267.

58. *Crisis* vol. 23 (December 1921): 83; *Negro Year Book*, 1922–24.

59. *Negro Year Book*, 1922–24, 70; Mary Church Terrell, *A Colored Woman in a White World* (Washington: Randsdell, Inc., 1940), 355–56; *Negro Year Book*, 1931–32, 92–93.

60. Resolution of the Colored Independent Political Association of Rhode Island, n.d., BGH Papers.

61. Terborg-Penn, "Discontented Black Feminists," 267-68; see Cynthia Neverdon-Morton, *Afro-American Women of the South,* chapter 10.

62. Terrell, *A Colored Woman*, first page of introduction.

8. The Nineteenth Amendment and Its Meaning for African American Women

1. Terborg-Penn, "Afro-Americans in the Struggle for Woman Suffrage," appendices.

2. Ibid.

3. HWS 4: 1051, 1083.

4. Allen, *Reluctant Reformers*, 154–55.

5. Benjamin Brawley, *Women of Achievement: Written for the Fireside Schools* (Nashville: American Baptist Home Mission Society, 1919), 14–17; Elizabeth Ross Haynes, "Two Million Negro Women at Work," *Southern Workman* vol. 15 (February 1922): 64–66.

6. Terborg-Penn, "Discontented Black Feminists," 268; for a discussion of Black domestic workers in the District of Columbia during the period, see Elizabeth Clark-Lewis, *Living In, Living Out: African American Domestics in Washington, D.C., 1910–1940* (Washington: Smithsonian Institution Press, 1994).

7. Terborg-Penn, "Discontented Black Feminists," 269–70.

8. Elliott Rudwick, *W. E. B. Du Bois: Propagandist of the Negro Protest* (New York: Atheneum, 1972), 232–33; Neverdon-Morton, *Afro-American Women of the South*, 199, 198–201.

SELECTED BIBLIOGRAPHY

Manuscript Collections

Susan B. Anthony Papers, Manuscript Division, Library of Congress, Washington, DC.
The Anti–Woman Suffrage Papers, Political History Division, National Museum of American History, Smithsonian Institution, Washington, DC.
John Bruce Papers, Schomburg Center for Research in Black Culture, New York, NY.
Nannie Helen Burroughs Papers, Manuscript Division, Library of Congress, Washington, DC.
Mary Ann Shadd Cary Papers, Moorland-Spingarn Research Center, Howard University, Washington, DC.
Angelina Weld Grimké Papers, Moorland-Spingarn Research Center, Howard University, Washington, DC.
Diary of Charlotte Forten Grimké, Moorland-Spingarn Research Center, Howard University, Washington, DC.
Bertha G. Higgins Papers, Rhode Island Black Heritage Center, Providence, RI.
NAACP Papers, Manuscript Division, Library of Congress, Washington, DC.
National Woman's Party Collection, Political History Division, National Museum of American History, Smithsonian Institution, Washington, DC.
Mary Church Terrell Papers, Manuscript Division, Library of Congress, Washington, DC.
Margaret Murray Washington Papers, Archives, Tuskegee Institute, Tuskegee, AL.
Ida B. Wells-Barnett Papers, Regenstein Library, University of Chicago, Chicago, IL.

Newspapers, Magazines and Journals

Colored American Magazine
Crisis
Los Angeles Eagle
Messenger
National Association Notes
Negro Year Book
New National Era
New York Age
New York Times
Revolution
Woman's Era
Woman's Journal

Published Sources

Alexander, Adele Logan. "Adella Hunt Logan, the Tuskegee Woman's Club, and African Americans in the Suffrage Movement," in *Votes for Women: The Woman Suffrage*

Movement in Tennessee, the South and the Nation, ed. Marjorie Spruill Wheeler. Nashville: University of Tennessee Press, 1995.

Aptheker, Bettina. *Woman's Legacy: Essays on Race, Sex, and Class in American History.* Amherst: University of Massachusetts Press, 1982.

Bearden, Jim, and Linda Jean Butler. *Shadd: The Life and Times of Mary Shadd Cary.* Toronto: NC Press, 1977.

Brawley, Benjamin. *Women of Achievement: Written for the Fireside Schools.* Nashville: Baptist Home Mission Society, 1919.

Brown, Elsa Barkley. "Negotiating and Transforming the Public Sphere: African American Political Life in the Transition from Slavery to Freedom," *Public Culture* vol. 7, no. 1 (Fall 1994).

Cooper, Anna J. *A Voice from the South, by a Black Woman of the South.* Xenia, OH: Aldine Printing House, 1892.

DuBois, Ellen Carol. *Feminism and Suffrage: The Emergence of an Independent Women's Movement in America, 1848–1869.* Ithaca, NY: Cornell University Press, 1978.

Harper, Frances Ellen Watkins. *Sketches of Southern Life.* Philadelphia: Ferguson Brothers, 1896.

Hendricks, Wanda. "Ida B. Wells-Barnett and the Alpha Suffrage Club of Chicago." In *One Woman, One Vote: Rediscovering the Woman Suffrage Movement,* ed. Marjorie Spruill Wheeler. Troutdale, OR: NewSage Press, 1995.

Higginbotham, Evelyn Brooks. *Righteous Discontent: The Woman's Movement in the Black Baptist Church, 1880–1920.* Cambridge, MA: Harvard University Press, 1993.

Hill, Ruth Edmonds, ed. *The Black Women Oral History Project,* 10 vols. Westport, CT: Meckler, 1991.

Kraditor, Aileen. *The Ideas of the Woman Suffrage Movement, 1890–1920.* Garden City, NY: Anchor Books, 1971.

Lebsock, Suzanne. "Woman Suffrage and White Supremacy: A Virginia Case Study." In *Visible Women,* ed. Nancy A. Hewitt and Suzanne Lebsock. Urbana: University of Illinois Press, 1993.

A Narrative of the Life and Travels of Mrs. Nancy Prince. In *Collected Black Women's Narratives.* Introduction by Anthony G. Barthelemy. New York: Oxford University Press, 1988.

Painter, Nell Irvin. *Sojourner Truth: A Life, a Symbol.* New York: W. W. Norton, 1996.

Painter, Nell Irvin. "Sojourner Truth in Feminist Abolitionism: Difference, Slavery, and Memory." In *An Untrodden Path: Antislavery and Women's Political Culture,* ed. Jean Fagan Yellin and John C. Van Horne. Ithaca, NY: Cornell University Press, 1992.

Quarles, Benjamin. *Black Abolitionists.* New York: Oxford University Press, 1969.

Quarles, Benjamin. "Frederick Douglass and the Woman's Rights Movement." *Journal of Negro History* vol. 25 (January 1940): 35–44.

Stanton, Elizabeth Cady, et al., eds. *The History of Woman Suffrage, 1848–1920,* 6 vols. New York: Arno Press and the New York Times, 1969.

Terborg-Penn, Rosalyn. "African American Women and the Woman Suffrage Movement." In *One Woman, One Vote: Rediscovering the Woman Suffrage Movement,* ed. Marjorie Spruill Wheeler. Troutdale, OR: NewSage Press, 1995.

Terborg-Penn, Rosalyn. "Discontented Black Feminists: Prelude and Postscript to the Passage of the Nineteenth Amendment." In *Decades of Discontent: The Women's Movement, 1920–1940,* ed. Lois Scharf and Joan M. Jensen. Westport, CT: Greenwood Press, 1983.

Terborg-Penn, Rosalyn. "Discrimination against Afro-American Women in the Woman's Movement, 1830–1920." In *The Afro-American Woman: Struggles and Images,* ed. Sharon Harley and Rosalyn Terborg-Penn. Port Washington, NY: Kennikat Press, 1978.

Terborg-Penn, Rosalyn. "Nineteenth Century Black Women and Woman Suffrage." *Potomac Review* vol. 7 (Spring-Summer 1977).

Terrell, Mary Church. *A Colored Woman in a White World*. Washington: Randsdell Inc., 1940.

Washington, Margaret, ed. *Narrative of Sojourner Truth*. New York: Vintage Books, 1993.

Wells-Barnett, Ida B. *Crusade for Justice: The Autobiography of Ida B. Wells,* ed. Alfreda M. Duster. Chicago: University of Chicago Press, 1970.

Wheeler, Marjorie Spruill. *New Women of the New South: The Leaders of the Woman Suffrage Movement in the Southern States.* New York: Oxford University Press, 1993.

Wheeler, Marjorie Spruill, ed. *One Woman, One Vote: Rediscovering the Woman Suffrage Movement.* Troutdale, OR: NewSage Press, 1995.

Woodbury, Helen Laura Sumner. *Equal Suffrage: The Results of an Investigation in Colorado, Made for the Collective Equal Suffrage League of New York State*. New York: Harper and Brothers, 1909.

INDEX

Simmons, Mrs., 148
Sketches of Southern Life (Harper, 1896), 67
Slowe, Lucy Diggs, 71, 74–75
Smith, Caroline, 87
Social reform, and Black woman suffragists, 10–11, 76, 161. *See also* Temperance
Socialism, and Black women as voters, 149
Sojourner Truth Club, 88
South: disfranchisement of Black women after 1920, 11–12, 136, 151–57; Civil War and status of Black women, 23–24; roots of Black suffragists in late 1900s, 61, 79; disfranchisement of Black men, 66–67; sexism, racism, economics, and politics, 78; Democratic Party and state governments, 85; Black women's clubs, 88, 104–106; anti–Black suffrage, 108–109; white supremacy and woman suffrage, 120; opposition to Nineteenth Amendment, 131; experiences of Black women trying to vote, 149–51. *See also individual states*
South Carolina: Black women and voting in 1870s, 24, 40; woman suffrage movement in, 44–46; disfranchisement of Black women after 1920, 153
South Carolina Federation of Colored Women, 77
South Carolina Woman Suffrage Association, 110
South Carolina Woman's Rights Association, 45–46, 83, 110
Southeastern Federation of Colored Women's Clubs, 77
Southern Federation of Colored Women's Clubs, 104
Southern States Woman Suffrage, 124
Southern Woman Suffrage Conference, 101
Spears, Charlotta, 140, 141
Spencer, Mrs. Eliza A., 47
Sprague, Rosetta Douglass, 47
Squire, Belle, 122, 123
Stanton, Elizabeth Cady, 6, 14–15, 21, 22–23, 27–28, 31, 32, 33, 37, 38, 49, 111, 112
State Federation of Women's Clubs, 119
States: status of woman suffrage in 1890, 9; states' rights and Black women as voters, 11. *See also* South; *individual states*
Steward, Susan McKinney, 94
Stewart, Georgia, 60
Stokes, Ora Brown, 154
Stone, Lucy, 20, 23, 28, 29, 30, 32, 34, 44
Suffragist, 6, 108, 132

Talbert, Mary B., 97, 144, 146, 154
Talbert, Naomi. *See* Anderson, Naomi Talbert
Teaching, and Black woman suffragists, 59–60, 74
Temperance: and Soujourner Truth, 48; and Black woman suffrage movement, 85–86,

93. *See also* Social reform, and Black woman suffragists
Tennessee: and woman suffrage at state level, 11; and Black women as voters in 1920, 162
Terrell, Mary Church, 63–64, 65–67, 68, 69, 70, 86, 88, 90, 95, 113, 116, 117–18, 119, 123, 130, 132, 137, 144–45, 156, 158, 164
Terrell, Robert, 64
Texas: woman suffrage and Black women's clubs, 105; and woman suffrage prior to 1920, 146–48
Theory, and historiography of Black women in woman suffrage movement, 3–7
Thomas, James C., Jr., 142
Thurman, Lucy, 95
Tilton, Theodore, 31
Tinkham Bill (1920), 154
Train, George Francis, 28, 32
Trout, Grace Wilbur, 122
Truth, Sojourner, 14, 15–16, 17, 18, 24, 26, 31, 33, 34, 35, 38, 40, 42, 48, 52, 61, 79, 88, 109, 159, 170n.15
Tubman, Harriet, 88
Turner, Lillian A., 114
Turner, Mary, 96
Tuskegee Institute, 57, 60, 77
Tuskegee's Woman's Club, 60, 88, 104–105
Twentieth Century Art and Literary Club, 103

Universal Negro Improvement Association, 165
Universal suffrage: schism in, 24–35; and anti–Black woman suffrage movement, 109–12
Upton, Harriet Taylor, 115
Utah, and woman suffrage at state level, 9

Valentine, Lila Meade, 130
Villard, Mrs. Henry, 100
Virginia: early woman suffrage movement in, 56; and anti–Black woman suffrage, 124–25; disfranchisement of Black women after 1920, 154
Virginia Federation of Colored Women's Clubs, 77
A Voice from the South (Cooper, 1892), 68
Voice of the Negro, 72
Voting and voting rights: statistics on Black women and, 5; and political activism of Black women before 1920, 138–43; and political activism of Black women after 1920, 143–48; South and disfranchisement of Black women after 1920, 151–57; ideological meaning for Black women, 159–64

Walker, Maggie, 151, 154
Washington, Booker T., 61
Washington, Mrs. Edward, 148
Washington, Margaret Murray, 16, 77, 84, 88, 90, 92, 95, 104, 118, 164, 173n.1
Washington, D.C.: and Black women during

Rosalyn Terborg-Penn is Professor and Coordinator of Graduate Programs in History at Morgan State University in Baltimore. A founder of the Association of Black Women Historians, she is a coeditor of *Black Women in America: An Historical Encyclopedia, The Afro-American Woman: Struggles and Images,* and *Women in Africa and the African Diaspora: A Reader.*